2009

NASPA JOURNAL ABOUT WOMEN IN HIGHER EDUCATION

VOLUME II ◆ WWW.NASPA.ORG/PUBS/JOURNALS/JAWHE

Scholarship about women faculty, students, and administrators in higher education

NASPA
Student Affairs Administrators
in Higher Education

About the *NASPA Journal About Women in Higher Education*

Published annually, the *NASPA Journal About Women in Higher Education* is a blind peer-reviewed scholarly journal that aims to deepen understanding of issues facing women faculty, students, and administrators. The journal publishes articles that focus on empirical research, pedagogy, and administrative practice. Intended for both practitioners and researchers, the journal is designed to increase interest in research about women faculty, students, and administrators in higher education, and to highlight current examples of this research. The *NASPA Journal About Women in Higher Education* offers research reflecting a variety of paradigms and issues affecting women in higher education in all their diversity.

Membership and Subscriptions

Information concerning application for membership in NASPA and subscriptions to the *NASPA Journal About Women in Higher Education* may be obtained from

NASPA
1875 Connecticut Ave., NW, Suite 418
Washington, DC 20009
telephone 202-265-7500 • www.naspa.org

Rate Type	One-Year Subscription (Print and Online)	Int'l Surface	Int'l Air
NASPA Member	$59	$78	$90
Nonmember	$89	$110	$120
Institution	$199	$240	$253

Manuscripts

Manuscripts submitted for publication should meet the requirements of the *NASPA Journal About Women in Higher Education's* "Guidelines for Authors." Visit www.naspa.org/pubs/journals/jawhe for complete submission information.

Ownership

The *NASPA Journal About Women in Higher Education* is published annually by the National Association of Student Personnel Administrators (NASPA), 1875 Connecticut Ave., NW, Suite 418, Washington, DC 20009.

POSTMASTER: Send address changes to: *NASPA Journal About Women in Higher Education,* National Association of Student Personnel Administrators, 1875 Connecticut Ave., NW, Suite 418, Washington, DC 20009

Permissions, Reprints, and Single Issues

Copyright © 2009 by the National Association of Student Personnel Administrators (NASPA), Inc. Printed and bound in the United States of America. All rights reserved. No part of this book may be reproduced in any form or by any electronic or mechanical means without written permission from the publisher.

NASPA does not discriminate on the basis of race, color, national origin, religion, sex, age, gender identity, gender expression, affectional or sexual orientation, or disability in any of its policies, programs, and services.

Additional copies may be purchased by contacting the NASPA publications department at 301-638-1749 or visiting http://bookstore.naspa.org.

ISSN 1940-7882

ISBN 978-0-931654-05-3

Table of Contents

vii	List of Reviewers
ix	Editors' Note

ARTICLES

1	Third Wave Feminist Undergraduates: Transforming Identities and Redirecting Activism in Response to Institutional Sexism by Annemarie Vaccaro
26	Colonial Sexism 101? Anthropological Teachings About Women Barbara Bonnekessen
39	Leading in the Borderlands: Negotiating Ethnic Patriarchy for the Benefit of Students Alicia Fedelina Chávez
66	Turning Away from Academic Careers: What Does Work-Family Have To Do with It? Kate Quinn, Elizabeth Litzler
91	Black Female Faculty: Role Definition, Critical Enactments, and Contributions to Predominately White Research Institutions Venice Thandi Sulé
120	Childcare Options in South Korea: Experiences and Perceptions of Female College Faculty Hae Ja Shin
140	Crossing Boundaries: Understanding Women's Advancement from Clerical to Professional Positions Susan V. Iverson
167	If You Don't Ask, You'll Never Earn What You Deserve: Salary Negotiation Issues Among Female Administrators in Higher Education Suzette Compton, Louann Bierlein Palmer

188	Women Higher Education Administrators with Children: Negotiating Personal and Professional Lives Sarah M. Marshall
222	Evaluation of Sexual Harassment Training Instructional Strategies Mary Pilgram, Joann Keyton

PROGRAM DESCRIPTIONS

241	The Alice M. Baldwin Scholars Program Colleen Scott, Duke University, North Carolina
243	REAL Collaborative: Research for the Educational Advancement of Latin@s Iliana Alanís, Kimberley K. Cuero, Mariela A. Rodríguez, The University of Texas at San Antonio
245	Young Women Leaders Program Edith Lawrence, Keonya Booker, Lauren Germain, The University of Virginia

BOOK REVIEWS

247	*Through the Labyrinth: The Truth About How Women Become Leaders* Reviewed by Paige Haber, University of San Diego
250	*Challenges of the Faculty Career for Women: Success and Sacrifice* Reviewed by Jeni Hart, University of Missouri
254	*Unfinished Agendas: New and Continuing Gender Challenges in Higher Education* Reviewed by Kathryn M. Moore, North Carolina State University

257	Guidelines for Authors

List of Reviewers

Editors

Barbara K. Townsend	University of Missouri – Columbia
Susan B. Twombly	University of Kansas

Editorial Board

Ann Blackhurst	Minnesota State University
Jill Carnaghi	Washington University in St. Louis
Johnetta Cross Brazzell	University of Arkansas – Fayetteville
Jeni Hart	University of Missouri
Susan Jones	University of Maryland
Sarah Marshall	Central Michigan University
Sharon McDade	George Washington University
Laura Perna	University of Pennsylvania
Robert Schwartz	Florida State University
Gail Short Hansen	American University
Bette Simmons	County College of Morris
Kathryn Tuttle	University of Kansas
Ed Whipple	Bowling Green State University

Other Reviewers

Elisa Abes	Miami University, Ohio
Elizabeth Allan	University of Maine
Merilyn Amey	Michigan State University
Roger Baldwin	Michigan State University
Bower Beverly	Florida State University
Bonita Butner	University of Missouri – Kansas
Rosa Cintron	University of Central Florida
Julia Colyar	University at Buffalo
Christine Cress	Portland State University
Brad Curs	University of Missouri

John Curtis	AAUP
Zaneeta Daver	NASPA
Joe Donaldson	University of Missouri
Molly Duggan	Old Dominion University
Pamela Eddy	Central Michigan University
Jennifer Fellabaum	University of Missouri
Susan Gardner	University of Maine
Joy Gaston Gayles	North Carolina State University
Judith Glazer Raymo	Columbia University
Seunghee Han	University of Missouri
Casandra Harper	University of Missouri
Rachel Hile-Bassett	Indiana University – Purdue University Fort Wayne
Philo Hutcheson	Georgia State University
Adrienne Hyle	Oklahoma State University
Holley Karri	University of Alabama
Kirsten Kennedy	University of South Carolina
Adrianna Kezar	University of Southern California
Dongbin Kim	University of Kansas
Jillian Kinzie	Indiana University
Jamie Lester	Old Dominion University
Angela Lumpkin	University of Kansas
Amy Metcalfe	University of British Columbia
Melinda Montgomery	University of Kansas
Nana Osei-Kofi	Iowa State University
Ibitola Pearce	University of Missouri
Peggy Placier	University of Missouri
Kate Quinn	University of Washington
Lori Reesor	University of Kansas
Kristen Renn	Michigan State University
Vicki Rosser	University of Nevada, Las Vegas
Elizabeth Rudd	University of Washington
Margaret Sallee	University of Southern California
Juanita Simmons	University of Missouri
Buffy Smith	University of St. Thomas
Robert Toutkoushian	Indiana University
MaryBeth Walpole	Rowan University
Kelly Ward	Washington State University
Lisa Wolf-Wendel	University of Kansas
Mimi Wolverton	University of Nevada, Las Vegas

Editors' Note

NASPA Journal About Women in Higher Education is a scholarly journal published annually. The journal examines issues affecting all women in higher education: students, student affairs staff, faculty, and other administrative groups. Intended for both practitioners and researchers, it includes articles that focus on empirical research, pedagogy, and administrative practice. Designed to increase interest in research about women faculty, students, and administrators in higher education and to highlight current examples of this research, the *NASPA Journal About Women in Higher Education* reflects a variety of paradigms and issues affecting women in higher education in all their diversity.

We are pleased to note that this, the second volume of *NASPA Journal About Women in Higher Education*, begins to fulfill NASPA's hopes for research on women and for the long-term contribution of the journal. As co-editors, we were not sure that after the flood of manuscripts we received for the first volume that there was enough good research on women students, faculty, and administrators to fill a second volume. Thankfully, we were wrong.

This second volume includes cutting-edge research on students, faculty, and administrators—research that one would be hard pressed to find in other journals and that should be of interest to a very broad audience. Annemarie Vaccaro leads this volume with an article based on her study of a new generation of undergraduate feminists. Her article is followed by Barbara Bonnekessen's reflection on her teaching practices. Alicia Fedelina Chávez describes how she actually negotiated her own identity on behalf of students in two positions, as dean of students at a major research university and then as a campus president.

Bridging the gap between students and faculty, Kate Quinn and Elizabeth Litzler report on their study of the influence of work-family issues on graduate student career choices. Venice Thandi Sulé's study of Black female faculty will contribute to our growing understanding of women's experiences in the academy. Much attention has been paid in recent years to issues of work-family balance in U.S. universities. Hae Ja Shin brings an international perspective and data to this discussion that will be of interest to faculty and administrators alike.

The final four articles focus on administrators. Susan Iverson tackles the topic of advancement from clerical to professional positions, while Suzette Compton and Louann Bierlein Palmer report on their study of salary negotiations among women administrators. Sarah Marshall examines the work-family balance issue for administrators—a topic that has received too little research attention, given administrators' extended work hours. Although not about administrators, Mary Pilgram and Joann Keyton write for administrators in their evaluation of campus sexual harassment training programs.

In this second volume we continue the practice of including innovative program descriptions of potential interest for their ability to affect women's lives. Three programs are highlighted: The Alice M. Baldwin Scholars Program at Duke University; the REAL Collaborative, which promotes the advancement of Latinas at the University of Texas at San Antonio; and the Young Women Leaders Program at the University of Virginia. This volume then concludes with reviews of three important new books on women: *Through the Labyrinth: The Truth About How Women Become Leaders,* written by Alice Eagly and Linda Carli and reviewed by Paige Haber; *Challenges of the Faculty Career for Women,* written by Maike Ingrid Philipsen and reviewed by Jeni Hart; and *Unfinished Agendas: New and Continuing Gender Challenges in Higher Education,* edited by Judith Glazer-Raymo and reviewed by Kathryn Moore.

Taken together, the works demonstrate that research on the diversity of women in higher education institutions is alive and well and is moving in interesting and innovative directions. We hope you enjoy the second volume.

Barbara K. Townsend
Professor and Director
Center for Community College Research
University of Missouri – Columbia

Susan B. Twombly
Professor and Chair
Department of Educational Policy
 and Leadership Studies
University of Kansas

January 2009

Third Wave Feminist Undergraduates: Transforming Identities and Redirecting Activism in Response to Institutional Sexism

Annemarie Vaccaro
Assistant Professor
Human Development and Family Studies
University of Rhode Island

This article shares the findings from an 18-month qualitative study of a vibrant, feminist student group at one midsized university in the West. Over the course of the study, the attitudes and behaviors of these women changed significantly as they experienced a chilly campus climate and encountered institutional sexism for the first time in their lives. Their third wave feminist identities transformed from a feminism of the future to the present, from a self-centered perspective to a focus on others, and from campus activism to community action.

Contemporary college undergraduates do not identify as feminists, at least that is what some literature suggests (Bellafante, 1998; Zucker, 2004). Studies show that young women reject the term "feminist" even when they advocate for women's rights (Gittel, Ortega-Bustamante, & Steffy, 2000). Yet, there is a growing body of literature that describes a vibrant, third wave feminist movement (Baumgardner & Richards, 2000; Findlen, 1995, 2001; Hernández & Rehman, 2002; Heywood & Drake, 1997; Walker, 1995). The purpose of this qualitative study was to document the experiences of an undergraduate group of third wave feminists at one midsized university. Feminist case studies are particularly useful in explaining "the process of development over time" (Reinharz, 1992, p. 167). Over an 18-month period, transformations in both the group behavior and the identities of 20 third wave feminists were documented.

LITERATURE REVIEW

North American feminism is often separated into three waves, or movements, with the first beginning in the late 1800s and lasting through suffrage, while the second wave had its height in the social movements of the 1960s and 1970s (Kezar & Lester, 2008; Taylor, Whittier, & Pelak, 2001). Even though most of the third wave literature focuses on the stories and experiences of young women who came of age in the 1980s and 1990s, some scholars argue that third wave sentiments and perspectives may be adopted by women of any age (Henry, 2004). For the purposes of this study, I focus on the third wave feminism of traditional age undergraduates.

Offering one concise definition or description of contemporary third wave feminism is nearly impossible, as third wave literature consists of a kaleidoscope of individual women's stories. However, these narratives reveal a number of consistent themes—three of which are described here. First, Findlen (2001) argues that third wave feminists did not create a new feminism, totally separate from their second wave mothers, but instead built upon their ideas, successes, and challenges to create a feminism that best met their needs. Heywood and Drake (1997) define third wave feminism as "a movement that contains elements of second wave critique of beauty, culture, sexual abuse, and power structures while it also acknowledges and makes use of the pleasure, danger, and defining power of those structures" (p. 3). Conversely, in her review of third wave literature, Henry (2004) argues that third wave identity is based not on continuation of second wave ideas, but instead upon a critique and disidentification with second wave feminism. Rebecca Walker, daughter of a famous second wave mother, believes that at the root of this disidentification are young women's fears that they will not measure up to what they believe is the second wave "strictly defined and all-encompassing feminist identity" (1995, p. xxxii). In short, the first prominent theme points to conflicting ideas about the relationship between second and third wave feminism.

A second theme in third wave literature is women's desire to be themselves, as individuals. Henry (2004) argues that third-wavers "want a shared connection through feminism, but they want their freedom and individuality too" (p. 42). The third wave desire for a feminist identity rooted in individuality is somewhat explained by generational research that reveals Generation Xers (or 13th generation) as fiercely independent and Millennials as somewhat focused on self (Howe & Strauss, 2003; Strauss & Howe, 1991). Overall, third wave literature is less about collective identities, than it is about women's pursuit of a feminism that meets their individual needs.

The third theme is that young feminists, especially third wave feminists of color, believe multiple identities are central to one's being. In her introduction to *Colonize This!,* an anthology of young feminists of color, Cherrie Moraga (2002) observes feminism for young women of color "requires cultural tradition invention (and) negotiating multiple worlds" (p. xiii). Third wave women of color write about complex and intersecting identities and their negotiation of these worlds (Hernández & Rehman, 2002). White third wave feminists purport to recognize, even more than their second wave predecessors, the vast diversity among women. However, some young feminists of color are weary of talk by White feminists without simultaneous recognition of their race privilege (Takagi, 1997). The complex nature of intersecting identities may be more or less of a reality for women with differential access to privilege, especially race privilege. Indeed talk of multiple identities is more prevalent in works written by women of color than White women.

Because of the complexity and individualistic nature of the third wave agenda, some authors suggest that a singular or simplistic third wave feminist identity may not actually exist (Gillis, Howie, & Munford, 2004; Johnson, 2003; Orr, 1997; Sowards & Renegar, 2004). Indeed, postmodernist feminism would problemitize the notion of a single category of feminists, or a uniform feminist identity. This is because women have such diverse experiences, especially in their access to power and privilege. It could be inferred that if third wave women cannot rally around a common identity, it is unlikely that they will engage in collective activism. However, some scholars suggest women's diverse needs and passions can be harnessed for the sake of group activism (Boonin, 2003; Heywood & Drake, 1997; Neuborne, 1995). Heywood and Drake (1997) suggest that "by using (women's) experiences as a starting point, we (third wave feminists) can create a diverse community and cultivate a meaningful response (to sexism)" (p. 7).

Instead of the collective action of the second wave feminist movement, Neuborne (1995) claims third wave feminists spend their daily lives doing everyday things to fight social injustice. She claims that theory was crafted and debated by their second wave feminist mothers and it is time for third wave feminists to act. Neuborne argues, "Now, let's talk about how to talk, how to work, and how to fight sexism here on the ground, in our lives" (p. 558). In her review of third wave literature, Catherine Orr (1997) concludes that young feminist communities may be radically different than those of the past, with more of a community presence in cyberspace than physical presence on campus. Given Orr's findings, have traditional forms of feminist activism disappeared from college campuses, or has feminist activism merely changed in form?

With the exception of Rhoads' (1998) discussion of the Mills College strike in 1990, the literature on campus women's groups dates back to the 1970s and is tied to the second wave of the women's movement (Cherniss, 1972; Farley 1970; Vollmer, 1974). Although historically significant, these studies do not shed light upon third wave activism on contemporary college campuses. A small body of recent literature describes student activism through women's studies courses, yet this research does not address women's collective activism outside of specific classroom assignments (Dean, 2007; Moane, 2006; Stake & Hoffman, 2000, 2001).

Lack of research on campus women's groups is surprising, given the power of consciousness-raising groups in the second wave of the women's movement and the empirical studies from the 1990s that show connections between feminist identity, feminist consciousness, and women's activism (Crosby, Todd, & Worell, 1996; Duncan, 1999; Kelly & Breinlinger, 1995). Additionally, higher education literature is replete with research about the importance of extracurricular campus involvement for student satisfaction, engagement, and success (Astin, 1984, 1993; Kuh, 2003). If collective activism is a hallmark of feminism, and involvement in campus groups is central to a traditionally engaged university experience, surely feminist groups exist on college campuses. Lack of documentation about such groups inspired an 18-month study of a vibrant, feminist, activist group at one midsized university in the West.

METHODOLOGY

Feminist methodology was used as a framework for this study, as it uses gender as a basic category of analysis, values the experiences of women, and recognizes women's behavior in the context of social settings (Hesse-Biber, Leavy, & Yaiser, 2004; Reinharz, 1992). The focus of this study was a third wave feminist, undergraduate group at one midsized university in the West. The Women's Undergraduate Group (WUG) was a university-recognized student group open to undergraduate women of any major. Archival records showed the group had been in existence for more than a decade.

The demographics of the group were as follows: 17 White, one Black, one Latina, and one Indian American woman. Four of the 20 women identified as lesbians or bisexuals at some point in the study. At the beginning of the study, the group was comprised of five first-year students, five sophomores, seven juniors, and three seniors. Women had a variety of majors including: communication, business, sociology, anthropology, and women's studies. By the end of the study each group member had taken at least one women's studies course.

Case study method was used in this research project. "A case study is an exploration of a bounded system or case over time through detailed, in-depth data collection involving multiple sources of information rich in context" (Creswell, 1998, p. 61). Reinharz (1992) argues that case studies are "essential for putting women on the map of social life" (p. 174). My hope is that this study will put one feminist group (and potentially other activist groups) on the radar screen of student affairs practitioners.

A case study must have clear boundaries in terms of time and location (Asmussen & Creswell, 1995). This case was bounded by a single campus location and group membership over a study period of 18-months. The study began in August and ended in January of the following academic year. Case study design works well when studying unique (or undocumented) phenomenon, such as a third wave feminist group on a college campus.

Data were collected via three venues: document analysis, individual interviews, and direct observations of group meetings and events. Group artifacts such as flyers, meeting minutes, and other relevant documents were reviewed as background material and provided historical and cultural context for the group. Access was granted to the WUG Listserve where members shared information, sent meeting reminders, posted minutes, and encouraged peers to attend various events. Occasionally, women shared personal experiences on the Listserv.

A large portion of the data for this paper was gleaned from in-depth interviews and participant observations. Trust and safety are paramount to feminist research. Before the study began, all the WUG members approved my observation at meetings and events. As a student affairs practitioner who held both administrative and part-time women's studies faculty roles at the institution, I built trusting relationships and used reflexivity to diffuse the power differentials between myself as the researcher, and the students as participants (Denzin & Lincoln, 1998).

I engaged in observation for the entire length of the study. A total of 78 hours of observation were completed: 48 hours at weekly meetings and 30 hours at group-sponsored events. In line with the feminist perspective of reciprocity, as the researcher, I offered my time and assistance to the feminist group under study. This included helping the group set up and clean up after meetings, taking tickets at events, and serving as an usher at a theatrical performance of the *Vagina Monologues*.

All members of the WUG were invited to engage in one, in-depth interview. Nine of the 20 members chose to participate in the interviews, which lasted between 60 and 90 minutes. It is important to note that the nine participants comprised the core group of women who consistently attended meetings, whereas the remaining 11 women subscribed to the Listserve and sporadically attended events. The racial backgrounds of the nine women who completed interviews were: seven White, one Indian American, and one Black woman. Interviewees also represented a mix of class years from first through senior.

Data Analysis

While this work is not presented in narrative format, narrative analysis was used to analyze the women's interview data. Narrative analysis has been described as "a placeholder for different ways of conceptualizing the storied nature of human development" (Daiute & Lightfoot, 2004). One of the strengths of narrative analysis is that it allows a researcher to holistically explore a person's identity, relationships, and emotions, all within a larger cultural and social context (Daiute & Lightfoot, 2004; Reismann, 1993). Hence, it was very useful for uncovering ways individual women's experiences intersected with the overall women's group, and with the larger university structure.

While narrative analysis allowed me to hear women's stories in a genuine manner, observation allowed me to "fill the inevitable gap between experience . . . and (women's) communication about it" (Reismann, 1993, p. 10). Similar to most qualitative methods, observation data were analyzed by a systematic coding of texts (Creswell, 1998). These codes were then used to cross-analyze and code the women's narratives. Three types of coding were used in this study (Creswell, 1998; Strauss & Corbin, 1998). First, open coding was used to determine initial themes of which there were 23. Second, axial coding provided interconnections between the themes such as: unique foci of feminist identity, time orientation, activism efforts, and activism locations. Finally, selective coding helped craft the formation of a model of feminist transformation presented in the next section and summarized in Figure 1.

FINDINGS

THIRD WAVE FEMINISM: IT'S ALL ABOUT ME AND MY FUTURE

The women's definitions of and identification with feminism varied as the third wave literature suggests (Gillis, Howie, & Munford, 2004; Johnson, 2003; Orr, 1997; Sowards & Renegar, 2004). However, through the women's stories, a unique image of third wave feminist activism emerged, one that evolved over the course of 18 months. At the beginning of the study, WUG participant definitions of feminism were a mix of traditional feminist concepts, third wave writings, and a host of other topics. However, the women's perspectives on feminism changed over the course of this study as they experienced a chilly climate and institutional sexism in response to their campus activism. At the beginning of the study, emergent themes included: individualistic perspectives on feminism, a futuristic time orientation, and a desire to engage in campus activism.

A Feminism of "Me"

During initial meetings and group events, undergraduate women talked about feminism in a very individualistic sense. Certainly, second wave feminists lived the idea of the "personal is political." But second wave feminists used that phrase to show the sexism individuals faced was part of a larger pattern of societal injustice toward women. The reverse seemed to be true for this group of young feminists. All but one of the 18- to 21-year-old women could not initially describe personal experiences with sexism. They were told stories of sexism by their mothers, aunts, and teachers, but never recognized or experienced it themselves. Nevertheless, their feminism was highly personal and focused on self. It was all about "me."

At the beginning of the study, when asked what feminism meant to them, WUG members gave highly personal definitions. For many women like Terry, feminism allowed them to be themselves.

> I don't think there are the feminist police, like you have to be a certain way to be a feminist. You can do whatever. It's really open.

Most women felt supported in their "personalized" pursuit of feminism. However, there were rare occasions when a woman felt feminism did not truly include everything. For instance, there were times when Erin had to rebel against fellow WUG members. She complained:

> A lot of the girls say, 'Oh you just want to be a housewife.' They feel like I'm limiting my possibilities; but that's what I want to do, and I think that is what my feminism is about.

Nevertheless, Erin continued to follow her individualistic path of feminism.

Janet described her entrée into feminism as a recent personal revolution related to her internal struggles with self-esteem. Janet's self-esteem was connected not only to her WUG leadership position, but also to other people's recognition of her success in that role.

> I have always had trouble with self-esteem and issues and I'm always so hard on myself, but this year . . . I'm proud of myself . . . and . . . how much of a leader I am now . . . [and] people recognize that.

Finally, Kallie was the sole member who talked about a personal experience with gender violence. It shaped both her ideas about feminism and reason for joining the group. She said:

> My desires are selfish and personal. I use [the group] as a way, after being victimized as a woman . . . to overcome those feelings to find support and strength in other women who are very empowered themselves.

When probed to talk more deeply about why they were feminists, only Kallie could talk about a personal experience with overt sexism.

While WUG women's sense of individualism fits nicely with third wave literature, their lack of recognition of multiple identities does not. While third wave literature stresses the significance of multiple and intersecting identities, I found the women in this study lacked such a focus. Through their narratives and behavior, it seemed like their identities as women (narrowly defined) were most salient. Callero (1985) argues that "when a role identity is salient, it is most representative of the self, and consequently one's self-definition will more likely reflect salient role identities." Indeed, the women's most salient identity was that of being a woman.

Certainly, cross membership of WUG members in the Gay-Straight Alliance suggests that these women were aware of the cross-cutting relationships of gender and sexual orientation, but issues of race and class went unacknowledged. Whiteness and class privilege were rarely recognized, especially by White WUG members. Instead, the women focused on the chilly climate and sexism they experienced without regard to race, class, or other identities. One of the contributing factors to their focus on a single identity may have been the group's connection to a women's studies department that encouraged women to bond together as women and sisters, without acknowledgement of multiple identities or women's differential access to privilege and power.

Feminism for My Future

In addition to their focus on the single identity of "me," another key aspect of WUG identity was their focus on the future. All of the interview participants talked abstractly about their desire to live in a future where they would not be held back as women. Their fear of the future, instead of their present or past experiences, inspired their feminism. For Sally, feminism was rebelling against potential barriers that might stop her from being who she wanted to be someday in the future.

> My feminism is about not stopping because I'm a girl. Not putting limits on myself, arbitrary limits, because of my chromosomal make up. . . . It's about not being afraid to speak up, and it's about fighting against all of these arbitrary rules that have been in place for so long.

While she had not yet encountered such rules, Sally believed she would someday.

For other WUG members, feminism was about having the opportunity to seek the specific career of their dreams in a future world of work where sexism would no longer exist. Jillian shared:

> I should not be allowed to be anywhere just because I'm a woman. I am intelligent enough and strong enough to hold any position. I could be a CEO or a teacher or whatever I want to be without being stigmatized for being a woman.

Like Jillian, Theresa was not sure of her career path, but it was obvious that she desperately wanted to "get paid equally" for the work she would do in the future. Anna, however, had her heart set on a future career in law.

I really want equality . . . With my possible dreams of going to law school knowing that I'll be treated the same as the men. Knowing that I'll be having the same education. . . . You know, education in law school is geared more towards men. I don't see why I should be excluded. I want equal pay for equal work, not just a theory, but an actual practice.

In sum, women described their feminism as highly personal. But, such personal notions of feminism were not rooted in lived experiences with gender discrimination. For most WUG members, their feminism was inspired by an eye toward their future. They were feminists today, so they could be treated equally in the future.

Third Wave Activism: Inside and Outside the Ivory Tower

Readers might conclude that with such highly personal, but futuristic definitions of feminism, WUG might struggle to engage in present-day, feminist activism. Yet, activism was part of the women's identity development as third wave feminists. When WUG women described, and the researcher observed, group activism, a fascinating pattern emerged. Early in the study, WUG women identified a number of health and safety issues on campus and worked to eradicate them, usually with little success. Archival and group advertising revealed the main goals of the group in the first year of the study as: focusing on health and safety, education and classroom issues, and women's empowerment on campus. Only when those campus activist efforts failed, did their sense of feminist identity and activism turn outward: outside themselves and outside the university.

Patriarchy Experienced Firsthand: University Bureaucracy and Institutional Sexism

Not long into the study, WUG women began to experience what they perceived to be present-day examples of sexism. Young women, who initially described feminism for their future, learned all too quickly what institutional sexism looked and felt like. At the meetings and in individual interviews, women argued that the university could easily accommodate their requests to increase women's health and safety on campus. Since WUG believed their requests would have been relatively easy to accomplish and inexpensive to the institution, they were forced to accept the idea that university rejection was a form of institutional sexism.

Anna specifically argued that other groups, especially those with predominately male members, were recognized and respected by the administration. She and her WUG peers felt the campus climate was warm for men, but chilly for women.

> I think they would be more responsive of men. I think a lot of it is (that we are) a women's group. I mean a year and a half to get garbage disposals in the bathroom was ridiculous! I mean it takes nothing. We [even] offered to go buy garbage pans or garbage pails and just sit them in there. That really bothers me.

Rejection was especially painful when WUG offered to cover the costs of their own requests, as with the sanitary disposals in women's restrooms. As the study progressed, seemingly small things like having tampon dispensers in restrooms became insurmountable obstacles mired in university bureaucracy. WUG members lamented that the university administration, comprised of men, rarely considered women's needs when making structural decisions. Terri asked:

> How long did it take to get tampon disposal things in the bathrooms? Good God! That's just, that's messed up. And then the fact that in the student center bathrooms, there is a condom machine, but there aren't any tampon or pad machines. Personally I would rather have a tampon or a pad than a condom. Male architects . . . come on! Help us out!

When women were specifically asked if they personally felt supported by the university, they provided a host of very animated responses. Many women, like Zoie, believed rhetoric from the university was nothing more than words to appease WUG.

> They might be somewhat responsive, but I think it takes a really long time for them to respond. If we are asking for anything that has to do with money or actual objects it's really hard to get them to be supportive. But if we're just asking for ideology, yeah they'll support this and yeah, they'll support that!

By ignoring seemingly simple requests, the university confirmed WUGs lowly status as a group of women. Tina remarked:

> We have gone to the chancellor about 100,000 times and he still won't do anything. . . . I feel like they are not out to make us feel like

we are a really super important group. . . . I feel like we're half of the population and we probably don't get half of the importance.

Lack of success in their activist efforts weighed heavy on the hearts and minds of these young feminists, especially when safety issues hit close to home. Janet was frustrated with the inability to travel across campus safely in the evening, saying "the whole saferide situation [is frustrating] because the schedules are secret and . . . it is hard to use." Women's frustration was heightened by a gang rape that allegedly happened on campus, but was never included in the university crime reports. Theresa explained:

> I am very upset [that] I found out about the rape that occurred in my dorm . . . I was even more upset by how the university handled it. . . . One of our (WUG) members overheard some administrative member talking [about a] cover up. NO! I think the university needs to tell people about it . . . so young women, we can empower ourselves and be informed and know how to make choices to protect ourselves. And I think that the statistics about sexual assault that happen on and around campus need to be more accurate and better publicized. You know, to be safe.

Not only did the women perceive the university administration to be secretive and unsupportive, but WUG also faced rejection and lack of support from others on campus.

Rejection from Other Women on Campus

In the course of the study, WUG sought the support from other women-only groups on campus. Specifically, 9 months into the study, three sorority presidents attended a WUG meeting to discuss potential collaboration on a take-back-the-night rally. When the sorority guests said that they would not commit to official plans until they got approval and support from their Greek brother fraternities, Becky exploded.

> I don't give a damn if men want to be there or support us. Why the *%$! do you need the approval of men to work for the women's safety!

As her frustration was echoed by other WUG members, the sorority members excused themselves and left the meeting, never to return. Alas, peer support, even from other female students, was low.

One place where WUG women expected to gain support was from

the university staff group for women. Theresa described the response from that women's group when WUG requested support for a first-ever, *Vagina Monologues* production.

> Representatives from the group were kind of . . . I don't want to say taken aback, but they weren't the first to jump in and say 'oh we'll help you do this' and 'we'll help you do that.'

Lack of, or lukewarm, support from other women on campus added to WUG's frustration. They used defense mechanisms, such as sarcasm and humor, to deal with the perpetuation of sexism, the lack of acceptable responses from the university, and the absence of support from other women on campus. Sarah said, "I don't joke around all of the time but I try to make it fun if we're all gloomy."

Forget the Academy: Fighting Injustice Outside the Ivory Tower

Instead of feeling consistently hopeless, WUG women took their energy, passion, and feminist activism outside the university. They refused to be activist failures! They wanted their feminist passion to mean something, so they engaged in a number of events to fight sexism outside of the Ivory Tower. The success of the *Vagina Monologues* and the pleasure women gained from volunteering at a women's shelter inspired a change in both the women's activist behaviors and their feminist identities. Their feminism became less about "me" and more about their felt connection to women locally and globally.

At a meeting 9 months into the study, WUG women were asked which WUG events or activities were most meaningful to them. First and foremost, participants talked about the *Vagina Monologues.* Paige explained that the *Monologues* were "a great example of getting the whole community involved." Yet, in this case, the whole community excluded most of the university community. Even though a small number of university members attended the *Monologues,* WUG women were incredibly proud of producing a successful performance. The *Vagina Monologues* provided a venue for women to exhibit their third wave feminist identity and connect, in spirit, to feminists around the world who also participated in similar productions. Equally as important, WUG members felt like successful activists, as they raised more than $1,000 for a local women's organization. Unlike their campus activism, which was unsupported by the university administration or other campus groups, the *Vagina Monologues* drew attendees from across the city. Community members donated not only money, but also vast amounts of praise to the young activists. Accolades from the nonuniversity community renewed their spirits and gave them a sense of pride in their feminist achievements.

Over the course of the study, WUG members became quite disconnected from the university. In their excitement about the Vagina Monologues production, they failed to heed a policy about registering "community" events on campus. Since the production was not considered a campus program, but a community event, official approval was required. After the performance, Charmaine, the WUG president, stated a university official:

> brought to their advisor's attention that we had not asked permission. . . . [But] no one stopped us from doing it. That would kind of be funny to see it if they were to try and stop us!

Embedded in Charmaine's comments was an underlying resentment of the unsupportive university administration. Underneath her anger was sadness; even in the glory of a successful production, the university administration used their power to remind the WUG of not just university policies, but also their place in the hierarchy. Charmaine wondered if the fraternities who violated university policies were treated similarly.

A second activity that most of the women were proud of was volunteering at a local women's shelter. Once a week, WUG members carpooled downtown to cook and serve meals to homeless women and children. Women agreed that purchasing food, which they then donated to the shelter, was a good use of their budget; even if it was against the university spending rules. In this case, as with the *Vagina Monologue* production registration, violation of university rules became a form of feminist resistance to perceived sexism in campus administration. Gilligan, Rodgers, and Tolman (1991) describe resistance as "psychological strength, as a potentially healthy mark of courage" (p. 2). WUG women were tired and drained from covert and overt forms of university oppression. By the end of the study, covert resistance such as diverting funds to the community was the most campus activism WUG engaged in. Such behavior was their version of resistance (Gilligan et al., 1991) or outrageous acts and everyday rebellion (Steinem, 1984). In her research with marginalized women, Trethewey (1997) found that a key element to women's resistance was their ability to redefine themselves. In effect, that is what many of the WUG members did. Instead of taking on identities as campus activist failures, these women redefined their identities to be feminists who supported their sisters locally and globally.

Transformations in Third Wave Feminist Identity

Women's identity transformations were directly tied to the changes in group behavior. At the beginning of the study, WUG documents and publicity talked about goals of campus safety and education, which went largely unfulfilled. Conversely, success in providing meals at the shelter and producing the *Vagina Monologues* inspired WUG women to continue their feminist fight off campus. By the end of the first academic year, both individual members, and the group itself, found outlets for their feminist activism in local organizations such as Planned Parenthood and The National Abortion Rights League. Through their volunteer experiences, WUG members connected with women activists in the local community, something they rarely did inside the university.

Since this study spanned 2 academic years, I had the opportunity to see WUG recruitment in August of the second academic year. WUG publicity looked markedly different than it did in the previous academic year. WUG now described itself as a group of feminist activists fighting for local and international justice. Their success at the local shelter and hosting the *Vagina Monologues* (an international phenomenon) inspired returning members to construct a group that met their needs, interests, and emerging feminist identities.

Cortazzi (1993) suggests that sociologically informed narrative analysis can draw attention to ways in which stories arise in interaction and are often . . . jointly produced by several people" (p. 3). Women's narratives revealed identities that were changing from an individualistic one focused on "me" to a more collective feminist identity. While women initially described their feminism as all about them and their own futures, women's perspectives were quite different a year later. WUG women now described their identity in terms of fighting sexism for all women, instead of merely doing it for themselves.

Three themes emerged in the women's newfound collective identities. First, women described sexism as a national and international issue, affecting women around the globe, not just themselves. Patti shared:

> I think patriarchy is a very big problem . . . we are still so far away, and yet my generation doesn't see that. . . . I'd really like to tackle those global issues.

Like Patti, many of the young women believed local and international activism was foundational to their third wave identity. While initially activism meant making campus change, a year later activism was steered toward the global problem of sexism. Even the WUG literature changed to reflect this. A recruitment flyer distributed in the second academic year described WUG as:

> a group of women . . . very strong minded and determined women out to make a difference, out to bring a little more justice to gender.

In short, WUG women's identity transformed to include a more global view of what it meant to be a "successful" feminist. By looking beyond the Ivory Tower, women changed more than their behavior, they changed their feminist identities.

The second theme is that women sought a feminist identity rooted in care for others. Women's newfound identities were about supporting other women in the community. They were becoming empowered to think beyond "me." Women described themselves and their group by saying things like, "we're a feminist group and we try to help people." Compassion for others manifested itself in their work in the local community. WUG women also felt a connection to the feminists who had come before them. Anna shared:

> I'm still trying to figure out my feminist identity but I think it is working towards equality for all people . . . and remembering women who have worked before us. . . . We still have a long way to go.

Through their local activism, women were able to see themselves as successful feminist activists who cared for their sisters in the local and global community. Like Anna, some women were still trying to figure out exactly what global, feminist activism looked like. Amanda described herself and peers as "a lot of really intelligent and inspiring young women . . . just hanging out trying to figure out what we can do as part of the third wave." Her identity, like those of her peers was rooted in "what we can do" for other women.

WUG's desire to be seen as successful activists speaks volumes about the interconnections between their activist behaviors and identities. Indeed, I found they could not be understood separately. In short, activist success and care for others were essential to their transformed feminist identities. Rhonda described this phenomenon eloquently when she shared:

> I think it is so important for people my age to get out there . . . I never knew how empowering activism can be. It really is. It really, like, puts a little light in your heart.

For Rhonda, third wave feminist identity was synonymous with "a little light" in her heart. The light in her heart, and those of her peers, was inspired by care for other women through successful activism.

A Model of Transformation of Third Wave Feminist Identity

Findings from this study reveal important information about third wave, feminist identities and activism. Narrative analysis combined with 18 months of observation revealed complex interplay between personal identity, experiences with sexism, and feminist activism.

The meaning and study of "identity" is complex and spans many disciplines. Yet, identity development is a cornerstone of student affairs. To make meaning of women's experiences and identities, I relied on different notions of identity at different stages of the study. At the outset of the study, symbolic interactionist (microsociology) perspectives on identity (Cerulo, 1997) informed the analysis. That school of thought, informed by sociologists like Cooley and Meade, focuses on how human-to-human interactions shape a person's sense of self. At the beginning of the study women described a "feminism of me." Many women described their feminism as highly personal, even though only one WUG member shared a lived experience with sexism. Toward the middle of the study, I observed that the women's experiences became less about "me" and more about a collective identity. Hence, ideas of socially constructed identities became salient. This change occurred when women began to band together around their collective experience with sexism in the Ivory Tower, and it continued as they engaged in community activism.

WUG's transformed feminist identity can be understood through a postmodern feminist lens—that which aims at "exposing and transforming oppressive power relations" in the social hierarchy (Hesse-Biber, Leavy, & Yaiser, 2004, p. 19). Initially, the study sought to document the activity of a feminist activist group, but issues of feminist identity emerged as the young women experienced institutional sexism and a chilly campus climate. Intensely personal campus health and safety issues like night lighting, safe-ride shuttles, and tampon disposals in women's restrooms were things that affected women individually as well as collectively. When WUG began to advocate for women's health and safety on campus, they felt an immediate and all-encompassing rejection from the university. Alas, sexism had become real and present. In their quest to counter sexist campus practices, WUG members felt ignored by individual administrators who refused to listen, peers who did not care, and other women on campus who were hesitant to support radical young feminists. Institutional sexism, steeped in what participants perceived to be an oppressive university hierarchy, became central to the study. Sexism within the Ivory Tower became foundational to understanding both the feminist identities and activist efforts of study participants.

These young feminists learned about the complexity of social injustice perpetrated by an institution of higher education. Sowards and Renegar (2004) suggest that young women who grew up believing that they were equal (or treated equally) may be "ill-equipped to deal with discrimination when confronted with it" (p. 539). In some ways WUG women were ill-equipped to deal with sexism at their institution. But, instead of letting failure on campus discourage their activism, WUG members altered their feminist tactics. While they engaged in some forms of feminist resistance on campus, they mostly refocused their feminist activism outside the Ivory Tower.

As opposed to getting burned out or giving up, WUG members directed their feminist passion off campus. Through community action, namely the *Vagina Monologues* and volunteering at a local women's shelter, WUG members continued their quest for feminist activism. In their community activism, women found new identities, ones rooted in collective action for the good of all women, not merely for themselves. In summary, this study highlights the phenomenon of women's third wave feminism transformed from feminism of the future to the present, from a focus on self to others, and from campus activism to community action. A visual image of this transformation is represented in Figure 1.

SUGGESTIONS FOR PRACTITIONERS

Student engagement and involvement (Astin, 1984, 1993; Kuh, 2003) are central to the field of student affairs. Students who are engaged in their education build "the foundation of skills and dispositions that are essential to live a productive, satisfying life after college" (Kuh, 2003, p. 25). Engagement, as Kuh and others define it, includes activities inside and outside the classroom. The goal of supporting feminist activists provides a perfect opportunity for student affairs professionals

Figure 1. Third wave feminist identity transformation.

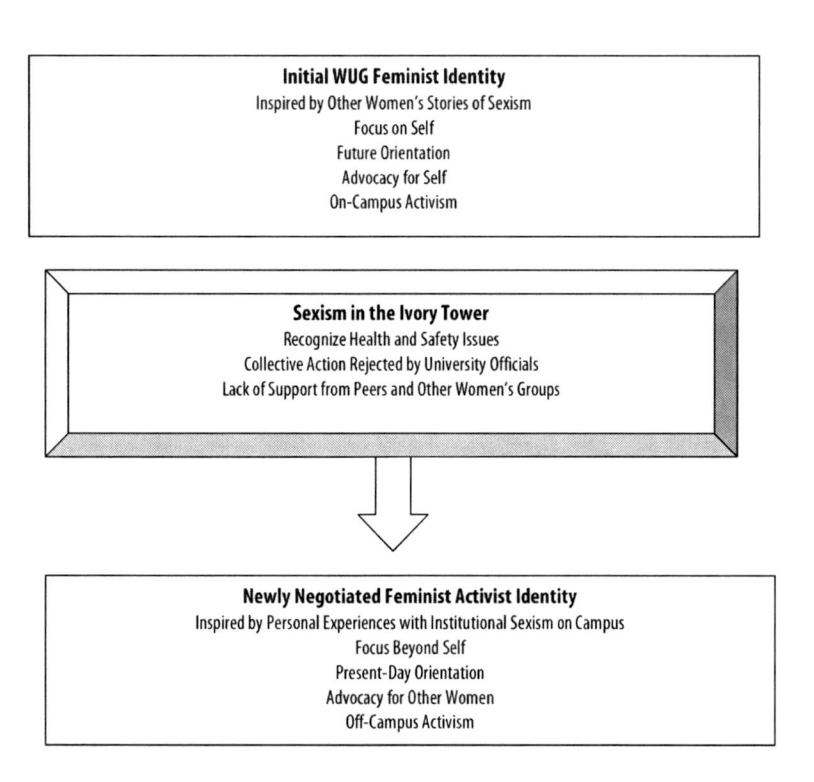

```
┌─────────────────────────────────────────────────┐
│          Initial WUG Feminist Identity          │
│     Inspired by Other Women's Stories of Sexism │
│                  Focus on Self                  │
│               Future Orientation                │
│               Advocacy for Self                 │
│              On-Campus Activism                 │
└─────────────────────────────────────────────────┘

┌─────────────────────────────────────────────────┐
│           Sexism in the Ivory Tower             │
│        Recognize Health and Safety Issues       │
│   Collective Action Rejected by University Officials │
│   Lack of Support from Peers and Other Women's Groups │
└─────────────────────────────────────────────────┘
                        ▼
┌─────────────────────────────────────────────────┐
│      Newly Negotiated Feminist Activist Identity │
│ Inspired by Personal Experiences with Institutional Sexism on Campus │
│               Focus Beyond Self                 │
│             Present-Day Orientation             │
│            Advocacy for Other Women             │
│              Off-Campus Activism                │
└─────────────────────────────────────────────────┘
```

to build bridges between academic and student affairs: a prominent goal of student affairs. Only by bridging this divide can student services professionals understand feminist curriculum and third wave activist efforts. Student affairs practitioners may find it incredibly useful to learn the ways women's studies faculty inspire feminist activism in classrooms, on campus, and through service-learning in the local community. Knowing such efforts only prepares practitioners to better understand the experiences and developmental needs of feminist students in residence halls, student organizations, judicial hearings, or other student affairs settings.

Additionally, student affairs practitioners can play an essential role in helping students navigate and resist sexist practices both on and off campus. First, however, practitioners must show students they are approachable and trustworthy. The most disheartening finding from this study was WUG's lack of communication with the division of student affairs. The few interactions WUG had with student affairs practitioners were not very positive. Not only were those practitioners seen by WUG as part of the bureaucracy, but they were also not considered feminist supporters. WUG felt the only people who truly understood their feminist perspectives were the women's studies faculty who spoke the language of feminism.

Women's refusal to seek support in student affairs suggests that, while student affairs graduate programs require certain levels of "multicultural competence" (Pope, Reynolds, & Mueller, 2004), such education may not suffice. For the sake of time, complex issues of gender, sexism, and feminism, may be omitted from student affairs preparatory programs. If practitioners do not adequately understand such issues, they may not be perceived by third wave feminists as useful or approachable resources. To be effective practitioners, student affairs staff should become familiar with feminism in general, and third wave feminism in particular. Learning about feminism can occur through: feminist program sessions at national and regional NASPA conferences, National Women's Studies Association conferences, reading third wave literature, or through dialogue with feminist faculty and staff.

Only when student affairs practitioners learn how to recognize sexism, can they effectively assist students in navigating sexist policies and practices on campus. As are many forms of modern-day oppression, sexism can be difficult to recognize, especially for practitioners with privilege. The following list of questions may be helpful to practitioners who want to resist sexism on campus. While it is not an all-inclusive list, it is a place to begin conversations about institutional sexism.

1. Does your campus literature, such as the code of conduct, use gender-inclusive language?

2. What are the images in your publications? Do they objectify women?

3. Who are the people in power in your division? Do female students see any powerful women role models on campus? How are those role models treated and respected by the university?

4. Are there basic safety features such as emergency lights and safe-ride shuttles? Do women have input into the placement of safety devices? What else do women need to feel safe? How often are they asked?

5. What health services, programs, and resources are available to women? How accessible are they? Do women students have input into health programs and services?

6. Are overtly sexist programs and events, such as "auction a date" supported? Does the university sponsor performers who use sexist remarks or images? Who selects campus performers? Have those individuals had any antisexist training?

7. How does your office, division, or university respond to claims of sexual harassment, rape, or sexism in decision making?

8. Do men, women, and transgender students receive differential treatment in campus offices?

The answers to some of these questions may uncover sexism at various levels of an institution. No matter what their student affairs position, staff members have more access to decision-making structures than students do. Being effective allies to young feminists means using our positions of power to make change at our institutions (Broido & Reason, 2005). By using positional power to make feminist-friendly decisions, student affairs practitioners can warm the chilly climate for women students.

Equally, if not more important, than answering the aforementioned questions is listening to women when they voice concerns about sexism. Whether practitioners see an issue, event, or policy as sexist or not, it is our duty to explore the issues students bring to our attention. The women in this study felt the university did not listen to their concerns. The institution's inaction to their pleas for increased health programs and safety devices had detrimental effects on the women's trust in their university. Listening to women and validating their concerns is among the most basic, but effective responses student affairs practitioners can offer. No matter how small something seems to administrators, nonresponse is never the answer. Findings from this study show that university inaction on a number of seemingly small requests amounted to an overwhelming pattern of rejection for women. Finally, after truly listening to women's concerns, student affairs practitioners have a responsibility to help students navigate the university hierarchy.

REFERENCES

Astin, A. W. (1984). Student involvement: A developmental theory for higher education. *Journal of College Student Personnel, 25,* 297–308.

Astin, A. W. (1993). *What matters in college: Four critical years revisited.* San Francisco: Jossey-Bass.

Asmussen, K. J., & Creswell, J. W. (1995). Campus response to a student gunman. *Journal of Higher Education, 66,* 575–591.

Bellafante, G. (1998, June 29). Feminism: It's all about me! *Time, 15,* 54–60.

Baumgardner, J., & Richards, A. (2000). *Manifesta: Young women, feminism, and the future.* New York: Farrar, Straus, and Giroux.

Broido, E. M., & Reason, R. D. (2005, Summer). The development of social justice attitudes and actions: An overview of current understandings. In R. D. Reason, E. M. Broido, T. L. Davis, & N. J. Evans (Eds.), *Developing social justice allies. New Directions for Student Services,* no. 110 (pp. 17–28). San Francisco: Jossey-Bass.

Callero, P. (1985). Role-identity salience. *Social Psychology Quarterly, 48*(3), 203–215.

Cerulo, K. A. (1997). Identity construction: New issues, new directions. *Annual Review of Sociology, 23,* 385–409.

Cherniss, C. (1972). Personality and Ideology: A personological study of women's liberation. *Psychiatry, 35,* 109–122.

Cortazzi, M. (1993). *Narrative analysis.* London, England: Falmer Press.

Creswell, J. W. (1998). *Qualitative inquiry and research design: Choosing among five traditions.* Thousand Oaks, CA: Sage.

Crosby, F., Todd, J., & Worell, J. (1996). Have feminists abandoned social activism? In L. Montada & M. Lerner (Eds.), *Current societal concerns about justice: Critical issues in social justice* (pp. 85–102). New York: Plenum.

Daiute, C., & Lightfoot, C. (Eds.) (2004). *Narrative analysis: Studying the development of individuals in society.* Thousand Oaks, CA: Sage.

Dean, A. (2007). Teaching feminist activism: Reflections on an activism assignment in introductory women's studies. *Review of Education, 29*(4), 351–369.

Denzin, N., & Lincoln, Y. S. (1998). *The landscape of qualitative research: Theories and issues.* Thousand Oaks, CA: Sage.

Duncan, L. (1999). Motivation for collective action: Group consciousness as mediator of personality, life experiences, and women's rights activism. *Political Psychology, 20,* 611–635.

Farley, J. T. (1970). *Women on the march again: The rebirth of feminism in an academic community.* Unpublished Doctoral Dissertation, Cornell University, New York.

Findlen, B. (1995, 2001). *Listen up: Voices from the next feminist generation.* New York: Seal Press.

Gilligan, C., Rodgers, A. G., & Tolman, D. L. (1991). *Women, girls & psychotherapy: Reframing resistance.* New York: Haworth.

Gillis, S., Howie, G., & Munford, R. (2004). *Third wave feminism: A critical exploration.* New York: Palgrave MacMillian.

Gittel, M., Ortega-Bustamante, I., & Steffy, T. (2000). Social capital and social change: Women's community activism. *Urban Affairs Review, 36*(2), 123–147.

Hassel, H., & Lourey, J. (2005). The dea(r)th of student responsibility. *College Teaching, 53*(1), 2.

Hernández, D., & Rehman, B. (Eds.). (2002). *Colonize this: Young women of color on today's feminism.* New York: Seal Press.

Henry, A. (2004). *Not my mother's sister: Generational conflict and third-wave feminism.* Bloomington, IN: Indiana University Press.

Hesse-Biber, S. N., Leavy, P., & Yaiser, M. L. (2004). Feminist approaches to research as a process. In S. N. Hesse-Biber & M. L. Yasser (Eds.), *Feminist perspectives on social research* (pp. 3–26). Oxford, England: Oxford University Press.

Heywood, L., & Drake, J. (Eds.) (1997). *Third wave agenda: Being feminist, doing feminism.* Minneapolis, MN: University of Minnesota Press.

Howe, N., & Strauss, W. (2003). Millennials go to college. *Strategies for a new generation on campus: Recruiting and admissions, campus life, and the classroom.* USA: The American Association of Collegiate Registrars and Admissions Officers and LifeCourse Associates.

Johnson, A. (2003, September/October). Seeking sisterhood: A voice from the third wave. *Off Our Backs,* 22–25.

Kadi, J. (Ed.). (1994). *Food for our grandmothers: Writings by Arab-American and Arab-Canadian feminists.* Boston: South End Press.

Kelly, C., & Breinlinger, S. (1995). Identity and injustice: Exploring women's participation in collective action. *Journal of Community and Applied Social Psychology, 5,* 41–57.

Kezar, A., & Lester, J. (2008). Leadership in a world of divided feminism. *NASPA Journal About Women in Higher Education, 1,* 49–73.

Kuh, G. D. (2003, March/April). What we're learning about student engagement from NSSE. *Change, 35*(2), 24–32.

Loeb, P. R. (2001). Against apathy: Role models for student engagement. *Academe, 87*(4), 42–47.

McTighe Musil, C. (2003, Spring). *Educating for Citizenship. Peer Review.* Washington, DC: Association of American College and Universities.

Moane, G. (2006). Exploring activism and change: Feminist psychology, liberation psychology, political psychology. *Feminism & Psychology, 16*(1), 73–78.

Moraga, C. (2002). Forward: The war path of greater empowerment. In D. Hernández, & B. Rehman (Eds.), *Colonize this! Young women on today's feminism* (pp. xi–xvi). New York: Seal Press.

Neuborne, E. (1995). Imagine my surprise. In B. Findlen (Ed.), *Listen Up: Voices from the next feminist generation*. New York: Seal Press.

Orr, C. M. (1997). Charting the currents of the third wave. *Hypatia, 12*(3), 29–45.

Pope, R. L., Reynolds, A. L., &, Mueller, J. A. (2004). *Multicultural competence in student affairs*. San Francisco: Jossey-Bass.

Reinharz, S. (1992). *Feminist methods in social research*. New York: Oxford University Press.

Rhoads, R. A. (1998). *Freedom's web: Student activism in an age of cultural diversity*. Baltimore: John Hopkins University Press.

Sowards, S. K., & Renegar, V. R. (2004). The rhetorical functions of consciousness-raising in third wave feminism. *Communication Studies, 55*(4), 535–552.

Stake, J. E., & Hoffman, F. T. (2001). Changes in student social attitudes, activism, and personal confidence in higher education: The role of women's studies. *American Educational Research Journal, 38*(2), 411–436.

Stake, J. E., & Hoffman, F. T. (2000). Putting feminist pedagogy to the test: The experience of women's studies from student and teacher's perspectives. *Psychology of Women Quarterly, 24,* 30–38.

Steinem, G. (1984). *Outrageous acts and everyday rebellions* (2nd ed.). New York: Henry Holt & Co.

Strauss, A. L., & Corbin, J. (1998). *Basics of qualitative research: Techniques and procedures for developing grounded theory* (2nd ed.). Thousand Oaks, CA: Sage.

Strauss, W., & Howe, N. (1991). *Generations: The history of America's future, 1584–2069*. New York: William Morrow and Company.

Takagi, D. Y. (1997). Maiden voyage: Excursion into sexuality and identity politics in Asian America. In E. Kim & L. V. Villanueva (Eds.), *Making more waves: New writing by Asian American women,* (pp. 142–149), Boston: Beacon Press.

Taylor, V., Whittier, N., & Pelak, C. F. (2001). The women's movement: Persistence through transformation. In L. Richardson, V. Taylor, & N. Whitter (Eds.), *Feminist frontiers* (5th ed.), 559–574.

Tretheway, A. (1997). Resistance, identity, and empowerment: A postmodern feminist analysis of clients in a human service organization. *Communication Monographs, 64*(4), 281–301.

Vollmer, B. M. (1974). *Psychosocial characteristics of college women involved in campus liberation groups.* Unpublished doctoral dissertation, University of Denver, Denver, Colorado.

Walker, R. (1995). *To be real: Telling the truth and changing the face of feminism.* New York: Anchor Books.

Zucker, A. N. (2004). Disavowing social identities: What it means when women say, "I am not a feminist, but…" *Psychology of Women Quarterly, 28*(4), 423–435.

Colonial Sexism 101? Anthropological Teachings About Women

Barbara Bonnekessen
Assistant Professor, Social Science,
   Cultural Anthropology & Women's and Gender Studies
Director, Women's Resource Center
Department of Humanities
New Mexico Tech

> *Images of "Third World" women fill the media: battered victims of starvation, with too many children, hidden behind burqas. Images of "Third World" businesswomen, female politicians, or academics are rare, as is the use of the "other" woman as a model. This attitude has a long history in Western thought, ranging from classical and medieval travel accounts about strange monsters and "bad" women, to the diaries and travel accounts of Western women engaged in colonizing the non-European world, and to contemporary media blips from Afghanistan and Iraq. The imagination of "other" women as powerless, dependent, or unfeminine may also be taught through academic textbooks in cultural anthropology, the only science dedicated to expand the knowledge of human diversity. This article explores how undergraduate students conceptualize the meaning of "Third World" woman and how three widely used textbooks used in undergraduate education could affect students' attitude through the ways in which they represent non-Western women.*

As yet another student mentions the ever-present *National Geographic Magazine* as her family's primary source of knowledge about the non-Western Other, I fervently groan the traditional prayer that each and every person ought to be sentenced to at least one class in cultural anthropology. This prayer used to be my response to the never-ending stream of student remarks about the "strangeness" of the Other, the frequent assertions that "we" (meaning U.S. women and ruthlessly excluding their instructor[1]) have it so much better and should serve as model to all other women, and the continuous surprised faces when I stress that women have been, and still are, always "working women." At one point, I replaced the prayer with a classroom exercise in the Introduction to Cultural Anthropology: "Close your eyes and tell me what comes to mind when I ask you to describe 'Third World women'[2]." I wrote the adjectives (usually they included poor, uneducated, too many children, and oppressed) on the board and listed the opposites next to them (rich, educated, too few children, oppressors). Then I asked the class if they really thought that they could be described in this manner; if not, would that make them "Third World," too? The uncomfortable squirming was answer enough: wanting to separate themselves from the Other, they had imagined themselves as what they knew they were not.

The students who participate in the above exercise are replaced by others in the Introduction to Cultural Anthropology that I teach every semester. For many, I will never know if any of the class discussions, lectures, or readings have made a lasting impact on their perception of global women and men. Globally engaged individuals do not need agents of change—they usually act as such agents themselves—but, over the years, many of my students have intentionally conceptualized themselves as provincial individuals only; in keeping with the overall population, few own a passport, have little intention to travel outside the United States, a strong hostility to non-U.S. media or international organizations, and frequently exhibit the "sense of superiority, mixed with [a] missionary attitude" reported by Hase (2002) for her students. As pessimistic as it may sound, I frequently doubt that one course out of the approximately 40 undergraduate courses for a bachelor's degree will have a lifetime impact, especially if the material is not reinforced by other courses, life experiences, and social expectations of critical global knowledge. The many students who continue to enroll in more classes with me, though, do encourage me. I have managed to make them curious; they now know that there is something to learn about "the Other" that is valuable, and they come back for more. Since I do want to teach for change, I must make sure that my lectures and all the supporting materials I use have this impact even when students do not return for more. For years, I focused my efforts on my lectures, but assigned standard textbooks to be read and showed standard ethnographic film in classes. While I critiqued yet another film in class (we *heard* that women provide up to 80% of the food supply of gathering-hunting societies, but *saw* them for about 10 seconds; then we watched a man hunt for almost 8 minutes),

I realized that images would stick in my students' minds much longer than my words, especially if such images supported long-held stereotypes and prejudices. I was struck—am I potentially boycotting my own efforts with the material I assign to support my teachings?

In this essay, I will explore some of the roots of Western thinking about non-Western women; consider how, in cultural anthropology, we might contribute to certain opinions; and what we might do as educators to teach our students about the varieties of women's lives and experiences.

I will begin by describing the experiential basis for this discussion. For over a decade, I taught cultural anthropology and women's and gender studies at a medium-sized Midwestern urban university. The student population was mostly local; European-American and African-American students were in the majority (while the University overall enrolled more White than Black students, my classes frequently showed an even balance), with a few Latino, Asian-American (very few Native American or Middle-Eastern Americans), and international students. Most students were working full time or had families and attended "school" to earn a bachelor's degree only. Neither anthropology nor women's and gender studies offered more than a minor; and most students majored in sociology, history, English, psychology, or communication Studies.

Over the years, I worked with two of the major textbooks used in the Introduction to Cultural Anthropology, and I had the opportunity to review many others. I also tended to show ethnographic films and other documentaries in classes. We discussed the films in class, and my students had an opportunity to verbally comment on the textbooks on the last day of class. One summer, a class also assisted me in a review for the next edition of the textbook with the publisher's permission. My subsequent remarks are based on my work with these students and materials.

Beginning in the 1990s, many scholars and consumers of scholarly work have taken issue with the representation of the Other in public media and in scholarly publications (see, for example, Ginsburg, 1994; Haas, 1996; Hervik, 1999; Lutz & Collins, 1993). But imagining the Other is nothing new, although the first roots of cultural anthropology in the writings of Herodotus of Halicarnassus in the fifth century BC (Hodgen, 1964, pp. 20–29) served not only to inform his contemporaries, but did so in a comparative and realistic manner. His impact was forgotten by the Middle Ages, when Peter Martyr (1455–1526) realized that fact-based descriptions could not hold the attention of his audience without the fantastic embellishments that would become the stuff of legends (Hodgen,

1964, pp. 30–31). Martyr's description of an island of women who "engaged in no feminine occupation" (in Hodgen, 1964, p. 31) declares the "other" woman as lacking proper "feminine" attributes.

European colonialism not only continued the unfavorable description of other women to Western women, it also added the nationalist appropriation of women as indicators of "us," "them," and "race"[3] to the mixture of Other and Western women. An excerpt from James Mill in his 1818 *History of India* illustrates his opinion about the difference of what we today call "Western" and "Third World" women:

The condition of women is one of the most remarkable circumstances in the manners of nations. Among rude people, the women are generally degraded; among civilized people they are exalted . . . As society refines upon its enjoyments, and advances into that state of civilization . . . in which the qualities of mind are ranked above the qualities of the body, the condition of the weaker sex is gradually improved, till they associate on equal terms with the men, and occupy the place of voluntary and useful coadjutors. (in Strobel, 1991, p. 49).

It becomes obvious that non-Europeans were not to be counted among the "refined" societies, when we turn to the letters and diaries of German colonial women in southwestern Africa around the turn of the 19th century. The major commentaries from the colonial women about local women centered on the latter's lack of cleanliness, beauty, intelligence, industry, honesty, and modesty (Mamozai, 1989). American women who traveled Latin America in the 19th century echoed these sentiments and were convinced that even the upper class women with whom they interacted had much less education or freedom than they themselves enjoyed (Hahner, 1998). And it was only because they needed their help that East Coast women migrating into the trans-Mississippian west in the 19th century finally came to see native women of the Plains as not only equally skilled and overworked, but also, in some cases, they even admired the women-centered domestic work that European-American women missed. But this admiration was hard-won after overwhelming complaints in which a lack of sanitation and general oppression played major roles (Riley, 1984).

The contemporary academy is not unaffected by these Western ideas of proper female roles and behavior. In the seemingly most harmless of all instances, in our self-imagination of our distant prehistory, we find Physical Anthropology imagining women of the Australopithecine doing manual labor on their knees, surrounded by children, while progressive males march toward becoming Homo sapiens (Wiber, 1998). This imagination has created some loathsome consequences in "the application of evolutionary theory to human behavior—particularly deplorable behavior, such as rape, sexual harassment, and aggression. . . ." (McCaughey, 2007, p. 2).

These images seem far distant from the contemporary campus. After all, we are now connected to the whole world through the World Wide Web, can receive images and eye witness accounts from all around the world, from all people. But how often do we talk with women? And how do we see women in the "Third World" of the New World Order? Most importantly, however, how does cultural anthropology inform contemporary students about the other woman and about themselves?

While teaching in the Midwest, many of my undergraduate students, irrespective of which "race"[/] or ethnicity they claimed, told me that they had never left the geographical area controlled by the United States[4], and many of them had not even left the Midwest itself. Some did not have the resources, others asserted loudly that the world held no interest for them, and many felt incapable of dealing with the assumed inconveniences of foreign travel. Given the realities of globalization, however, it is likely that many students will soon be employed by a transnational company and may find themselves quickly moved outside of the United States, or that those who work for any agency or organization will find that many of their clients are an Other. Despite this lack of preparation, compounded by the almost guaranteed future need, students enter my classes in cultural anthropology with very definite opinions about the people inhabiting the world around them. Some students trace these opinions back to Human Geography classes at the elementary and junior high school level; others point to newspapers, television, and the ever-present *National Geographic Magazine;* and a few even refer to conversations with foreign fellow students. But most shrug and claim not to remember the source of their information. Interestingly enough, opinions about Others are more detailed and varied about men; while non-U.S. women are frequently homogenized and dismissed invariably as poor, oppressed, and "just taking care of children."

For many students, the fact that we are cultural anthropologists makes us experts in Other humans,[5] and they are likely to accept the information presented in assigned books as well as that expressed in lectures as "scientific"[6]. Ethnographic film, although removed from the exoticizing imagery of television, still allows the viewer to consume without engaging. And in end-of-semester discussions, my students shared how much they enjoyed the pictures used in their textbook. This is particularly interesting, since images are often absorbed without a conscious examination of the

Colonial Sexism 101?

content and "most students view[ed] educative illustrations in a relatively uncritical way" (Wiber, 1998, p. 82). This uncritical reception is rather disquieting, since "[w]e live in a world in which, increasingly, people learn of their own and other cultures through a range of visual media . . . that have emerged as powerful cultural forces. . . ." (Ginsburg, 1994).

Scanning some of the most widely used textbooks introducing cultural anthropology, we realize that women are shown as a human minority, including some difference made by class between women and men, for example by showing mostly men engaged in income-producing activities, especially those that students recognize from their own environment (e.g., in one, the New York Stock Exchange is shown as a male space). But there are also few pictures that show women as poor, uneducated, or oppressed (one book's chapter on family shows a battered White woman in the midst of pictures of happy nuclear and extended heterosexual families). The students' idea that women are invisible and hidden is strengthened in the manner in which the textbooks hide women. This becomes especially obvious in one example where women in a picture are identified as the women of a named male—a tradition of hiding women's personhood that is present in many traditional monographs (e.g., Balikci, 1989, where a male is named and a woman and child are only referred to as "his"; or Chagnon, 1997, where women are named, but also identified in relation to a male, whereas men are named but not identified in relation to women). While naming practices have improved, the bulk of ethnographies available to our students in academic libraries were written and published before ethnographies included women as persons (see Mukhopadhyay & Higgins, 1988, for a documentation of the first decade of change).

When I asked a class to write down adjectives to describe first and third world women, as well as "self," it became obvious that the students constructed themselves in opposition to their perception of Third World women. While there were many overlapping adjectives, the weight of negatives rested on Third World women (poor and oppressed), while the majority of positive adjectives were used for First World women and self (caring, determined, educated, and independent). This result can be analyzed through two lenses. Both the tradition of Western dichotomizing and the early socialization of the current student population in an era of "we're number one!" may not allow my students to perceive the Other as anything but a lesser opposite. Despite a clear participation in the world market and a global political system, and despite the openly heterogeneous character of the U.S. population and cultures, the nationalist myth of

"American" still seduces students into the creation and maintenance of a homogenous group defined by nothing more than a passport (which many do not own). Supporting the creation of such a group must include the creation of an Other, for how else would one delineate oneself? That women play an important part of this nationalist creation is often demonstrated by the students (mostly White and Black) in the internal racist creation of Latinas as suffering from "machismo," and of Black women as abandoned by Black men because of the still cherished myth of the "Black matriarchy." These creations and the invisibility surrounding Asian-American and Native American women (consider also Mohanty's "[c]orresponding analyses of 'matriarchal' black women on welfare, 'illiterate' Chicana farm workers, and 'docile' Asian domestic workers. . . .", Mohanty, 2003, pp. 47–48) only serve to highlight White women as "American" women—women who, according to media headlines, have crashed through the glass barrier and "have come a long way." If even the "other" American woman doesn't measure up to the White, middle-class success story, how much worse must it be for those women worldwide who do not even have access to the hyphenated "American" to elevate their status! Combining "race," class, and gender in the creation of the model woman of the 21st1st century, all other women must be sacrificed to uphold the myth of the West as progressive world leader and to continue the 19th century ladder of progress that made Western societies into the self-described apex of civilization.

But there is another, more alarming possibility. In many classes, it has become obvious that current students do not know much anymore about women's status in the United States (after all, on paper all are equal now) and certainly know very little about their global environment. This could lead a cynical observer[7] to conclude that American students are misinformed about global women to appreciate better what little they have. If other women are poor and oppressed, that must mean that American women are rich and free—if we finish the classroom exercise mentioned at the beginning. That this is not so is readily observable in women's poverty, lack of access to jobs if there are young children, and especially in the increased pressure on women to become Martha Stewart-educated housewives as soon as they are mothers—unless one is unmarried, Black, and poor. In contrast to the ever-present trope of the 1950s, it is not anymore through legislation and education that women are pushed to supply society's reproductive labor for free—now it is supposed to be a voluntarily made choice in the interest of the children. Constructing White American women as free and well-off encourages them to stop asking questions; and one certainly should not complain about the glass ceiling when there are "other" women who are poor and oppressed—discussions of Western gender stratification and segregation can be relegated easily to be dismissed as childish whining in the face of "real" suffering[8]. That American women are subject to a fierce backlash has been documented throughout the 1990s (best known among those is Faludi, 2006) and the increasing volume of publications about "other" women's plight (e.g., Okin, 1999; Moghissi, 1999) might just become another tool in a process where "'cultural differences' between Western and non-Western women are heavily emphasized" (Mies, 1998, p. 11). In the meantime, so-called "Third World women" are not necessarily content with being represented as the helpless victims of patriarchy—a young South African woman at the 1999 Third World Studies conference (Omaha, NE) was adamant that the achievements of "other" women are long overdue to be recognized and celebrated. Unfortunately, it is still rare that we recognize that "other" women are not only doing well, but that Western women might actually use them as models (Bonnekessen, 1998). But then we have a history of seeing women's equality as "uncivilized" when "others" show a better grasp of human rights (Mies, 1998, pp. 93–94), and it is still a rare occurrence when feminists come together globally to follow Mohanty's leadership in "building a noncolonizing feminist solidarity across borders" (Mohanty, 2003).

It lies within the purview of teaching the complexity of "race," class, and gender to break through the Western dichotomies as well as gender stratification and segregation. We cannot continue to allow our students to imagine homogenized groups of people as either well-off or not, without stressing the heterogeneous reality behind the simplifying population labels. We cannot allow women to be hidden again without consequence; after all, what is important about human beings cannot be demonstrated with male examples only.

The primary responsibility for the creation and maintenance of information about human beings lies with the science that claims expert knowledge; after all, anthropology studies and knows about humans. Since our beginnings in scattered travel logs and during the long process of institutionalization, we have claimed knowledge and expertise about all human beings. Although we now know that such a claim is based more on hubris than on reality, the fact remains that cultural anthropology is indeed the only science with a database extensive enough to create knowledge about all humans—the question is, of course, if we make appropriate use of it. That anthropology has not lived up to its potential when it comes to describing and analyzing half of the population has been admirably documented elsewhere (Morgen, 1989; Reiter, 1975; Ward, 1999); but how far have we come in rectifying that insight, and how much have we adjusted that material that we present to students who might never again take another class with us or read any of our publications?

My students have demonstrated convincingly that, without reading the diaries of their 19th-century ancestors, they still hold the same ideas about non-Western women. Many of the adjectives used today were used then; and despite our self-congratulation about the increased standards of knowledge and access to information, we appear to have been very selective about what we want to learn. Using negative stereotypes of others in an ethnocentric attempt to elevate oneself may be tolerable outside of the academy, but my students count among that minority of human beings who have access to tertiary education, and what may be tolerable on the street becomes a paralyzing problem in the classroom.

Representing the "Third World" in our classrooms creates an ethical dilemma: With only 16 weeks available in the semester, which of the three large categories of human ordering—"race," class, or gender—do we stress? Attempting to bring out the interconnectedness of the first and third worlds in a world system's approach can often lead to an overemphasis of the Third World as poor, exploited, and helpless—exactly the attitude my students already bring into the classroom. Pointing out that all economic classes in the first and Third World are very similar to their respective counterparts may lead the students to turn away from any willingness to support foreign aid and to recognize our responsibility in the poverty of others. In fact, this often leads to the remark that "we should help our own first!" Demonstrating women's advances in other countries can mean that students now completely dismiss the global feminization of poverty—emphasizing the latter means that students are again supported in the mistaken belief that Western women have reached utter equality and should now missionize all others (this, of course, draws with it the racist beliefs that non-Western men all abuse and exploit "their" poor helpless women).

In short, there is no failsafe single strategy that would promise success. Over the years, I have realized that it is specifically that insecurity that provides the best strategy. Stereotypes are powerful blinders; that which confirms is visible, that which does not is obscured. As we teach students about the Other, the simple use of the singular exacerbates an assumed homogeneity. "Others" come in as much variety as any imagined "we" and, with just a little more attention to detail and critical honesty about ourselves, we realize that similarities and differences must be stressed simultaneously and that any attempt to reduce humans to just one category (may that be sex, "race," religion, and similar) is intellectual laziness at best.

What may remain for us to do is to continue on that complex path that forces us and our students to look at all human issues through the triple-lens of "race," class, and gender. There is no area of human experience where this lens will fail to deliver different experiences. And it is only when we look through this lens that we will stop imagining women and will begin to talk to and maybe even learn from each other.

REFERENCES

Balikci, A. (1989). *The Netsilik Eskimo.* Prospect Heights, IL: Waveland Press.

Bonnekessen, B. (1998). *Selective blindness: An anthropological query into the meaning of development.* Paper presented at the Third World Studies Conference, University of Nebraska, Omaha, Nebraska.

Chagnon, N. (1997). *Yanomamö* (5th ed.). Forth Worth: Harcourt Brace College Publishers.

Faludi, S. (2006). *Backlash: The undeclared war against American women* (15th anniversary ed.). New York: Three Rivers Press.

Ginsburg, F. (1994). Culture/media: A (mild) polemic. *Anthropology Today, 10*(2), 5–15.

Haas, J. (1996). Power, objects, and a voice for anthropology. *Current Anthropology, 37* (Supplement February), S1-S22.

Hahner, J. E. (Ed.). (1998). *Women through women's eyes: Latin American women in nineteenth-century travel accounts.* Wilmington, DE: Scholarly Resources.

Harding, S. (1986). *The science question in feminism.* Ithaca, NY: Cornell University Press.

Hase, M. (2002). Class conflict: Student resistance and nationalism in the classroom. *Women's Review of Books, 19*(5), 9–11.

Hervik, P. (1999). The mysterious Maya of National Geographic. *Journal of Latin American Anthropology, 4*(1), 166–197.

Hodgen, M. T. (1964). *Early anthropology in the sixteenth and seventeenth centuries.* Philadelphia: University of Pennsylvania Press.

Lutz, C., & Collins, J. (1993). *Reading National Geographic.* Chicago: University of Chicago Press.

Mamozai, M. (1989). *Schwarze Frau, Weisse Herrin.* Hamburg: Rowohlt.

McCaughey, M. (2007). *The caveman mystique: Pop-Darwinism and the debates over sex, violence, and science* (1st ed.). New York: Routledge.

Mies, M. (1998). *Patriarchy and accumulation on a world scale: Women in the international division of labor.* London: Zed Books.

Moghissi, H. (1999). *Feminism and Islamic fundamentalism: The limits of postmodern analysis.* London: Zed Books.

Mohanty, C. T. (2003). *Feminism without borders: Decolonizing theory, practicing solidarity.* London: Duke University Press.

Morgen, S. (Ed.). (1989). *Gender and anthropology: Critical reviews for research and teaching.* Washington, DC: American Anthropological Association.

Mukhopadhyay, C. C., & Higgins, P. J. (1988). Anthropological studies of women's status revisited: 1977–1987. *Annual Review Anthropology, 17,* 461–495.

Okin, S. M. (1999). Is multiculturalism bad for women? In J. Cohen, M. Howard & M. C. Nussbaum (Eds.), *Is multiculturalism bad for women? Susan Moller Orkin with respondents* (pp. 7–24). Princeton: Princeton University Press.

Reiter, R. R. (Ed.). (1975). *Toward an anthropology of women.* New York: Monthly Review Press.

Riley, G. (1984). *Women and Indians on the frontier, 1825–1915.* Albuquerque: University of New Mexico Press.

Strobel, M. (1991). *European women and the second British empire.* Bloomington: Indiana University Press.

Struck, D. (2007, January 13). Canadians fear fallout of U.S. passport rules. *Washington Post.*

Ward, M. C. (1999). *A world full of women* (2nd ed.). Boston: Allyn and Bacon.

Wiber, M. G. (1998). *Erect men/undulating women: The visual imagery of gender, "race" and progress in reconstructive illustrations of human evolution.* Waterloo, Canada: Wilfrid Laurier University Press.

ENDNOTES

1. I am German by birth, socialization, and nationality, which tempts many Americans to classify me as "White" until I speak and my accent clearly recasts me as "foreign." Admittedly, I tend to overplay

the "foreign" in many interactions with Americans (both inside and outside the classroom), intentionally claiming the "stranger" locus that is unique to the practice of cultural anthropology, while at the same time exemplifying that "international" and "global" populations are never only "outside."

2. The terms "Third World" and "First World" are not used here to validate them; there are no satisfying terms to distinguish the colonizer/industrialized countries from their colonized/nonindustrialized source countries that do justice to the extreme internal discrepancies that have led to the use of "North" and "South" in the development literature. The hierarchical terms are employed here because my students were most familiar with these terms and could identify the large population groups imagined behind the shorthand label in the popular discourse.

3. While "sex" and "gender" are useful in separating the biological and cultural aspects of women's and men's identifications, there is only "race" available for the classification of population groups by imagined appearance. Throughout this paper, I refer to "race" in quotation marks to stress its invention and use as a cultural construct.

4. According to a *Washington Post* article, 27% of American citizens hold a passport (Struck, 2007). The local applicability of this national percentage varies by region; my former students in the Midwest held steady at around 10% of each class asked (mainly international students), while my current students (in a location approximately 3 hours away from an international border) have an approximately 75% positive response rate per class (the students with passports are either international students or travel to Mexico exclusively).

5. I would deny that on two counts: (1) both feminism and postmodernism have shown that no individual can ever hope to adequately know or represent people located in other social spaces; and (2) "we" are a human group, too—and anthropology has rarely consented to exempt any human group from our curiosity.

6. "Scientific" in the sense of self-acclaimed neutrality and tested truth—a misinterpretation of the value of scientific results that has been rightfully criticized (see Harding, 1986).

7. In the current postmodern tradition in cultural anthropology, I have already deconstructed myself above as such an observer since I am a European resident in and participant observer of "American" culture since 1984.

8. This does not mean to imply that women's problems worldwide are not "real;" but the public discourse seems to focus on other women's issues only in negative comparisons to Western women's, thereby hiding non-Western women's achievements as successfully as Western women's problems.

Leading in the Borderlands: Negotiating Ethnic Patriarchy for the Benefit of Students

Alicia Fedelina Chávez
Assistant Professor
Department of Educational Leadership
  and Organizational Learning
University of New Mexico

This article draws from a 7-year autoethnographic study of a Mestiza (female Spanish/Native American) leader negotiating ethnic patriarchies while serving as dean of students at a large Midwestern university and then as senior executive officer for a small southwestern campus. Professional teaching stories derived from study findings illuminate leadership dilemmas in navigating situations across gender and culture in higher education. Values, norms, beliefs, priorities, and behaviors of various ethnic patriarchal leadership environs are explored using anthropological techniques to understand how one female leader of color moves effectively, though not without challenge, to negotiate for the benefit of students. Recommendations are provided for leaders, allies, and those working to develop beyond gender-cultured boundaries in higher education.

> *Because I, a* mestiza, *continually walk out of one culture and into another, because I am in all cultures at the same time . . . alma entre dos mundos, tres, cuatro, me zumba la cabeza con lo contradictorio . . . a soul between two worlds, three, four. My head buzzes with the contradictory; I am disoriented by all the voices that talk to me simultaneously.*
> —*Gloria Anzaldúa*

My first reaction is intense anger, rage . . . and I am usually so very slow to anger. This response is prompted by headlines announcing the first female president of Harvard; an article on first female Native, Asian, and Hispanic American presidents of 4-year colleges (Turner, 2007); and my own return to faculty after 4 productive yet physically and psychically exhausting years as a woman of color leading a college campus. I am shocked at my visceral reaction yet perhaps my response is intense because even after 25 years in various collegiate leadership and faculty roles, I am still painfully negotiating the gender-cultured borderlands of higher education almost as deeply as when I started as a college freshman. As a former dean of students of a Midwestern big ten university and former executive campus director for a small rural southwestern campus, I felt compelled to turn this anger into something positive and decided to analyze 7 years of autoethnographic leadership field notes on negotiating ethnic patriarchies in academe. Though my second reaction is elation at these milestones by women and especially women of color, I cannot help but wonder how in current times there are still so many of these firsts. My anger originates in this question, this reality of academe as still bounded and defined by specific identities and norms that make it profoundly difficult on a daily basis for those who are "other" (Chávez, Guido-DiBrito, & Mallory, 2003; Ibarra, 2001).

As a woman of color and a leader, scholar, and teacher in higher education I shouldn't be surprised at this paucity of women of color in the highest levels of leadership. Though in student affairs, we have many more women and persons of color as senior student affairs officers, there are few women of color in dean, provost, or presidential positions. We are certainly not present in numbers to match the almost majority ratios of people of color and women in much of the United States (U.S. Census Bureau, 2000). Of the 186,505 executive/administrative/managerial professionals in postsecondary education, only 33,875 are from one or more of the four ethnic minority groups designated as underserved (National Center for Education Statistics, 2006). This number shrinks drastically as you move up the executive ranks and narrow to women of color (Turner, 2007). Unfortunately census and department of education statistics separate ethnicity and gender, making it difficult to gauge the national numbers of women of color in executive level collegiate leadership. Though we have made important progress, we are still far from representing the ratios of women of color in higher education to women of color in the larger society. I have mourned as one after another of my friends who are women of color have left professorships and collegiate leadership exhausted from the experience of working in cultural and gender environs not their own.

Individually and institutionally women of color navigate ethnic patriarchies every moment of our professional lives (Rich, 1993). Since decision makers at executive levels hold much influence in the academy, it is important that we continue to diversify this professional group and culture (Tierney & Bensimon, 2000). It is also important that we continually transform from a very homogeneous practice of academe based on specific cultural and gender norms to a more diverse practice based on ways of being among many cultures and across gender (Ibarra, 2001; Ng, 2000; Wolgemuth & Harbour, 2007).

This article adds to the literature about women in higher education by illustrating leadership norms I faced as a woman of color and some ways I was able to negotiate them in service to students. It is an individual exploration from a diverse epistemological orientation to negotiate culture and gender in the transformation of practice. My hope is that readers will find both inspiration and practical ideas from my experience as a woman of color negotiating leadership environs founded on cultural and gender norms unnatural to me. I have organized the article into sections including discussions about ethnic patriarchy, borderlands, identity and leadership, a summary of the research process, findings illustrated through professional "teaching stories" about leading as a woman of color in academe, and recommendations. Leaders and other practitioners in higher education may find it useful to draw insights from these stories and recommendations to continue transforming their own practice toward a more diverse epistemology. I dedicate this article to women of color in academe and those who wish to enter, for we need to trust in our own ways of being as cultural translators; as role models; and as leaders, teachers, and scholars.

ETHNIC PATRIARCHY AND BORDERLANDS

Ethnic patriarchy is a term I use to refer to ways that patriarchy and culture intersect. As a woman of color I experience cultural- and gender-differentiated treatment and treatment that is a fusion of the two. Gender roles and expectations are defined differently within various cultural groups (Lorde, 1984; Green, 2007). The way I am perceived and treated by a group of Hispanic males is often very different than by Native American males or by males from a mix of Caucasian European origins. Institutionally, policies, structures, and practice are also framed differently across cultures and gender (Fried, 1995; Ibarra, 2001; Mihesuah & Wilson, 2004). To negotiate ethnic patriarchy as an executive leader, I must walk as effectively as possible in the borderlands of gendered cultural norms of academe and among external groups influencing higher education. My leadership experience includes negotiating predominantly Caucasian male presidential/provost cabinets, regents, and dean's councils; Native American male tribal councils; and Hispanic male community groups. It is an often uncomfortable challenge to critique gender issues in groups that are already facing stereotypes and oppression, yet the reality of sexism within Hispanic, Indigenous, and other ethnic communities is very real, is differentiated in its manifestation of norms, and benefits from critique because women of color face challenges in different ways within as well as outside of culture (Lorde, 1984; Cannella & Manuelito, 2008; Green, 2007).

Negotiating borderlands of identity, organizations, and society is not a new concept. Borderland literature describes the profound experiences of existing in the borders between identity cultures as one who is different from the prevailing culture. Borderland scholars study and illustrate the experiences of those living across identity differences in many areas of society often through intense personal narrative. These studies include both the internal border interactions of multiple underserved identities such as being a woman and a person of color, as well as the experiences of entering into organizations and societal arenas as an identity "other" (Chávez, Guido-DiBrito, & Mallory, 2003; Fried & Associates, 1995; Ibarra, 2001). There are deep literatures out of gender studies (Anzaldúa, 1990; Frankenberg, 1993; Kipnis, 1991); lesbian, gay, bisexual, and transgender studies (Rhoads, 1994; Sanlo, 2005); ethnic studies (Garrod & Larimore, 1997; Borrego & Manning, 2007; Mihesuah & Wilson, 2004; Rochlin, 1997); ability studies (Gerber & Reif, 1991; Strange, 2000); and studies on class (Borrego, Guido-DiBrito, & Chávez, 2008; Dews & Law, 1995; Schwartz, Donovan, & Guido-DiBrito, 2008) to draw understanding of how individuals negotiate these borderlands. There has also been an explosion of research on identity in student development literature (Evans, Forney, & Guido-DiBrito, 1998; Guido-DiBrito & Chávez, 2003) and some exploration of the experiences of women of color as leaders in higher education (Turner, 2007; Valverde, 2003). Scholars of indigenous knowledge, philosophy, and scholarship urge us to incorporate many venues, methods, and ways of knowing to explore scholarly questions and transform education (Cajete, 1994; Mihesuah & Wilson, 2004; Wolgemuth & Harbour, 2007) The falling ratings of U.S. higher education within worldwide contexts (U.S. Department of Education, 2006) are important indicators that the evolution of collegiate culture and practice across these borderlands is critical. This study adds to the literature on identity and leadership borderlands by delving into deep autoethnographic analysis of the self in negotiating gender-cultured contexts.

INTERSECTIONS OF IDENTITY AND LEADERSHIP

I became a reluctant role model to other women of color at the age of 22 when I began my first professional leadership position as a residence hall manager at New Mexico State University. A young student who described herself as Spanish and Native American asked me about my professional experiences and if I thought she could be a leader. I spent the next hour listening to and sharing stories. I felt humbled when she shared that she hadn't thought she could be a leader until she saw my very Spanish female name listed at the front office. This experience made real for me the responsibility of intersecting roles of identity and leadership. For you see, I am *Mestiza*, a Spanish and Native woman from the high desert mountains of northern New Mexico. This cultural blending has roots in New Mexico from the mid-1500s when 16 families traveled from Spain and intermarried with Native peoples (Beck, 1962; Chávez, 1989). The term *Mestiza* signifies a blended and distinct culture that draws from both Latin and Indigenous cultural norms (Anzaldúa, 1987). Travelers who visit my hometown often feel they have entered another country and indeed, many cultural rhythms remain from long ago. It is often said that we stayed put and the border moved . . . and moved . . . and moved again . . . and we never knew.

Those of us whose identities and ways of being are not common in higher education walk in borderlands (Anzaldúa, 1987) between our own ways of being in the world and those of academe. After getting to know me, a supervisor once told me he "didn't envy the reality that I would always have to walk as a leader with feet in two worlds" (Schwartz, 1988). Differences can be so foundational and unconscious that even now I am often unable to recognize them until gender-cultured barriers rise up between me and what I am working to accomplish. Because so many of our students, faculty, and staff reside in these borderlands, we need to continually recraft academe from a more diverse epistemology of norms, values, assumptions, and beliefs (Ibarra, 2001). Unfortunately, as Kaylynne Two-Trees states, "privilege of any kind can act as a learning disability" (Personal Communication, 1996). Privilege enables individuals to move through situations with little challenge to their beliefs about the world or to norms they propagate (Hurtado, 1996). When one has the privilege of being normative by identity, it is not as necessary to study others to survive in everyday life (Strange, 2000). I believe this leads to less motivation for ethnic patriarchies to transform or to make the way easier for those outside these norms. Since most executive leaders in higher education are not women of color (Turner, 2007; Valverde, 2003), studies from within the highest echelons of higher education leadership are essential to transformation.

THE STUDY

This study is drawn primarily from 7 years of autoethnographic field notes and interpretive reflections of my experiences as an executive-level leader at two very different institutions of higher education. One of the institutions is a very large, Midwestern research institution in the state's capital. Students of color make up about 13% of the overall enrollment. I served as dean of students while at this institution. The other is a small rural branch campus of a large southwestern research university and is located in the mountainous northern region of the state. Students of color, mostly Hispanic and Native American, make up over 49% of enrollment. I served as the executive campus director [senior executive officer] for this campus. To help protect individuals in my research, I have chosen not to name the specific institutions.

METHODS

I chose autoethnography as the research approach for this study to analyze dilemmas of negotiating gender-cultured leadership arenas as a woman of color in higher education and illustrate through professional teaching stories. Autoethnography is an analysis of the self in contexts of dynamic tension using an anthropological research lens to deconstruct, compare, and contrast values, beliefs, behaviors, artifacts, and assumptions (Holman Jones, 2005). "Autoethnography refers to writing about the personal and its relationship to culture; it is an autobiographical genre . . . that displays multiple layers of consciousness" (Ellis, 2004, p. 37). To increase trustworthiness of the study within an autoethnographic approach, I chose three primary methods of data collection: (1) participant observation of myself and others in a variety of contexts, keeping extensive field notes as often as possible during or just after meetings and other administrative activities; (2) daily journals of my reflections, feelings, and interpretations; and (3) initiated conversations with leaders about culture and gender. Using multiple methods made it more likely that I would minimize overly romantic or frustrated interpretations of the data, remain open to unexpected findings, and develop depth in understanding (Marshall & Rossman, 2006).

For this study, I focused on strategies and insights that proved effective in negotiating for students inside and outside collegiate institutions and was careful to analyze the challenges within these situations. Two research questions served as my guide: (1) How does a woman of color negotiate groups of leaders dominated by males of similar and different cultures than her own? and (2) What strategies show effectiveness in negotiating across culture and gender with leaders in high-level positions of academe and in external groups impacting the institution?

DATA ANALYSIS

To develop thick description (Geertz, 1973) and gain a deep understanding of my experiences of gender-cultured aspects of leadership, I first utilized thematic analysis (Huberman & Miles, 1994), categorizing specific gender-cultured dynamics and strategies common across my experiences. Second, I developed systematic coding (Marshall & Rossman, 2006) to analyze and reduce data according to identified themes and to search for outlying themes. Third, I analyzed data to identify professional teaching stories that each illustrated and brought to life several of the thematic findings.

THE POWER OF TEACHING STORIES

I use teaching stories to make sense of and illustrate findings of this study. Teaching stories are both the creation of metaphorical stories to teach larger lessons and the telling of real events to illustrate a concept or idea. They are a tradition in my family and a primary way that learning takes place and knowledge is transferred in both of my cultures. This tradition stems from a belief that it takes the heart, mind, body, and spirit to fully understand any phenomenon (Anzaldúa, 1987; Gunn Allen, 1989; Pelias, 2004). The use of storytelling is a strong ethic of Indigenous, Latina, and critical race feminisms (Parker, Deyhle, & Vellenas, 1999) and of indigenous knowledge traditions (Villegas, Rak Neugebauer, & Venegas, 2008). Teaching stories are distinctive in going beyond typically shorter and fragmented interview quotes often used to illustrate qualitative findings to tell a story with some type of dynamic tension and learn from how the issue was resolved (Cajete,

1994; Pelias, 2004). A lesson is often embedded within the story, usually about deeper wisdoms in life, and is a way of passing on insights to those who follow after us (Gunn Allen, 1989). I have always found strength in hearing the stories of others with similar experiences. Somehow this makes me feel less "other" and less alone as a woman from cultures less common in higher education leadership. I also find in my work with those from different backgrounds that it is helpful to hear their stories so that we can find ways to work effectively together.

I write this article as one way to connect with others through stories of our experiences that may assist us in continuing to transform higher education. By choosing professional teaching stories selectively from analyzed autoethnographic field notes and journal reflections, I am able to illustrate key study findings to the reader in ways that have influenced human choices throughout history (Cajete, 1994; Grande, 2004). I relate experiences from my own leadership as a gender-cultured outsider (Merriam, Johnson-Bailey, Lee, Ntseane, & Muhamad, 2001) to engage readers cognitively and emotionally.

FINDINGS: LEARNING FROM PROFESSIONAL TEACHING STORIES

Themes emerged strongly from the data, which was only somewhat of a surprise to me after facing numerous cultural and gender challenges as a leader of many years. I was surprised at the depth of institutional norms and was reminded of Lukes' (1974) three levels of power, in which he describes the most insidious barrier to social justice as the power to define underlying norms, values, and definitions within any context. To compound this, most leaders I've worked with, whether having altruistic or self-serving intentions, seem completely unaware that their professional norms and priorities have a basis in their own identities. This makes the burden of leading across differences quite challenging for identity outsiders. Many we work with assume that their practices, values, and beliefs are normative rather than originating in specific cultural or gender constructs and at best are often irritated when others act from different foundational norms and beliefs (Chávez, Guido-DiBrito, & Mallory, 2003). The following professional teaching stories each illustrate two or more of the major findings of this study—remaining ourselves; bringing together heart, mind, body, and spirit; learning yet pushing the edges of cultural and gender rhythms; identifying and seeking advice from cultural translators; and learning to speak the language and priorities of those you wish to persuade. I chose each teaching story as an important example of working across subtle yet powerful gender- and culture-related norms for the overall benefit of students. I find in my own professional life that it is usually these subtle rather than more overt situations that prove the most difficult to negotiate, because especially as gender-cultured outsiders it is so tempting to question ourselves rather than directly resist or confront institutional norms.

September 11—Heart, Mind, Body, and Spirit

I chose to share this story from my field notes, though it is often a role of deans of students to serve as the "heart of a campus" responding to crisis with words of compassion. I learned from responses to the speech I gave that going a step further and admitting that professionals might be feeling fear and confusion, emotions not typically associated with strong leaders, seems uncommon even and perhaps especially when there is a crisis. This story illustrates the importance of 'remaining ourselves' and leading authentically amidst gender–cultured constructs of leadership. On September 11, after a long day of emergency operations leadership as dean of students, I was asked to speak at an evening vigil and had 45 minutes to prepare. I sensed intuitively that it was up to me as a leader to go beyond an official measured response of compassion to something I find rare in the public selves of collegiate leaders. As I reflected on what had been happening on our campus, the beauty and the ugliness of responses, the personal mixed with the official, the grief, anger, and confusion, I knew it would be critical to connect to both positive and negative emotions, to inspire goodness in others, and to offer empathy and reassurance. A brief excerpt from my speech follows:

> It is at tragic and frightening times such as we are faced with today, when we are called upon most clearly to rise to our highest character. At times like this, we are faced with many emotions—anger, fear, helplessness, sadness. . . . Please know that we as administrators, service providers, teachers, and scholars are with you in heart and in spirit. We too are hurting and confused and questioning, and we will be turning our energy to assisting you and our community to cope during this difficult time. . . . We will be with you along the way.

In the weeks and months following, I learned that excerpts—especially my words "We too are hurting and confused and questioning . . . and we will be with you along the way"—had been broadcast around the world via Internet. I received hundreds of e-mails thanking me for speaking so clearly about emotions, spirituality, and connection as a collegiate leader. Most individuals I heard from told me that by admitting to feelings of fear, anger, and confusion I connected with them in ways that they had not experienced among leaders in academe. One male student shared that he was experiencing strong feelings of hate, and hearing that faculty and administrators also might feel strong negative emotions kept him from lashing out against others. He felt that his emotions must be normal if professionals might feel the same. Along with the thanks, I also received a number of negative responses from male executive leaders on the campus including my own supervisor, a male leader of color, who expressed concern that I should focus on positive emotions so as not to encourage acceleration of negative ones. In this instance and in many of my other interactions in academe, I find that leaders and professors are often expected to separate and not acknowledge certain emotions, body, and spirit. This is one of the very controversial dilemmas of being a woman and especially a woman of color in academe. We are often pressured to choose between the integrated selves encouraged as beneficial in our gendered cultures and the emotionally separated expectations of leadership in academe.

This seemed to gain in normative power as I climbed the executive ranks of leadership, as did the levels of disapproval I experienced from other leaders for the practice of acknowledging, discussing, or sharing, especially emotions considered weak or otherwise negative. I understand some of the reasons for these choices, based on the danger inherent in opening yourself to personal attacks. High-level leaders receive so much scrutiny and challenge that it is not surprising so many choose to show only a positive or neutral public face. Yet, there are many times when our campuses need the personal; and when showing how we feel and what we believe helps calm, reassure, and heal our college communities. I have seen many collegiate leaders respond to student racial protests with removed, measured, legalistic words that triggered even greater negative responses when some statement of feeling, of empathy, and of personal connection and commitment would be helpful. It takes a kind of moral courage as a leader (Kidder, 2005) to share ourselves in more personal ways in times of crisis, in the classroom, the boardroom, and in our work around the campus. Though we have come a long way because of scholars and leaders who push the edges of practice, the foundations of higher education are still based very substantively in only parts of ourselves as human beings and in gender-cultured constructs from specific origins. I believe it is our role to show a more holistic and authentic face as leaders.

BECOMING PATRONA: BALANCING MATRIARCHY AND MACHISMO

As the executive campus director for an emerging college only 12 years old, a primary role in my leadership was to garner funds for and facilitate the building of a physical campus so that our primarily very low-income students could travel to one campus proper instead of between seven rented locations around the county. To do so, one of my challenges was to negotiate the predominantly Hispanic male arena of public leadership and construction professions. I was able to achieve this by "identifying and seeking the advice of local cultural and gender translators" and "learning yet pushing the edges of cultural and gender rhythms." In keeping with norms of the Spanish American public sphere in this region, Hispanic male leaders, architects, contractors, and craftsmen tended to approach me with great formality, kindness, and a kind of patronizing brotherly or fatherly protectiveness. From the beginning, these Latinos showed a greater comfort in working with the Hispanic male business operations manager for our campus than with me. I decided to contact several elders in the community for advice and to consider the historical roles of men and women within the Spanish cultures of this region (Beck, 1962; Chávez, 1989). The following excerpts serve to illustrate.

> Today I met for the first time with a number of public officials, architects, contractors, and craftsmen who will be involved in the design and construction of our next campus building. Most of these individuals are local Hispanic males, and I was the only woman at the meeting. I noticed that each of these professionals greeted me in the highly formal, courtly, and relational way that is common to this region and traces to social traditions brought from Spain in the 1500s. Each individual made a point to find some way to connect with me in a personal way, sharing that we had gone to high school together, they had high respect for my grandfather, or they shopped at my sisters' store. Each also with a flourish of a hat or quick bow tried to reassure me that they would take care of things so that I did not need to "trouble my mind or dirty my graceful hands."

This is a common phrase by men to women in this region, often spoken in Spanish. I decided at the time to listen, observe and to contact some individuals longer in the community to process some of these gender-cultured constructs and how to best lead amidst them. An excerpt from later that week reads:

> I met today with my father for his advice in leading within the highly Spanish male context of construction professions in this area. I explained what I had experienced; and my father, who has served as a public official, smiled and suggested that the trick would be to find ways to honor their courtliness and to translate their protectiveness to partnership by connecting my experience to theirs.

Later that week, I sought the advice of an elder in our community who is a Mexican American female building contractor and well-known artist. She suggested from her own experiences within this professional community that I invoke aspects of a Latina matriarchal role to lead within this machismo context, explaining that patriarchal roles had shifted with colonization from equal matriarchal and patriarchal roles to this machismo version with patriarchy taking the main stage. She pointed out that Latina women showed much leadership and power in more informal ways, often as voices for our service to community and family. She encouraged me to find ways to bring the power of this matriarchal leadership to bear as I led these men. I knew that I was likely to experience some polite and possibly some hostile responses to my bringing this leadership into realms not typical for Spanish females in this region. An excerpt serves to illustrate what I chose to do.

> Yesterday, I met for the second time with the building team for our newly funded project. To begin signaling leadership I made a point to call the meeting through my office rather than having this done by my business operations manager as I had for the first meeting. I chose to start the meeting on a knoll of land overlooking what would become the center of campus, knowing that the energy of the land would help us come together. I invoked our partnership by speaking of the great honor in building a college together that is already making a profound difference in our community. I spoke as well of knowing the hard work of construction from my own and my sisters' experiences of crafting adobe [mud] bricks for our family home as a child and again more recently with members of the congregation to repair our church. I then outlined generally how I would lead the work, getting

us together bimonthly to facilitate larger decisions and review budgets while encouraging more targeted meetings led by the business, facilities, and project managers to handle daily decisions. When I finished, there was a moment of silence when I noticed some nods of approval as well as some angry and uncomfortable shuffling and glances. An elderly member of the group broke the silence, saying, "Patrona, we are here with you to serve our community."

I heard later that another individual grumbled about the Chávez family's inability to contain their women, and I did eventually lose one individual from the team who said that he would not work for a woman. Yet most of these men seemed to come around. By invoking the power of matriarchal leadership already existing in Spanish traditions and honoring our mutual dedication to the community, I was able to successfully lead in a very Spanish male context. Over time, I learned that many on campus and in the community had begun to refer to me as *patrona*, a female version of a male term for leader-employer-landowner in many Hispanic communities. Unlike many stereotypes of Hispanic and Native women, my early and current experiences are of women who are simultaneously fierce, assertive, and compassionate. By leading through these characteristics, which are often considered opposing in U.S. culture but are often interwoven in my experience of Native and Spanish American women, I have been able to negotiate for a variety of student needs. It is also my hope that I have been able to dispel myths of the "passive Latin women of color" for a few of those with whom I have worked. However, this has never come without the challenges of being patronized or undermined.

HEALING THE UNFORGIVABLE: TROUBLING CHOICES BY GOOD PEOPLE

I chose this professional teaching story to further illustrate the concept of "remaining ourselves," learning yet pushing the edges of cultural and gender rhythm," and "learning to speak the language and priorities of those you wish to persuade." By listening to and responding from my own ways of being while working to understand someone else's way of being, I was able to facilitate some healing during a difficult time. While serving as a dean of students, the university where I worked made headlines when someone noticed photographic discrepancies on the cover of a marketing publication. It was revealed that a photo of an African American student had been inserted into a photo of a crowd of Caucasian American students, and reporters descended on the University. As dean, I contacted the African

American student to offer assistance, fielded some of the media, and offered support to groups of justifiably upset students of color. In addition, I chose to offer support, assistance, and accountability to a decision maker in the situation. Journal reflections follow from that time.

> Today I met with an African American student whose photo was inserted into another photo for a marketing publication. He has been hounded by reporters and is struggling to cope with unasked for and unwanted national attention, the use without permission of his image, and trying to keep up with academics in the midst of turmoil. It is heart wrenching to know that all I can offer is empathy and a bit of support on campus. I am so very impressed with his graceful dignity and compassion in dealing with all of this.

An excerpt a few days later:

> Yesterday, I heard calls for firing of the leader who decided to portray diversity by altering a photograph in a University publication. Though I am angry too, my reaction has been far different. I want this White male leader to stay and make reparation to the campus! It is too easy to walk away, and in my cultural traditions it is important for all to consider longer term relations, regain dignity, and make amends by being held responsible for repairing the damage of our actions.

An excerpt a few weeks later:

> Today I had lunch with the leader who made decisions about the photograph. It has been a difficult 3 weeks, and I can see that he is down. I asked him if he would find it helpful to know what I have been hearing from students of color and others on campus. He seemed distraught as he spoke of meeting with minority students and feeling like they hated him. He spoke of how he was trying so hard to build the student diversity of the campus and was dedicated to advocating for students of color to improve retention. I asked him a few questions about what behaviors from students made him feel that he was hated, then reflected for a moment on how I might assist him in finding healing and in continuing with this priority. I told him that I didn't believe these student behaviors showed hatred. They were clearly frustrated, angry, and hurt about being used and not served well; and their main concern in my experience is to work with us as leaders to improve the campus for those who come after them. I spoke of how misinterpretations are often made across cultures when there are differences in how much

Leading in the Borderlands

we show emotions and asked if part of what he was feeling might also be from an upbringing of low public displays of emotion. He looked startled and said that yes; he had been raised to show mostly positive emotions and had been taken aback at the strong emotions shown by these students. He asked me how he might go about working through this; and I suggested he meet with some of these students, share how he was feeling, ask for their assistance in significant ways, and work to apply as many of their ideas as possible.

By putting aside my own frustrations and empathizing with this leader from a *Mestiza* framework of lifelong relationships, accountability, and healing, I was able to facilitate shifting his focus toward understanding, connecting with students as partners, and finding solutions. In a small way I assisted a well-meaning person to overcome a profound misjudgment. It was important in this situation for me to draw from the concepts of Spanish and Indigenous cultures to frame every relationship as a lifelong one, healing beyond mistakes, and making reparation to those we harm. It was also important to work at understanding some of the cultural and gender perspectives of this leader and to assist him to reconsider his assumptions about students of color. As I began to urge others on campus to support this leader in making reparation, I found that ethnic patriarchy manifested also among cultures with long-term relational orientations like mine. Many continued to call for his firing, some becoming angry at my call for us to work through this together. My greatest ally in this instance proved to be the African American student who had been added to the photograph. He came out in a very public way to offer forgiveness and urge the campus to work with this and other leaders to heal the community and learn from this mistake. In this way, we were able to negotiate some of the individualistic, quick-solution orientations of White ethnic patriarchy (Ibbara, 2001) that can prevent healing, reparation, connection, and longer-term solutions within the diversity of our campus communities.

ROLE DANCING: COLLABORATING WITH NATIVE AMERICAN MALE TRIBAL COUNCILS

Perhaps one of my greatest challenges as the leader of a campus in the southwest was to gain entrance and start collaborative partnerships with Native American male tribal governors. This teaching story illustrates three concepts of negotiating ethnic patriarchy suggested by this study, "learning yet pushing the edges of cultural and gender rhythms," "seeking the advice of cultural translators," and "learning to speak the language and priorities of those you wish to persuade." There are 22 distinct tribes in this state, and this small institution serves two tribal pueblos. Both of these tribes are highly patriarchal in public aspects of government, and only men sit in governorships and councils. Women hold important roles in other aspects of tribal life but are rarely permitted in this public aspect of government. To complicate matters, most of the Native American students we served at that time were women, and even before my arrival many of these women were beginning to make demands to become leaders and have a role in the more public aspects of their tribal governments. Excerpts from this time read:

> Today I met with the Governor of the Pueblo after a series of meetings and discussions with the tribal secretary, the tribal administrator, and several friends who are members of the tribe. Though I have much Native ancestry, I was not tribally raised and it is with great care that I need to proceed. Knowing that women are not typically allowed in tribal council meetings, I considered sending our male dean of instruction in my place but decided that my leadership as a woman would be important to Native women and to the college. After consultation with tribal members about cultural and governmental protocol, I determined that calling upon relationships I have with individuals near the governor would be critical to gaining entry. I walked into a room filled with Native American male council members, introduced myself with my family and clan names, and spoke of my wish to serve the tribe. We had much discussion about collaborations that would benefit the tribe. I was treated with great formality and respect as a leader in education. This surprised me to some extent since I had observed Native women of the tribe reprimanded publicly on a number of occasions for speaking up.

I was told by several leaders including a pueblo governor that few community leaders ever approached the tribe except to ask for something and my very formal and respectful leadership demeanor, attention to protocol, and offer of assistance and collaboration made a difference in garnering partnerships between the tribe and the college. In the almost 4 years I served as campus leader, we built needed academic programs, negotiated policy changes concerning credit for tribal languages, developed courses in Native Studies, held retreats to boost student success, and collaborated on sustainability initiatives. By taking the time to learn appropriate protocol, build long-term relationships, and take on the activist stance of entering all male domains as a woman, I was able to serve as a catalyst for collaborative endeavors between the campus and tribes. As I look back now on that first meeting I am humbled that I gained entry into this male world and yet troubled that this is such a rare occurrence for women in the tribe. I believe as well that some of my own stereotypical beliefs about male and female tribal roles would have gotten in the way if I had not contacted several individuals within the tribe for advice and assistance in gaining entry. As an outsider to this tribe, my influence was mostly leading by example as a woman of color, and it is hard to say if my actions evoked transformation.

Building Relationships and Forming Allies: Proactively Developing Cultural Translators

In situations such as those described earlier, I identified and contacted individuals to serve as cultural translators on negotiating ethnic patriarchy. I find that it is helpful to do this on an ongoing basis so when needs arise there is already a relationship. One way that I have often applied the practice of gathering over food common in my cultures is to invite campus leaders to coffee, tea, or lunch to ask about their beliefs and priorities. I find that individuals are often startled when asked what is important to them. I long ago lost track of the added benefits of this technique, yet two stories serve to illustrate—one in targeting specific cultural translators and the second in looking for these individuals through daily activities. While serving as a part of the dean's council, I was told that a particular academic dean at the university was difficult to know and I noticed that he was often contentious in meetings. It took me awhile to arrange a meeting with him, but he finally agreed to a walk for coffee on campus. Excerpts from my field notes illustrate.

> Today I met with an academic dean to start building our relationship. I took the opportunity to ask him how he came to be a dean. He looked at me strangely and sighed, launching into a fascinating account of his dislike for administrators and yet his passion for student learning and the development of knowledge. On our return toward his building, I asked how I might be of service to him, and he told me that he would have to think about this.

I left it at that but then began to notice that he would seek me out at deans' meetings to chat about many things including identity privilege and how we might each use our own privilege to benefit others. A few months later my field notes read:

> I spoke up passionately today in dean's council for the needs and contributions of students of color and drew a blank look from almost everyone. I have become used to having my ideas ignored as one of the few women and the only person of color on the council. I paused for a moment in frustration and suddenly, this dean stood up and spoke. He urged everyone that student learning and the development of new knowledge would be benefited if we paid attention to the diverse ways of our students. He then spoke of his esteem for me and that with me in the council and my extensive background in working with diverse students, we might have a chance even in this state of making progress. He turned to me saying "Dr. Chávez, we would be honored if you would continue."

Though I could have been upset that it took a White older male to get the attention of this council about the needs of students of color, instead I felt so very grateful to have found a way to connect and ally with someone who already had the influence to persuade an important group on campus. When I thanked him later he responded that conversations we'd had taught him that he had a responsibility to use his White male privilege to make a difference among his peers. Though my struggles within this very White, older male council continued, I felt less alone in standing up for students.

As a dean of students, I often met with groups outside the university to garner their support for students. While having lunch with a group of Chinese American businessmen, one individual caught my eye and silently motioned to how he was holding his teacup to be served. When the waiter served me, I too bowed my head and held the cup with one hand while placing finger tips of my other hand beneath. When I looked up, I noticed nods of approval from around the table and the leader began to invite me directly into conversation and ask how he could be of assistance to the University. After the luncheon, the man who had motioned to me shared that this one small act signaled that I was a leader who paid attention to the importance of small things, was willing to go beyond my own comfortable rhythms to work with others, and who would be a person of honor even in difficult times. I was amazed that my small act had communicated these important messages. I began to seek this individual's advice in continuing to work with this group over time in support of the University. This was often a bumpy road as a woman working with an all-Chinese male group.

I often encountered disdain, dismissing of my words, and sometimes was completely ignored, yet this cultural translator allied with me consistently to understand and work through these barriers. By taking a proactively relational stance with other leaders, I have been able to continually form critical allies and cultural translators for the work of advocating for and serving students.

DISCUSSION AND RECOMMENDATIONS: NEGOTIATING ETHNIC PATRIARCHY

In this section, I discuss key recommendations illustrated in the professional teaching stories for those working across culture and gender to benefit students. Developing cultural competence as leaders is essential if we are to continue transforming education within a highly diverse country and global society (Lindsey, Nuri Robins, & Terrell, 1999; Pope, Reynolds, & Mueller, 2004). Remaining ourselves, learning and yet pushing cultural and gender rhythms of others, seeking advice from cultural translators, and learning to speak the language and priorities of those you wish to persuade are primary strategies I find critical as a woman of color leading in higher education. These are not easy practices, and we must each find our own ways to push gender-cultured boundaries of identity in higher education.

REMAINING OURSELVES: BRINGING HEART, MIND, BODY, AND SPIRIT

Recently, I had yet another experience of individuals becoming irritated with my cultured professional norms while simultaneously receiving strong positive remarks from others who believe that my cultured ways have had a profound effect on them. I reached out for help to a longtime friend and partner activist and asked her how I might make sense of these opposing messages. She explained that *I am the same person in both situations*; and the same qualities that some may see as wise, compassionate, and helpful to education are seen by others as problematic, irritating, disruptive, and even dangerous to the status quo of academe. She explained that those who actively transform organizations and who by our very identity have a transformative impact are often seen negatively by those who are happy and comfortable with the current culture of education (Chagnon, 2006). I have to admit that I was stunned by her interpretation. As someone who is very introspective and constantly trying to improve myself, it had never occurred to me that the same qualities could attract such opposite responses. I kept thinking that if I could just improve or get rid of my "bad qualities," things would be fine.

Though I will always strive to discern which of my professional traits and behaviors might be problematic and need improvement, this was a freeing revelation to me as a *Mestiza* whose essence in many ways is opposite to much of academic culture (Ibarra, 2001; Mihesuah & Wilson, 2004). One of the most powerful social tools in pushing for conformity to identity norms is to make others feel as though their ways are problematic, and it is when those who are different and their allies stand up and give voice that this begins to change (Anzaldúa, 1990; Lorde, 1984; Lukes, 1974). So how do we as women and especially women of color negotiate this tension of opposites? How do our allies work with us to transform academe so that many ways of being are welcomed, encouraged, and garnered as assets to our work? Audre Lourde provides perhaps one of the best guides in her now famous urging not to dismantle the master's house with the master's tools (1984). With these words, she was urging African American women not to respond to ethnic patriarchy with White male strategies and norms, cautioning that these would reinforce the status quo rather than transform systems. As a leader, teacher, and scholar, I strive to avoid the competition, individuality above collectivity, power over others, and the separation of parts of myself as a leader that are all too common in collegiate culture (Ibarra, 2001). In keeping with tenets of indigenous and Latina feminisms that urge a balance of ways among differences (Garcia, 1995; Green, 2007), I purposefully contemplate and experiment with ways to integrate my own ways while honoring the ways of others. I do this by striving toward behaviors that are congruent with my beliefs and discarding those that derive from what I believe are destructive institutionalized forms of "the master's tools." Though I sometimes face negative reactions and consequences from other leaders, these practices allow me to act in small and large ways as a transformative leader and educator (Rhoads & Black, 1995). It is not only others who serve as barriers. I find I also have to struggle to deconstruct and critique my own stereotypes, gender-role expectations, and cultural values. This is one of the reasons that as a leader and teacher, I also urge professionals to make time regularly for purposeful contemplation and self-assessment.

Learning yet Pushing the Edges of Cultural and Gender Rhythms

Individuals who work effectively in other nations such as international educators, military personnel, and global corporate employees know the power of constantly staying vigilant in their study of the language, etiquette, mannerisms, and rhythms of others while remaining true to their own ideals (Torbiörn, 1994). This is true within the United States as well. Learning and respecting others' social and cultural norms is an important sign of respect. Yet to transform higher education toward a diverse epistemology and practice we must continually push these norms. I respect as well as push cultural and gender norms by including my ways while paying attention to and practicing at least some ways of others. Integration is a way of showing respect practiced by women in both of my cultures. In this way I am able to remain true to who I am while respectfully negotiating another's cultures. This seems to be one of the most contested aspects of feminist theory across cultures (Green, 2007). Indigenous and Latina feminists originate in collaborative cultures where it is considered healing to work toward solutions that are in balance for everyone (Canella & Manuelito, 2008; Mihesuah & Wilson, 2004). This often leads to questions about our authenticity in remaining true to ourselves. Yet by working collaboratively across differences and honoring ourselves even as we honor others, we are staying true to our deepest gender-cultured ideals.

Identify, Form Relationships with, and Seek Advice from "Cultural Translators"

As noted in most of the professional teaching stories in this article, I have been blessed to identify, cultivate, learn from, and partner with many cultural translators in my professional life. This in part comes from my own gender-cultured tendencies toward relational strategies and lifelong relationships. This is a kind of leadership activity I consider highly essential to negotiating ethnic patriarchy successfully enough to truly benefit students across campus. I encourage leaders and other practitioners to purposefully make time to cultivate relationships on a regular basis, to remain on the lookout for those who might be empathetic and helpful within a group needing influence, and to seek targeted cultural translators for assistance with distinctive gender-cultured situations. I continue to be thankful for individuals willing to assist when I approach them with a sincere desire to learn. Yet even in the caring atmosphere common in student affairs, I often received disapproving comments over the years about my highly relational working style. More than one supervisor has cautioned me to spend greater time on projects and less time relationship building even if they also express that my productivity level is at 150%! I was always amazed that this kind of feedback usually came from women and that these leaders didn't seem to understand that my productivity was a direct result of my relational style. We still have a ways to go even within ourselves to transform gender-cultured campus norms.

Learn to Speak the Language and Priorities of Those You Wish to Persuade

I am often struck by frustrations I see as individuals in higher education try to persuade those from other professional or cultural groups using their own professional jargon and priorities. Voices rise, words are repeated, and the group is often blamed for not understanding or caring. I learned long ago that to persuade effectively I must learn the language and frame things in both my own and the priorities of others. I often add differentiated language to persuade faculty, administrators, student affairs professionals, donors, and regents. For example, the language of knowledge, autonomy, and governance are common among faculty while the language of student development, community, accountability, and leadership are some of the strong terms and priorities of student affairs. When I first moved from student affairs to faculty environs, then again from faculty to central administration, I found that if I was going to benefit students widely it was critical for me to learn professional language and priorities of many constituency groups. Even when priorities are similar, different professional language or jargon is often used to describe the same things. I find that I must be innovative in making connections based in the professional language of different groups and framed to support their priorities as well as my own. Similarly, various ethnic and gender groups often share language and priorities. Since I do not have a background in every subculture, I find it useful to learn from group insiders and to observe groups prior to trying to persuade them of something. I have spent countless highly productive hours attending meetings of groups I need to persuade such as faculty senates, student organizations, city councils, and regents. In addition, I gain insight toward assisting in their mission. The key for me to do this authentically is to offer rationale from my own priorities mixed with rationale that I believe is in line with theirs.

CONCLUSION

Since I began writing this article, we have been through a historic time when a White woman became speaker of the house and a Black man has been elected as president. Though I see how much race and gender were exploited in the process and wonder how long before we see a woman of color as contender, I find hope in this progress. I also find great hope in the subtle and overt activism I see on college campuses, in the courage of students and colleagues who continue struggling in gender-cultured environs not their own, and in my own mixed *Mestiza* blood . . . *La Sangre* running through my veins and through the diverse blood of this country. Ethnic patriarchy is something we must acknowledge and deconstruct in higher education as we serve a global society. There is much to be done within ourselves, in working with others, and in recrafting our collegiate institutions toward a more diverse set of identity-based epistemologies and practices.

Crafting our own ways of leading authentically within the borderlands of identity is an ongoing endeavor. While remaining true to ourselves, we must continually learn to negotiate the cultures of others if we are to serve students in the halls of academe. A quote by Susan Wooley shared by a longtime friend and colleague as we negotiated across our cultural differences provides powerful testimony.

> We have lifetimes of undigested, unassimilated experience to be unpacked, catalogued, and crafted into theory, providing the foundation from which to later speak with men. The only way to stop being outlaws is to become lawmakers . . . at last trusting our own experience.

I often imagine the marvelous possibilities of research, leadership, and teaching if we would use our full, complex, and integrated selves in each moment, each endeavor. Perhaps our most radical and important daily act is to be fully ourselves so that we can collectively imagine a more diverse epistemology of higher education and work together to transform.

REFERENCES

Anzaldúa, G. (1987). *Borderlands, la frontera: The new Mestiza* (2nd ed.). San Francisco: Aunt Lute Books.

Anzaldúa, G. (Ed.). (1990). *Making face, making soul, haciendo caras: Creative and critical perspectives by feminists of color*. San Francisco: Aunt Lute Books.

Beck, W. A. (1962). *New Mexico: A history of four centuries*. Norman, Oklahoma: University of Oklahoma Press.

Borrego, S. E., & Manning, K. (2007). *Where I am from: Student affairs practice from the whole of student's lives.* Washington, DC: National Association of Student Personnel Administrators.

Borrego, S. E., Guido-DiBrito, F., & Chávez, A. F. (2008). *A critical qualitative exploration of class culture.* Unpublished manuscript.

Cajete, G. (1994). *Look to the mountain: An ecology of indigenous education.* Ashville, NC: Kivaki Press.

Cannella, G. S., & Manuelito, K. D. (2008). Feminisms from unthought locations: Indigenous worldviews, marginalized feminisms, and revisioning anticolonial social science. In N. K. Denzin, Y. S. Lincoln, & L. Tuhiwai Smith, *Handbook of critical and indigenous methodologies* (pp. 45–59). Thousand Oaks, CA: Sage.

Chávez, A. F., Guido-DiBrito, F., & Mallory, S. (2003). Learning to value the "other": A model of diversity development. *Journal of College Student Development, 44*(4), 1–17

Chávez, F. A. (1989). *Chávez: A distinctive American clan.* Santa Fe, NM: William Gannon.

Dews, C. L. B., & Law, C. L. (1995). *This fine place so far from home.* Philadelphia: Temple University Press.

Ellis, C. (2004). *The ethnographic I: A methodological novel about autoethnography.* Walnut Creek, CA: Alta Mira Press.

Evans, N. J., Forney, D. S., & Guido-DiBrito, F. (1998). *Student development in college: Theory, research and practice.* San Francisco: Jossey-Bass.

Fried, J., & Associates (1995). *Shifting paradigms in student affairs: Culture, context, teaching and learning.* Lanham, MD: American College Personnel Association.

Frankenberg, R. (1993). *White women, race matters: The social construction of whiteness.* Minneapolis: University of Minnesota Press.

García, A. M. (1995). The development of Chicana feminist discourse. In A. Kesselman, L. D. McNair, & N. Schniedewind (Eds.), *Women images and realities: A multicultural anthology* (pp. 406–416). Mountain View, CA: Mayfield.

Garrod, A., & Larimore, C. (1997). *First person, first peoples: Native American college graduates tell their life stories.* Ithaca, NY: Cornell University Press.

Gerber, P. J., & Reif, H. B. (1991). *Speaking for themselves: Ethnographic interviews with adults with learning disabilities.* Ann Arbor, MI: University of Michigan Press.

Geertz, C. (1973). *The interpretation of cultures: Selected essays*. New York: Basic Books.

Grande, S. (2004). *Red Pedagogy: Native American social and political thought*. Lanham, MD: Rowman and Littlefield Publishers.

Green, J. (Ed.) (2007). *Making space for indigenous feminism*. Black Point, Nova Scotia: Fernwood Publishing.

Guido-DiBrito, F., & Chávez, A. F. (2003). Understanding the ethnic self: Learning and teaching in a multicultural world. *Colorado State University Journal of Student Affairs, XII*, 11–21.

Gunn Allen, P. (1989). Grandmother of the sun: The power of women in Native America. In J. Plaskow & C. P. Christ, *Weaving the visions: New patterns in feminist spirituality*. San Francisco: Harper & Row.

Holman Jones, S. (2005). Autoethnography: Making the personal political. In N. K. Denzin & Y. S. Lincoln, *The SAGE handbook of qualitative research*, 3rd ed. Thousand Oaks, CA: Sage.

Huberman, A., & Miles, M. (1994). Data management and analysis methods. In N. K. Denzin & Y. S. Lincoln (Eds.), *Handbook of qualitative research* (pp. 428–444). Thousand Oaks, CA: Sage.

Hurtado, A. (1996). *The color of privilege: Three blasphemies on race and feminism*. Ann Arbor, MI: The University of Michigan Press.

Ibarra, R. (2001). *Beyond affirmative action: Reframing the context of higher education*. Madison, WI: University of Wisconsin.

Kidder, R. M. (2005). *Moral courage*. New York: Harper Collins Publishers.

Kipnis, A. R. (1991). *Knights without armor: A practical guide for men in quest of masculine soul*. New York: Putnam.

Lorde, A. (1984). *Sister outsider: Essays and speeches by Audre Lorde*. Trumansberg, NY: The Crossing Press.

Lukes, S. (1974). *Power: A radical view*. London: MacMillan.

Lindsey, R. B., Nuri Robins, K., & Terrell, R. D. (1999). *Cultural proficiency: A manual for school leaders*. Thousand Oaks, CA: Corwin Press.

Marshall, C., & Rossman, G. B. (2006). *Designing qualitative research* (4th ed.). Thousand Oaks, CA: Sage.

Merriam, S. B., Johnson-Bailey, J., Lee, M. Y., Ntseane, G., & Muhamad, M. (2001). Power and positionality: Negotiating insider/outsider status within and across cultures. *International Journal of Lifelong Education, 20*(5), 405–416.

Mihesuah, D. A., & Wilson, A. C. (2004). *Indigenizing the academy: Transforming scholarship and empowering communities.* Lincoln, NE: University of Nebraska Press.

National Center for Education Statistics. (2006). *Digest of education statistics, 2005* (NCES 2006-030), chapter 3. U.S. Department of Education. Retrieved July 9, 2008 from http://nces.ed.gov/fastfacts/display.asp?id=61

Ng, R. (2000). A woman out of control: Deconstructing sexism and racism in the university. In J. Glazer Raymo, B. K. Townsend, & B. Ropers-Huilman (Eds), *Women in higher education: A feminist perspective* (pp. 360–370). Boston: Pearson Custom.

Parker, L., Deyhle, D., & Vellenas, S. A. (Eds.). (1999). *Race is . . . race isn't: Critical race theory and qualitative studies in education.* Boulder, CO: Westview Press.

Pelias, R. J. (2004). *A methodology of the heart.* Walnut Creek, CA: AltaMira Press.

Pope, R., Reynolds, A., & Mueller, J. (2004). *Multicultural competence in student affairs.* San Francisco: Jossey-Bass.

Rhoads, R. A. (1994). *Coming out in college: The struggle for a queer identity.* Westport, CT: Bergin & Garvey.

Rhoads, R. A., & Black, M. A. (1995). Student affairs practitioners as transformative educators: Advancing a critical cultural perspective. *Journal of College Student Development, 36*(5), 413–421.

Rich, A. (1993). Toward a woman centered university. In J. Glazer, E. Bensimon, & B. Townsend, *Women in higher education: A feminist perspective* (pp. 121–134). ASHE Readers Series. Needham Heights, MA: Ginn Press.

Rochlin, J. M. (1997). *Race & class on campus: Conversations with Ricardo's daughter.* Tucson, AZ: University of Arizona Press.

Sanlo, R. (Ed.) (2005). Gender identity and sexual orientation: Research, policy, and personal perspectives. *New Directions in Student Services, 111.* San Francisco: Jossey-Bass.

Schwartz, J., Donovan, J., & Guido-DiBrito, F. (2008). Stories of social class: Self-identified Mexican male college students crack the silence. Unpublished manuscript.

Strange, C. (2000). Creating environments of ability. *New Directions for Student Services, 91.* San Francisco: Jossey-Bass.

Tierney, W. G., & Bensimon, E. M. (2000). (En)Gender(ing) socialization. In J. Glazer Raymo, B. K. Townsend, & B. Ropers-Huilman (Eds),

Women in higher education: A feminist perspective (pp. 309–325). Boston: Pearson Custom.

Torbiörn, I. (1994). Dynamics of cross-cultural adaptation. In G. Althen, *Learning across cultures.* NAFSA Association of International Educators.

Turner, C. S. V. (2007). Pathways to the presidency: Biographical sketches of women of color firsts. *Harvard Educational Review, 77*(1), 1–38.

U.S. Department of Education. (2006). *A test of leadership: Charting the future of U.S. higher education.* Commission Report. Washington, DC: U.S. Department of Education.

U.S. Census Bureau. (2000). Profiles of general demographic characteristics: National summary, Retrieved July 9, 2008 from http://www.census.gov/prod/cen2000/dp1/2khus.pdf

Valverde, L. A. (2003). *Leaders of color in higher education: Unrecognized triumphs in harsh institutions.* Walnut Creek, CA: Alta Mira Press.

Villegas, M., Rak Neugebauer, S., & Venegas, K. R. (2008). *Indigenous knowledge and education: Sites of struggle, strength and survival.* Harvard Educational Review Reprint Series, no 44. Boston: Harvard Review Publishing.

Wolgemuth, J. R., & Harbour, C. P. (2007). A man's academy? The dissertation process as feminist resistance. *NASPA Journal About Women in Higher Education, 1,* 181–201.

Turning Away from Academic Careers: What Does Work-Family Have To Do with It?

Kate Quinn
Project Director for Balance@UW
Office of the Provost
University of Washington

Elizabeth Litzler
Director for Research
Center for Workforce Development
University of Washington

> *This study explores factors in graduate students' decisions to turn away from their academic career aspirations to determine the role of work-family concerns. An original survey instrument was designed to collect information about individual characteristics, experiences in graduate school, career aspiration, and perceptions of the family-friendliness of academic careers. This paper focuses on 238 PhD students in the science, technology, engineering, and mathematics (STEM) fields and the arts, humanities, and social science (AHSS) fields. Analysis includes bivariate correlations and multiple logistic regression. Findings are mixed regarding the influence of work-family concerns on the decision to turn away from academic career aspirations. Additionally, net of other variables, gender has no impact on the decision to turn away from academic career aspirations.*

The underrepresentation of women among the faculty of prestigious research universities has caused speculation about reasons for women's "lack of interest" in these positions (Richmond, 2005; Rimer, 2005; Sears, 2003; Wilson, 2004, 2005). Factors such as "chilly climates" and sexism may influence the decision to avoid academic careers for some women graduate students (Wilson, 2004, 2005), but it is believed that perception of the ability, or lack thereof, to simultaneously have children and a competitive academic career plays a large role (Richmond, 2005; Rimer, 2005; Sears, 2003; The Associated Press & The New York Times, 2005; Wilson, 2004, 2005). In fact, it has been suggested that some PhD recipients are selecting careers based on the perceived potential to achieve work-family balance and not on factors related to their original academic career aspirations (Golde & Dore, 2001; Nyquist et al., 1999; Wolf-Wendel & Ward, 2001). If this is happening, some brilliant scholars could be turning away from their academic career aspirations out of the desire for a balanced life that combines a successful career and a satisfying family life—a life they do not perceive as possible in academe.

If institutions of higher education are to remain competitive, they must be able to recruit and retain the best and brightest faculty members (American Council on Education, 2005; Committee on Maximizing the Potential of Women in Academic Science and Engineering, 2006). Consequently, considerable attention is being given to whether potential faculty are turning to private practice, industry, or government careers and away from the academy because of concerns for work-life balance (Ashburn, 2007; Bickel & Brown, 2005; Gappa, Austin, & Trice, 2007). But, are work-family concerns a primary reason why potential future faculty, especially women, turn away from academic careers?

The purpose of this paper is to explore the role of work-family concerns in graduate students' decisions to turn away from their academic career aspirations. By the time students reach this decision, considerable time and resources have been invested—both by the students and by their institutions and faculty members. A better understanding of why graduate students turn away from their academic career aspirations could assist universities in retaining potential future faculty in the pipeline. In many fields, the lack of women faculty is more pronounced than is the lack of men (Wilson, 2004), but some fields are experiencing challenges recruiting and retaining junior faculty of both genders (Bickel & Brown, 2005).

Researchers (Golde, 1998; Rice, Sorcinelli, & Austin, 2000; Sears, 2003) have found that many graduate students believe that faculty careers are not conducive to balancing work and family roles. Golde (1998) identified a relationship between desire for work-family balance and graduate students' decisions to leave graduate school. Rice, Sorcinelli, and Austin (2000) found that work-family balance was a common stressor for both graduate students and early career faculty. Sears (2003) discovered that women graduate students in science and engineering fields "downgrade" their academic career aspirations and express concern for work-family balance more frequently than men in the same fields do. However, none of these studies controlled for other factors occurring in graduate school to explore the unique influence of work-family concerns on a student's decision to turn away from his or her academic career aspirations.

CONCEPTUAL FRAMEWORK

This study uses graduate student socialization theory (Weidman, Twale, & Stein, 2001) as an integral part of an Input—Experiences—Outcome conceptual model. In the model (Figure 1), graduate students' attributes, their experiences in graduate school, the opinions they form about whether there is a bias against work-family flexibility in academic careers and whether they are confident in their career preparation, are all directly or indirectly related to their decision to turn away from an academic career. The model indicates that student attributes are related to student experiences in graduate school, which in turn are related to student opinions. The model has the decision to turn away from academic career aspirations as the outcome. Additionally, two theories related to work-family are added to the model: Life Role Priority (LRP) (Friedman & Greenhaus, 2000) and bias avoidance (Drago et al., 2004).

Figure 1. Conceptual framework of factors in graduate student decisions to turn away from academic career aspirations.

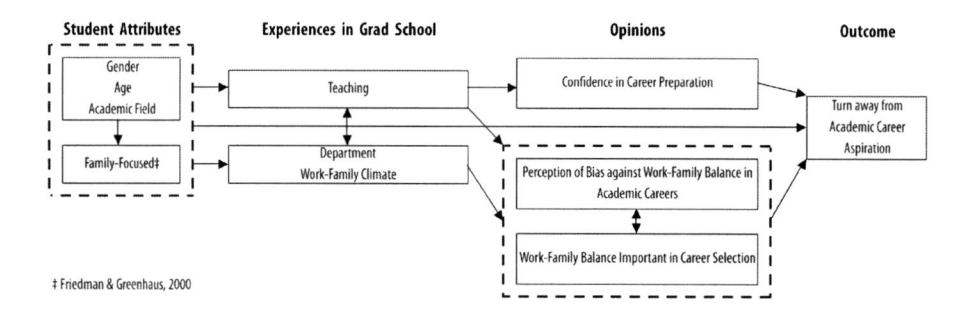

‡ Friedman & Greenhaus, 2000

Socialization theory, as it pertains to graduate students, posits that the attributes with which graduate students enter their programs influence the experiences students have in graduate school and whether they continue toward the careers they wanted when they started graduate school (i.e., the target role) (Weidman et al., 2001). Similarly, experiences in graduate school influence students' opinions about the target career and their level of confidence in their preparation for it, as well as their subsequent career decisions. Through socialization, students learn the norms of academic life and make decisions about whether to adopt attitudes in line with the norms or to change career aspirations. In graduate school, students engage in *acquisition* of the knowledge relevant to the target role, *investment* in the target role, and *involvement* with the target role both within the department/university and in national professional/disciplinary associations.

Institutional culture, at various levels including the college, department, and research group or lab, provides students with information about whether work-family balance is appropriate or permitted, or if the ideal worker norm is rewarded. Similarly, at the national/disciplinary level, students attend conferences or work with practitioners and learn about the overall field's perception of work-family, and expectation of work-family balance. Through socialization, students begin to identify with the target role. They either see themselves performing the role, or they turn away from the original target. For example, if students perceive their department climate to be unwelcome to the kinds of work-life balance they desire or a bias against work-family flexibility in academic careers, they may determine that academic careers are not conducive to the lives they want and may turn away from academic career aspirations.

LRP (Friedman & Greenhaus, 2000) refers to how individuals rank the importance of four areas to their overall feelings of success in life. Individuals who rank family and personal relationships as most important to feelings of life success are considered "family-focused." Those who rank career success as most important are "work-focused." Those who rank family and career equally are "work-family focused." Individuals who rank aspects of community, civic, or religious service/activities or personal recreation and leisure as most important are identified as "self/society focused." In a study of MBA recipients' satisfaction with work and life, Friedman and Greenhaus (2000) found that all four LRPs correlated either positively or negatively with the level of satisfaction both with work and with life outside of work (including family). This study is the first to look at how this theory plays out for graduate students, exploring whether having the LRP "family-focused" influences students' experiences in graduate school, their opinions, and the decision to turn away from academic career aspirations. The LRP "family-focused" was selected for this study because we predict that graduate students who prioritize family and personal life are the best indicator of whether potential future faculty members see academic careers as incompatible with satisfying family and personal lives.

Bias avoidance (Drago et al., 2004) is based on the assumptions that: (1) "Ideal Workers" (Williams, 2000), or those individuals who can devote a lifetime of undistracted commitment to their careers, are rewarded highly; (2) individuals who occasionally miss work for caregiving responsibilities or who appear to put family concerns ahead of their careers are not "ideal workers" and are therefore not rewarded and, in fact, may be penalized; and (3) individuals will hide attributes that potentially identify them as caregivers in order to appear to be ideal workers, thereby avoiding potential career repercussions. In other words, according to the theory of bias avoidance, individuals with family commitments will try to hide these characteristics in order to avoid having their commitment to career questioned. According to this theory, if the environment is supportive of work-family balance, caregivers will not exhibit bias avoidance behaviors or fear career repercussions (Drago et al., 2005). To explore the effect of bias avoidance, this study measures if students indicate fear of career repercussion if they use a flexible policy option, an affirmative response means that they perceive a bias to be avoided. Prior studies of bias avoidance have examined faculty behaviors and perceptions. This is the first study to explore bias avoidance within the context of graduate education and look specifically at graduate student socialization to work and family in academic careers.

METHODS

The research questions that guide this study are: (1) What student attributes, experiences, and opinions affect graduate students' decisions to turn away from their academic career aspirations?; (2) To what degree do each of the influential factors play a role in this decision?; and (3) Do work-family concerns play a significant role in the decision to turn away from an academic career aspiration?

SAMPLE

The data for this study come from a larger sample of 1,190 graduate and professional students from a large, public, research extensive institution that is a member of the American Association of Universities (AAU) and shares many characteristics in both faculty and graduate student body with other AAU universities of comparable size and ranking. This university grants 600+ PhD degrees annually, is a leader among public universities for federal research and training grants, and many of its research doctorate programs rank among the best in the country, according to the National Research Council's study on research doctorate programs (Goldberger, Maher, & Flattau, 1995).

This paper focuses on a subset of 238 PhD students, (57.6% female, 42.4% male) in the science, technology, engineering, and mathematics (STEM) fields and in the arts, humanities, and social science (AHSS) fields. As the focus of this paper is on factors influencing graduate student decisions to turn away from academic career aspirations, these fields were selected due to the high proportion of potential academic careers. Tables 1 and 2 provide the comparisons between sample and population by gender and field and by age bracket and field for all STEM and AHSS respondents. Analysis is restricted to respondents who indicated their gender, whether they changed career aspirations during graduate school, and had valid values on all relevant variables (Table 3). Of this subset, 32.8% indicate turning away from academic career aspirations.

TABLE 1. Comparison of population and sample proportions by gender and field.

Gender	AHSS [a] Population ($n = 1519$)	AHSS [a] Sample ($n = 159$)	STEM [b] Population ($n = 2624$)	STEM [b] Sample ($n = 315$)
Men	45%	36%	63%	44%
Women	55%	64%	37%	56%

[a] $\chi^2(1, N = 1678) = 5.13, p = .024$
[b] $\chi^2(1, N = 2939) = 41.70, p = .000$

TABLE 2. Comparison of population and sample proportions by age and field.

	AHSS[a]		STEM[b]	
Age	Population ($n = 1519$)	Sample ($n = 159$)	Population ($n = 2624$)	Sample ($n = 315$)
16–20	<1%	<1%	<1%	<1%
21–25	19%	19%	29%	28%
26–30	38%	43%	43%	44%
31–35	22%	22%	16%	16%
36–40	10%	7%	6%	5%
41–45	4%	4%	3%	4%
46–50	3%	2%	2%	2%
51 or older	4%	1%	1%	1%

[a] $\chi^2(7, N = 1680) = 4.80, p = .684$
[b] $\chi^2(7, N = 2939) = 3.48, p = .837$

Procedures

Data for this paper are derived from a larger study of graduate and professional student socialization regarding work and family in higher education. Data were gathered June 2005 through a Web-based survey designed for the study. The entire population of students matriculated in a graduate or professional program at the selected University received an e-mailed invitation to take the survey, which included the endorsement of the graduate student senate and the dean of the graduate school, as well as the URL to the consent form. Consenting subjects continued to the online questionnaire. Nonrespondents received one reminder e-mail message 2 weeks after the initial invitation to participate. The 1,190 respondents represent an 11.2% response rate to the survey. While this response rate was lower than desired, the sample size is large enough to permit statistical analyses and the characteristics of the sample only differ from those of the population by gender, with female respondents overrepresented in the sample.

The survey was developed through a pilot study in which graduate students were interviewed about their perceptions of the family-friendliness of their departments and of academic careers in their fields. Data from the pilot were used to establish relevant items and wordings for the survey instrument. The survey instrument was tested item by item with a sample of 10 graduate and professional students to verify that questions were worded appropriately to obtain the intended data. Based on feedback from

TABLE 3. Descriptive statistics.

	Total		AHSS				STEM			
			Female		Male		Female		Male	
	Mean	SD	Mean	SD	Mean	SD	Mean	SD	Mean	SD
DV: Turn away from academic aspirations	0.33	0.47	0.31	0.47	0.29	0.46	0.44	0.50	0.23	0.42
Female	0.58	0.50	1.00	0.00	0.00	0.00	1.00	0.00	0.00	0.00
Family-Focused	0.29	0.45	0.27	0.45	0.19	0.40	0.33	0.47	0.29	0.46
Gen Y	0.18	0.39	0.04	0.20	0.10	0.30	0.26	0.44	0.21	0.41
Gen X	0.71	0.45	0.82	0.39	0.67	0.48	0.67	0.47	0.69	0.47
Older	0.11	0.31	0.14	0.35	0.24	0.44	0.07	0.26	0.10	0.30
In STEM Field	0.70	0.46	0.00	0.00	0.00	0.00	1.00	0.00	1.00	0.00
Experience gained in teaching	0.83	0.38	0.88	0.33	0.86	0.36	0.83	0.38	0.79	0.41
Hostile department climate for W-F balance	3.16	1.05	3.37	0.92	2.81	1.12	3.28	1.05	2.99	1.07
Am confident in career preparation	3.62	0.97	3.57	1.20	3.67	1.11	3.50	0.95	3.76	0.77
Perception of bias against W-F flexibility	0.00	1.00	0.08	1.00	0.06	1.25	0.20	1.03	-0.28	0.83
W-F balance important in career selection	0.84	0.36	0.80	0.40	0.67	0.48	0.95	0.21	0.80	0.40
Valid N (listwise)	(n=238)		(n=51)		(n=21)		(n=86)		(n=80)	

these beta tests, the survey instrument was modified. Finally, the survey instrument was sent to two senior scholars, one in graduate education and one in work-family, to obtain expert feedback on the appropriateness of survey items. Their feedback was used to further modify the instrument.

Measures

The survey instrument was designed through pilot interviews to collect information about individual characteristics, experiences in graduate school, career aspiration, perceptions of the family-friendliness of academic careers, and opinions on the appropriateness of work-family flexibility for faculty. This paper focuses on how student characteristics, experiences, and opinions relate to the decision to turn away from academic career aspirations. Independent variables include four student attributes (gender, age, academic field type, and LRP is family-focused), two measures of graduate school experiences (teaching and perception of the work-family climate of the home department), and three measures of student opinions (student confidence in career preparation, the importance of work-family balance in career selection, and perception of bias against work-family flexibility in academic careers). The measures are explained in detail in the following subsections. Descriptive statistics for all variables are provided by academic field and gender in Table 3.

Turn away. The dependent variable in this study is the decision to turn away from an academic career aspiration. Respondents who indicate turning away from academic career aspirations during graduate school are coded 1. Respondents who indicate that they did not change career aspirations during graduate school, or who indicate a change toward academic career aspirations, are coded 0.

Female. This binary variable is coded so that females = 1 and males = 0.

Age. The variable for age was created by coding those who self-identified as being 36 or older at the time of the survey as Older = 1 and everyone else as Older = 0.

Academic field type. The variable "STEM" was created by sorting all academic programs within the STEM areas and coding them 1. Respondents from the AHSS areas are coded STEM = 0.

Family-focused. The measure LRP is used with permission and was designed by Dr. Stewart Friedman and Dr. Jeffrey Greenhaus for the study "Work and family—allies or enemies? What happens when business professionals confront life choices" (2000). It is calculated by taking the responses from 3 survey questions pertaining to the kinds of activities that give individuals the "most satisfaction" and the relative importance of both career and a long-term relationship in overall satisfaction with life. The LRP "family-focused" is coded 1 = family-focused and 0 = not family-focused.

Teaching experience. The measure for experience with teaching comes from a single-item question in the survey. Respondents were asked to indicate areas in which they had "already gained experience" in their current academic program, including teaching. Respondents indicating experience in an area are coded 1, and respondents who did not indicate experience in that area are coded 0. Experience with teaching is a measure of university/department-level socialization to academic careers through the processes of "acquisition" and "involvement." Experience with research would have been helpful to include but only nine members of the sample had no research experience, effectively making the variable a constant.

Hostile department climate for work-family. This variable represents student perception of the work-family climate of the home department. The values range from 1 = strongly disagree to 5 = strongly agree for the survey item: "In my academic department, faculty who put their family or personal needs ahead of their jobs are not looked on favorably." This variable measures what students are learning about the norms of work-family balance (acquisition) for faculty.

Confidence in career preparation. This variable was taken directly from the survey item: "I am confident that my graduate program will prepare me for my chosen career." Respondents could answer on a 5-point scale from 1 = strongly disagree to 5 = strongly agree. In the language of socialization theory, this variable measures student "identification" with the target role.

Work-family balance important. On the survey, respondents were asked, "What THREE factors are MOST important to you in selecting a career?" The respondents who chose "Ability to balance work and personal life" are coded 1, and respondents who did not choose this option are coded 0.

Perception of bias against work-family flexibility. Based on the theory of bias avoidance, the survey included items about whether respondents would be afraid to use various flexible policy options for fear of career repercussions. Again, not using a flexible policy option out of fear of repercussion (i.e., exhibiting bias avoidance behaviors) is a proxy for perceiving that there is a bias with corresponding career repercussions to be avoided. Based on the pilot interviews, not all graduate and professional students are aware of the various flexible policy options, but all indicated that they understood that these options were not part of the "standard" or "traditional" faculty career path. This understanding enabled the pilot participants to talk about whether they predicted that they would fear using a flexible policy option or whether they would take advantage of available policy options to help them achieve work-life balance. This variable measures what students are learning (acquisition) at the national or disciplinary level about the appropriateness of work-family balance for faculty in their field. Principal component factor analysis with Varimax rotation was used to develop the measure of student perception of work-family bias in academic careers. Only one factor with an eigenvalue above 1.0 rotated out of the 5 survey items. Table 4 shows the items and associated factor loadings that comprise the perception of bias measure. The alpha score for perception of bias against work-family is acceptable at .72.

TABLE 4. Factor analysis results for perception of bias against work-family flexibility.

	Loading
Factor 1: Perception of bias	(.72)
If I were a faculty member, I would be afraid to utilize [flexible policy option] because I want to be taken seriously as an academic.	
Department granted teaching release for family reasons	.77
Transitional support program for personal or care-related emergencies	.77
Tenure clock extension for caregiving purposes	.70
Family or medical leave	.72
Part-time tenure track	.50

ANALYSIS

Bivariate correlations explored relationships between the variables. Multiple logistic regression was used to analyze the effects of the influential factors on the decision to turn away from academic career aspirations. Logistic regression is appropriate for this analysis because the dependent variable is a binary outcome variable, and using this type of dependent variable in ordinary least squares regression would result in biased estimates of the slope. The probability level of .05 was used for all statistical tests.

FINDINGS

Several factors are associated with the decision to turn away from an academic career. Bivariate correlations are measured by Pearson's R. Table 5

TABLE 5. Pearson correlations and significance levels for variables expected to be associated with turning away from academic career aspirations ($n = 238$).

	1	2	3	4	5	6	7	8	9	10
1 Turn away from academic career	1									
2 Female	0.165 *	1								
3 Family-focused	0.264 **	0.043	1							
4 Older	-0.130 *	-0.054	-0.135 *	1						
5 In STEM Field	0.031	-0.177 **	0.058	-0.121	1					
6 Teaching experience	0.176 **	0.059	0.022	-0.019	-0.082	1				
7 Hostile climate for work/family	0.253 **	0.172 **	0.115	0.075	-0.031	-0.005	1			
8 Confidence in career prep	-0.306 **	-0.111	-0.025	-0.015	0.014	-0.065	-0.126	1		
9 Perception of bias against W-F	0.170 **	0.177 **	-0.026	-0.023	-0.047	0.089	0.157 *	-0.204 **	1	
10 W-F balance important	0.127	0.171 **	0.095	-0.036	0.147 *	-0.011	-0.012	-0.061	0.074	1

* Correlation is significant at the 0.05 level (2-tailed).
** Correlation is significant at the 0.01 level (2-tailed).

shows the variables that were expected to have a relationship with turning away from academic career aspirations.

The dependent variable, the decision to turn away from academic career aspirations, is significantly associated with being female, not being in the older age category, being family-focused, experience with teaching, perception that the department climate is hostile toward work-family balance, lower levels of confidence in career preparation, and perception that there is a bias against work-family flexibility in academic careers.

Among our sample, we find that female respondents are less likely than male respondents to be in STEM fields, and are more likely to perceive a hostile department climate toward work-family balance, perceive bias against work-family flexibility in academic careers, and feel that work-family balance was important to them in selecting a career. In terms of age, older respondents are less likely than other respondents to indicate that they are family-focused. Respondents in STEM fields are more likely than those in AHSS fields to indicate that balance was important to them in selecting a career.

Based on the findings in the correlations table, a step-wise logistic regression is used to analyze the effect of the seven influential factors on the decision to turn away from academic career aspirations (Table 6). The step-wise regression is useful in this project because it provides a window to see how effects change when additional variables are added to the model. Being in a STEM field and the importance of work-family balance in career selection are included in the regression as control variables.

TABLE 6. Logistic regression of student attributes, experiences, and opinions formed in graduate school on the decision to turn away from academic career aspirations ($n = 238$).

	Model 1			Model 2			Model 3		
	B	s.e.	exp(B)	B	s.e.	exp(B)	B	s.e.	exp(B)
Female	0.76	0.31	2.13 *	0.55	0.33	1.74	0.32	0.35	1.38
Family-focused	1.13	0.31	3.10 **	1.03	0.32	2.80 **	1.10	0.35	2.99 **
Older	-0.82	0.58	0.44	-1.08	0.63	0.34	-1.28	0.65	0.28 *
In STEM field	0.18	0.33	1.20	0.26	0.35	1.30	0.19	0.37	1.21
Teaching experience				1.25	0.49	3.48 *	1.23	0.52	3.43 *
Hostile dept. climate				0.55	0.16	1.73 **	0.52	0.17	1.69 **
Confidence in career preparation							-0.66	0.18	0.51 **
Perception of bias against W-F flexibility							0.19	0.17	1.21
W-F balance important in career							0.66	0.51	1.94
Constant	-1.61	0.38	0.20 **	-4.34	0.81	0.01 **	-2.29	1.11	0.10 *

*$p < .05$ **$p < .01$

In Model 1 of the logistic regression, the effects of student attributes female, family-focused, older, and STEM are analyzed. After the other variables are controlled for, being female increases the odds of turning away from academic career aspirations by 113%. Being family-focused significantly increases (by 210%) the odds of turning away from academic career aspirations.

In Model 2, student experiences are added to the regression: teaching experience and perception of department-level hostility to work-family balance. These two variables negate the effect of being female, but not of being family-focused. Increased perceptions of hostile department climate for work-family result in a 73% increase in the odds of turning away from academic career aspirations. Having teaching experience results in a 248% increase in the odds of turning away from academic career aspirations.

Model 3 adds in three student opinion variables: confidence in career preparation, perception of bias in academic careers against work-family balance, and the importance of work-family balance in career selection. The addition of these variables causes the age variable to become significant such that older students are 72% less likely to turn away from academic career aspirations. Of the three opinion variables, only confidence in career preparation is significantly predictive of turning away from academic career aspirations. Increased confidence in one's career preparation results in a 49% decrease in the odds of turning away from academic career aspirations.

The implications of these results are discussed in more detail in the next section.

DISCUSSION

This study used socialization theory in an Input—Experiences—Outcome model to explore the role of work-family concerns in graduate students' decisions to turn away from their academic career aspirations. As discussed in the conceptual framework, graduate students enter their programs with certain attributes that influence their experiences in graduate school, the development of opinions, and career decisions. Likewise, their experiences in graduate school and socialization to the norms of academic careers influence student opinions about academic careers and the decision to turn away from academic career aspirations. While scholars have focused on faculty careers and graduate students' career decisions specifically at research universities (e.g., Austin, 2002; Creamer, 2006; Finkel & Olswang, 1996; Golde & Dore, 2001; Johnsrud & Des Jarlais, 1994;

Quinn, Lange, & Olswang, 2004; Ward & Wolf-Wendel, 2004, 2005), we believe that there is a larger problem facing American institutions of higher education if potential future faculty are turning away from their academic career aspirations *entirely*. Research universities make up only 6% of all institutions of higher education in the United States and serve 28% of all enrolled college students (Carnegie Foundation for the Advancement of Teaching, 2008). Work-family scholars are beginning to examine faculty experiences at a range of institutions (Wolf-Wendel & Ward, 2006), but no one else has explored the faculty pipeline for all kinds of academic careers.

What did the model show about how student attributes and experiences in graduate school relate to the decision to turn away from academic career aspirations? On its own, gender seems to affect the decision to turn away from academic career aspirations. When all other variables are controlled, however, being in the older age group, being family-focused, having teaching experience, and perceiving a hostile department climate toward work-family balance are more influential on the decision to turn away from an academic career aspiration than is being female. That is, net of other variables, men and women have no differences in their propensity to change from academic career to nonacademic career aspirations. The lack of significance of the variable female is significant in itself. While the public is beginning to understand that work-family balance is not just a woman's issue, this study provides one more piece of evidence that this gender stereotype is false. There is a relationship between gender, type of program and perception of bias. Women in STEM perceive the most bias of all the respondents, men in STEM perceive the least bias, and neither men nor women in AHSS indicate strong relationship with perception of bias. This is an interaction that we were not able to test given the small sample size. Future research should examine this possible interaction and address its impact on recommendations for STEM and AHSS programs.

Controlling for other factors, there are five main variables associated with turning away from academic career aspirations. Being family-focused and having teaching experience are highly associated with turning away from academic career aspirations. Perceiving a hostile department climate for work-family is moderately associated with turning away from academic career aspirations. Being older and having high levels of confidence are associated with not turning away from academic career aspirations. These are each discussed below in the context of prior studies and with their respective implications for policy and practice.

Being family-focused. Respondents who prioritize family and personal relationships in their assessment of life satisfaction (i.e., the LRP "family-focused") are more likely to turn away from their academic career aspirations than other respondents. This is the first study to explore LRP in the context of graduate education, as well as the first to examine LRP impact on career decisions. A prior study of MBA recipients several years into their postgraduate careers found that individuals with the LRP "work-family focused" had the highest satisfaction levels with both work and family of all the LRPs (Friedman & Greenhaus, 2000). It is logical that (1) if academic careers are seen as threatening to the ability to have a family and (2) personal satisfaction and perceptions of life success depend on having a family, then academic careers would be undesirable. Studies such as "Do Babies Matter?" (Mason, Goulden, & Wolfinger, 2006) indicate that academic careers do jeopardize marriage and children for women academics. For institutions of higher education to be able to recruit and retain potential future faculty, it will be necessary to demonstrate that faculty can have rich, satisfying family and personal lives. If institutions of higher education can make academic careers flexible enough to appeal to family-focused individuals, then they should be able to keep a diverse population of graduate students in the pipeline for academic careers. Disseminating research such as "Academic Motherhood" (Ward & Wolf-Wendel, 2004) may help showcase the benefits of balancing academic careers and parenthood. The number of institutions offering "family-friendly" policies for faculty has been increasing (Lester & Sallee, in press; Raabe, 1997), and ideally this will increase the number of faculty who can be role models for balanced lives.

Experience with teaching. It is interesting that teaching experience is associated with turning away from academic career aspirations. Prior studies have found that graduate students are motivated to become faculty out of the love of teaching (Golde & Dore, 2001). Teaching typically involves a major time commitment and can detract from time available for research and other activities (Staton & Darling, 1989), so it is possible that experience with teaching has called into question the ability to balance the work requirements of an academic position.

Through experience with teaching, students may learn that academic careers require a greater time commitment than they are willing to give. It is not uncommon for graduate students to be teaching with little to no institutional or departmental support (Golde & Dore, 2001; Nyquist et al., 1999) and when students have high teaching responsibilities, their personal research can progress slowly (Wulff, Austin, Nyquist, & Sprague, 2004). Given that research productivity tends to be the yardstick by which academic success is measured, questioning one's ability to perform research while juggling the demands of teaching might cause some graduate students to turn away from academic careers. Additionally, the time burdens of teaching may call attention to other time-based conflicts—including work and family (Wulff, Austin, Nyquist, & Sprague, 2004), but this was not measured in this study. To help mitigate the effects of teaching experience on turning away from academic career aspirations, institutions should ensure that graduate students with teaching responsibilities have access to supports for teaching, time management workshops, and supports for both work-life balance and research/writing while teaching.

Perceiving a hostile department climate for work-family balance. Prior research has demonstrated the connections between departmental work-life climate and the ability to recruit and retain faculty, including how department climate can undermine university or college-level attempts to make faculty careers flexible (Drago, Crouter, Wardell, & Willits, 2001; Gappa, 2002; Gappa et al., 2007; Gappa & MacDermid, 1997) and how department level leadership is needed to create climate change (Gappa et al., 2007; Tierney & Bensimon, 1996). However, this is the first study to find a connection between departmental work-life climate and graduate students turning away from their academic career aspirations.

This connection is explained by the theory of graduate student socialization (Weidman et al., 2001). Through socialization, students learn the norms of their target profession and make decisions about assimilating to those norms or turning away from the profession. The connection between departmental work-life climate and graduate students turning away from their academic career aspirations has serious ramifications for the pipeline of future faculty. If departments cannot demonstrate supportiveness of work-life balance—both for faculty and graduate students who may become faculty—many potential future faculty of both genders may turn away from their academic career aspirations.

Thanks to the research on department-level work-life climate change that has been done to improve conditions for faculty, many best practices and recommendations for department chairs exist that can be easily replicated to improve department climate for everyone. These include tips and strategies for improving the "family-friendliness" of departments (Frasch, Mason, Stacy, Goulden, & Hoffman, 2007; Quinn, 2008; Quinn, Yen, Riskin, & Lange, 2007) and how chairs can communicate effectively and overcome resistance to change (Higgerson & Joyce, 2007; Wergin, 2003). Creating a department climate that supports work-life flexibility is crucial to keeping future faculty in the pipeline as they finish their graduate training and to recruiting and retaining faculty.

Being older. The finding that older respondents are less likely than their younger counterparts to turn away from their academic career aspirations may be reflective of a lower prioritization of work-life balance. Scholars of generational difference have shown that younger generations desire work-life balance more highly than do older generations and that older generations are more likely than younger generations to be willing to 'pay their dues' and make personal sacrifices for career success (Lancaster & Stillman, 2003). It is also possible that older students are more committed to their choices as a result of scaling back their lifestyle to return to school. This sacrifice could be a proxy for their commitment to their educational goal. However, it is possible that other unmeasured factors related to being older are in operation, such as financial security. Older students may be returning to graduate study after working and saving money, may be in committed relationships with professionals who can cover the bills, and may therefore have less concern over accruing and paying back student loans. Departments and universities should not be wary of bringing older students into their doctoral programs—our research shows that these students are good investments and are likely to continue to academe.

Having higher levels of confidence in career preparation. It is hardly surprising that higher levels of confidence in career preparation reduce the odds of turning away from an academic career. According to socialization theory, the more students self-identify with their target role, the less likely they are to turn away from it. Therefore, feelings of confidence in one's career preparation (academic) would help deter against turning away from academic career aspirations. Institutions that develop confidence-building exercises or workshops, or that find ways to help graduate students to develop their identification with the faculty role, will reduce the likelihood that potential future faculty will turn away from their academic career aspirations. Given other study findings, increasing teaching opportunities for graduate students is not the answer. Research has addressed "re-envisioning the PhD" and improving doctoral education; many tips are available for developing programs to prepare doctoral students for faculty careers (Golde & Dore, 2001; Wulff, Austin, & et al., 2004).

The primary goal of this paper was to determine if work-family concerns play a significant role in the decision to turn away from an academic career aspiration. Only two of the four work-family relevant variables, being family-focused (i.e., prioritizing family and personal relationships in overall feelings of life success) and perceiving a hostile department climate for work-family, have an impact on the decision to turn away from academic career aspirations, controlling for other measured factors. The other two work-family relevant variables are not significant in the multivariate regression, although perception of bias against work-family flexibility had a significant bivariate association with the dependent variable, lending some support for the bias avoidance perspective. Given the strong influence of the LRP "family-focused" on the decision to turn away from academic career aspirations, it is surprising that the other work-family measures (i.e., the importance of work-family balance in career selection and the perception of bias against work-family flexibility in academic careers) are not predictive of this career decision. These findings do not support the literature suggesting that desire for balance and perceptions that academic careers are not family-friendly are major factors why PhD recipients do not become faculty (Golde & Dore, 2001; Rice et al., 2000; Sears, 2003). The decision to turn away from an academic career aspiration is complex, as are most decisions involving family and career.

Some of this complexity is apparent in the relationship between perceiving both bias against work-family flexibility in academic careers and a hostile departmental climate for work-family. It is surprising that the bivariate relationship is not stronger (although it is significant) between these two variables. Based on graduate student socialization theory (Weidman et al., 2001), it was predicted that students would learn to fear work-family career repercussions primarily as a result of their experiences in and perceptions of their home department. Therefore, perceiving a hostile department climate for work-family was expected to explain more of the variance in perception of bias against work-family flexibility in faculty careers than was found. It is possible that students are being socialized to work-family norms both at the local level (i.e., the work-family climate of their home department) and through experiences at national conferences or other professional opportunities outside of their department. In other words, students may be learning the norms of their academic fields separately from the norms of their home departments. As it is conceivable that some academic fields may be more family-friendly than is evidenced by the climate of any given department, the perception of work-family climate of a department should not be considered a proxy for work-family climate in the academic field. This would explain why these two variables are not more highly associated. Still, a statistically significant, positive relationship was found between these variables.

Another complex finding is that confidence in career preparation is negatively associated with perceptions of a hostile department climate for work-family and bias against work-family flexibility. This represents a relationship between self-identifying with the target role and perceiving academic careers as reasonably friendly to work-life balance. This might suggest that the more confident people are in their career preparation, the less likely they are to perceive a hostile climate or bias against work-family flexibility. Perhaps this is because those who are confident have not had to experience hardship or negative experiences related to work-family during graduate school. Conversely, it is possible that perceiving a hostile department climate or bias against work-family flexibility undermines feelings of confidence in career preparation. It is also possible that respondents who do not perceive hostility or bias are in academic departments and fields that are supportive of work-life balance and that this supportiveness promotes confidence in one's career preparation. Further research is needed to explore fully these dynamics.

LIMITATIONS

This study is limited by the sample, which was drawn from a single institution. While studies of multiple universities may be more generalizable to the general graduate student population, this study can only be considered representative of PhD-granting universities with very high research activity. More work should be done to verify whether these findings are maintained in other university settings. Additionally, many of the variables are single-item measures, which provide a one-dimensional measure of constructs and may limit the validity of the findings. In general, when multiple items measuring different aspects of the same thing are combined into an index, the variable is more likely to be a well-rounded, valid measurement of the construct. The survey used by this study did not always have more than one measure of a particular construct and so single-item measures were necessary. Lastly, this is a quantitative study that cannot provide the depth of information about the mechanisms and processes by which graduate students experience bias and choose to leave academe. Qualitative analysis is necessary to fully understand the underlying processes at work.

CONCLUSION

This study differs from previous quantitative studies (Anderson & Swazey, 1998; Golde & Dore, 2001) that investigated the effect of graduate students' experiences on select outcomes but did not focus on the role of work-family concerns. The lenses of LRP and bias avoidance provided a new perspective on and understanding of how work-life concerns influence graduate student experiences and career decisions. Additionally, while studies of graduate students' experiences have gone beyond marginal distribution analyses to explore how multiple factors of the graduate experience simultaneously influence outcomes (e.g., Litzler, Edwards Lange, & Brainard, 2005; Zhao, Golde, & McCormick, 2007), this is the first study of graduate socialization and work-family to do so.

This study moves the literature one step forward in understanding the process and factors that affect whether graduate students go on to become faculty. This is especially a concern for women and underrepresented groups because their proportions are lower in faculty positions than in graduate school. Interestingly, this study finds that net of other factors, gender is not associated with turning away from academic career aspirations. Instead, turning away may be indicative of the changing priorities of the generation currently in graduate school, rather than a gender-specific phenomenon as is sometimes suggested. In fact, there is evidence here that older graduate students are much less likely to turn away than younger students. While the findings are mixed regarding the impact of work-family on turning away from academic career aspirations, this study provides evidence to university administrators that issues of work and family are of concern to everyone. Therefore, this study has implications for the ways that universities and colleges think about and deal with work-family for all their graduate students and faculty—not just the women, because there are clear pipeline repercussions to allowing hostile work-family climates to persist.

REFERENCES

American Council on Education. (2005). *An agenda for excellence: Creating flexibility in tenure-track faculty careers.* Washington, DC: Author.

Anderson, M. S., & Swazey, J. P. (1998). Reflections on the graduate student experience: An overview. *New Directions for Higher Education, 101*, 3–13.

Ashburn, E. (2007). Survey identifies colleges that know how to keep junior faculty members happy. *The Chronicle of Higher Education, 53*(22), A6.

Austin, A. E. (2002). Preparing the next generation of faculty. *The Journal of Higher Education, 73*(1), 94–122.

Bickel, J., & Brown, A. J. (2005). Generation X: Implications for faculty recruitment and development in academic health centers. *Academic Medicine, 80*(3), 205–210.

Carnegie Foundation for the Advancement of Teaching. (2008). Carnegie classifications data file, June 11, 2008.

Committee on Maximizing the Potential of Women in Academic Science and Engineering. (2006). *Beyond bias and barriers: Fulfilling the potential of women in academic science and engineering.* Washington, DC: National Academies.

Creamer, E. G. (2006). Policies that part: Early career experiences of coworking academic couples. In S. J. Bracken, J. K. Allen, & D. R. Dean (Eds.), *The balancing act: Gendered perspectives in faculty roles and work lives.* Sterling, VA: Stylus.

Drago, R., Colbeck, C., Stauffer, D., Varner, A., Burkum, K., Fazioli, J., et al. (2004). *The avoidance of bias against caregiving: The case of academic faculty* (Population Research Institute Working Paper 04-06). College Park, PA: The Pennsylvania State University.

Drago, R., Colbeck, C., Stauffer, K. D., Pirretti, A., Burkum, K., Fazioli, J., et al. (2005). Bias against caregiving. *Academe, 91*(5), 22–25.

Drago, R., Crouter, A. C., Wardell, M., & Willits, B. S. (2001). *Final report of the faculty and families project.* University Park, PA: The Pennsylvania State University.

Finkel, S. K., & Olswang, S. G. (1996). Child rearing as a career impediment to women assistant professors. *The Review of Higher Education, 19*(2), 123–139.

Frasch, K., Mason, M. A., Stacy, A., Goulden, M., & Hoffman, C. (2007). *Creating a family friendly department: Chairs and deans toolkit:* UC Faculty Family Friendly Edge.

Friedman, S. D., & Greenhaus, J. H. (2000). *Work and family—allies or enemies?: What happens when business professionals confront life choices.* Oxford ; New York: Oxford University Press.

Gappa, J. M. (2002). Academic careers for the 21st century: More options for new faculty. In J. C. Smart & W. G. Tierney (Eds.), *Higher education: Handbook of theory and research* (Vol. XVII, pp. 425–475). New York: Agathon Press.

Gappa, J. M., Austin, A. E., & Trice, A. G. (2007). *Rethinking faculty work: Higher education's strategic imperative.* San Francisco: Jossey-Bass.

Gappa, J. M., & MacDermid, S. M. (1997). Work, family, and the faculty career. *New Pathways: Faculty Career and Employment for the 21st Century* (Working Paper Series, Inquiry #8). Washington, DC: American Association for Higher Education.

Goldberger, M. L., Maher, B. A., & Flattau, P. B. (Eds.). (1995). *Research doctorate programs in the United States: Continuity and change.* Washington, DC: Committee for the Study of Research-Doctorate Programs in the United States, National Research Council.

Golde, C. M. (1998). Beginning graduate school: Explaining first-year doctoral attrition. *New Directions for Higher Education, 101,* 55–64.

Golde, C. M., & Dore, T. M. (2001). *At cross purposes: What the experiences of today's doctoral students reveal about doctoral education.* Washington, DC: The Pew Charitable Trusts.

Higgerson, M. L., & Joyce, T. A. (2007). *Effective leadership communication: A guide for department chairs and deans for managing difficult situations and people.* Bolton, MA: Anker Publishing.

Johnsrud, L. K., & Des Jarlais, C. D. (1994). Barriers to tenure for women and minorities. *The Review of Higher Education, 17*(4), 335–353.

Lancaster, L. C., & Stillman, D. (2003). *When generations collide: Who they are, why they clash, how to solve the generational puzzle at work.* New York: HarperBusiness.

Lester, J., & Sallee, M. (Eds.). (In press). *Establishing a family-friendly campus: Insights on success.* Sterling, VA: Stylus Publishing.

Litzler, E., Edwards Lange, S., & Brainard, S. G. (2005). Climate for graduate students in science and engineering departments. *Proceedings of the 2005 American Society for Engineering Education Annual Conference & Exposition.*

Mason, M. A., Goulden, M., & Wolfinger, N. H. (2006). Babies matter: Pushing the gender equity revolution forward. In S. J. Bracken, J. K. Allen, & D. R. Dean (Eds.), *The balancing act: Gendered perspectives in faculty roles and work lives.* Sterling, VA: Stylus.

Nyquist, J. D., Manning, L., Wulff, D. H., Austin, A. E., Sprague, J., Fraser, P. K., et al. (1999). On the road to becoming a professor. *Change, 31*(3), 18–27.

Quinn, K. (2008). *The chairperson's role in work-family flexibility for faculty.* Paper presented at the 25th Annual Conference on Academic Leadership: Defining Departmental Leadership: Engaging Academic Communities for Success, Orlando, FL.

Quinn, K., Lange, S. E., & Olswang, S. G. (2004). Family-friendly policies and the research university. *Academe, 90*(6), 32–34.

Quinn, K., Yen, J., Riskin, E. A., & Lange, S. E. (2007). Leadership development workshops for department chairs: A model for enabling family-friendly cultural change. *Change, 39*(4), 42–47.

Raabe, P. (1997). Work-family policies for faculty: How "Career- and family-friendly" Is academe? In M. Ferber & J. Loeb (Eds.), *Academic couples: Problems and promises* (pp. 208–225). Chicago: University of Illinois Press.

Rice, R. E., Sorcinelli, M. D., & Austin, A. E. (2000). Heeding new voices: Academic careers for a new generation. *New Pathways: Faculty Career and Employment for the 21st Century* (Working Paper Series, Inquiry #7). Washington DC: American Association for Higher Education.

Richmond, G. (2005, Feb 6, 2005). Gender debate ignores real issues. *The Register - Guard,* p. B.3.

Rimer, S. (2005, Apr 15, 2005). For women in the sciences, the pace of progress at top universities is slow. *New York Times,* p. A.15.

Sears, A. W. (2003). Image problems deplete the number of women in academic applicant pools. *Journal of Women and Minorities in Science and Engineering, 9*(2), 169–181.

Staton, A. Q., & Darling, A. L. (1989). Socialization of teaching assistants. In J. D. Nyquist, R. D. Abbott, & D. H. Wulff (Eds.), *Teaching assistant training in the 1990s* (pp. 15–22). San Francisco: Jossey-Bass.

The Associated Press, & The New York Times. (2005, January 21). Educator regrets comments on women. *St. Louis Post - Dispatch,* p. A.3.

Tierney, W. G., & Bensimon, E. M. (1996). *Promotion and tenure: Community and socialization in academe.* Albany: State University of New York Press.

Ward, K., & Wolf-Wendel, L. (2004). Academic motherhood: Managing complex roles in research universities. *The Review of Higher Education, 27*(2), 233–257.

Ward, K., & Wolf-Wendel, L. E. (2005). Work and family perspectives from research university faculty. *New Directions for Higher Education, 2005*(130), 67–80.

Weidman, J. C., Twale, D. J., & Stein, E. L. (2001). *Socialization of graduate and professional students in higher education: A perilous passage? ASHE-ERIC Higher Education Report, 28*(3). Washington, DC: The George Washington University, Graduate School of Education and Human Development.

Wergin, J. F. (2003). *Departments that work: Building and sustaining cultures of excellence in academic programs.* Boston: Anker Publishing.

Williams, J. (2000). *Unbending gender: Why work and family conflict and what to do about it.* Oxford: University Press.

Wilson, R. (2004, December 3). Where the elite teach, it's still a man's world. *The Chronicle of Higher Education,* p. A.8.

Wilson, R. (2005, January 19). A tough lesson: Despite efforts, women still outnumbered in top faculties. *Chicago Tribune,* p. 1.

Wolf-Wendel, L., & Ward, K. (2001). *Academic motherhood: Managing complex roles in research institutions.* Paper presented at the annual meeting of the Association for the Study of Higher Education, Richmond, VA.

Wolf-Wendel, L., & Ward, K. (2006). Faculty work and family life: Policy perspectives from different institutional types. In S. J. Bracken, J. K. Allen, & D. R. Dean (Eds.), *The balancing act: Gendered perspectives in faculty roles and work lives.* Sterling, VA: Stylus.

Wulff, D. H., Austin, A. E., & et al. (2004). *Paths to the professoriate: Strategies for enriching the preparation of future faculty.* San Francisco: Jossey-Bass.

Wulff, D. H., Austin, A. E., Nyquist, J. D., & Sprague, J. (2004). The development of graduate students as teaching scholars: A four-year longitudinal study. In D. H. Wulff, A. E. Austin, & Associates (Eds.), *Paths to the professoriate: Strategies for enriching the preparation of future faculty.* San Francisco: Jossey-Bass.

Zhao, C. M., Golde, C. M., & McCormick, A. C. (2007). More than a signature: How advisor choice and advisor behavior affect doctoral student satisfaction. *Journal of Further and Higher Education, 31*(3), 263–281.

Black Female Faculty: Role Definition, Critical Enactments, and Contributions to Predominately White Research Institutions

Venice Thandi Sulé
Research Fellow
University of Michigan

> *This paper explores how Black female faculty (BFF), the largest community of women of color faculty, simultaneously define their professional role and contribute to predominately White research institutions (PWRIs) through a series of critical enactments. The sparse research on BFF at PWIs focuses on barriers to social integration yet places less emphasis on factors that promote negotiation of barriers and organizational change. Analysis of qualitative data shows that the participants actively challenged structural constraints through service and research. In doing so, they used their positions as vehicles for institutional transformation. Thus, their role extended beyond the mundane expectations of faculty to one that emphasized commitment to social equity. Their work facilitated the incorporation of diverse communities into PWIs and broadened disciplinary knowledge.*

John (1997) calls Black women the Queens of Multiple Juxtapositions. She asserts that they simultaneously perform divergent roles as a means of survival:

> We have known that we had to pick and choose battles that we have had to confront and defer and that none of these ploys defined our essence. They were merely the crazy rules of an unfair game, and if we wanted to play—that is, work and support our families—then we had to temporarily be *down with the madness*. (p. 60)

In essence, enacting multiple juxtapositions means that one seemingly endorses hegemonic practices while working to undermine those very practices. Thus, as a survival tool and resistance strategy, juxtapositions challenge structural inequities. Furthermore, they allow individuals to thrive within institutions that they are attempting to transform. Accordingly, the *juxtaposition* manifests as one's ability to enact roles that signify acceptance and disapproval of institutional norms. This paper inadvertently captures juxtapositions through the way that Black female faculty (BFF) define their professional role and contribute to predominately White research institutions (PWRIs).

There exists a long history of Black women employing juxtapositions as resistance strategies within and outside of the academy (Benjamin, 1997; Collins, 2000; Evans, 2007; Hine, 1995; John, 1997). They are useful because they disarm people who would subvert any obvious attempts to dismantle a system that creates inequitable access to power. Also, they give practitioners of juxtapositions access to resources to make incremental changes that destabilize unjust norms. Thus, embedded within juxtapositional practice is a commitment to promoting social equity.[1] Drawing from this premise, I suggest that PWRIs represent spaces where hegemony is both practiced and legitimated as evidenced by the long tradition of systemic exclusion in regard to structural access and scholarship for women and people of color. Therefore, as the antithesis of the White male norm, Black women who find themselves within these spaces must determine how to negotiate constrictive assumptions and practices.

This paper focuses on the aforementioned negotiation process by revealing how BFF members simultaneously define their role and contribute to PWRs. With the ever growing anti-affirmative action presence at public higher education institutions, the way that the women function within these premier schools illuminates institutional norms that both undermine and elevate diversity efforts.[2] Equally as important, this study concretizes ways that historically underrepresented faculty members reflect citizenship through the interrogation and diversification of the teaching and learning environment.

LITERATURE REVIEW

BLACK FEMALE ADVOCACY THROUGH EDUCATION

Since the U.S. enslavement period, Black women have been instrumental in facilitating education within the Black community. They founded schools, served as teachers, and advocated for Black education (Giddings, 1984; Hine, 1994; Perkins, 1990). Although teaching was the only major occupational choice for Black women beyond domestic service until the post-Civil Rights Era, many Black female educators used their positions to promote social equity. As such, Black women became visible leaders in education (Giddings, 1984; Hine, 1994; Hine, Brown, Patterson, & Williams, 1990; Hine & Thompson, 1998).

Educated Black women, in particular, challenged the race and gender caste system through social service intervention. This is no more evident than with the establishment of the National Association of Colored Women (NACW) in 1896. Led by such luminaries as Mary Church Terrill and Mary McLeod Bethune, NACW was the first Black national organization that addressed the social well-being of African Americans. In addition to founding schools, NACW engaged in community development by creating college scholarships, resettlement programs, day care programs, and healthcare facilities among other activities. In addition to NACW community development projects, educated Black women actively defended their morality, advocated for suffrage, and publicly challenged sexual violence (Giddings, 1984; Hine, 1994). In essence, these women expressed their dissatisfaction with institutionalized discrimination by engaging in capacity-building within the Black community. They were pivotal in defending the worthiness of Black womanhood because they had more resources and a broader platform than average Black women who struggled to survive as domestics or agricultural laborers. Fundamentally, history reveals that educated Black women were instrumental in the fight against social injustice (Giddings, 1984).

BLACK FEMALE FACULTY AT PREDOMINATELY WHITE RESEARCH INSTITUTIONS

Although Black women have been involved in higher education since the 1860s and the first Black women received PhDs in 1921, BFF were virtually nonexistent at predominately White institutions until social movements in the 1960s resulted in legislation that addressed race and gender discrimination (Evans, 2007; Giddings, 1984). However, within these institutions Black women's rank, tenure, retention and compensation is among the lowest (Gregory, 1999; Moses, 1997). Narratives from these women are replete with accounts of systemic marginalization (Benjamin, 1997; Gregory, 1999; Moses, 1997; Myers, 2002). Black women feel isolated from key social networks, undervalued by peers attacked by students, and used as representatives of diversity (Moses, 1997; Myers, 2002; Turner et al., 2002). Despite these challenges, many Black women remain in predominately White institutions because of their commitment to teaching, mentoring and promoting diversity in higher education. Also, they have a genuine love for scholarly pursuits (Benjamin, 1997; Berry & Mizelle, 2006).

During a time when affirmative action and diversity programs are being scrutinized and dismantled, higher education institutions are challenged with demonstrating how underrepresented faculty members contribute to and define their roles in the academy. Although there is a growing body of literature that shows that diversity facilitates cognitive development and interracial engagement (Gurin, 1999; Gurin, Dey, Hurtado, & Gurin, 2002; Milem & Hakuta, 2002), there still remains a gap in knowledge about how underrepresented faculty define their professional role and how such role definition alters the teaching and learning environment. Therefore, this study provides further insight into how one group of underrepresented faculty, Black women, negotiate and contribute to the academy.

RESEARCH DESIGN

THEORETICAL FRAMEWORK

The fundamental interpretive lens for this study is Black Feminist Thought (BFT). As an epistemological perspective it asserts Black women have a unique standpoint because of a shared social location rooted in race and gender subordination. Their unique standpoint challenges White male norms as well as feminist and racial solidarity ideologies. In turn, BFT rearticulates the everyday experiences and standpoints of Black women. Furthermore, BFT acknowledges that Black women have experiences that reflect the intersection of being a member of a nondominant race and gender group. In using the experiences of Black women as an example, Crenshaw (2003) contends that:

> Black women are sometimes excluded from feminist theory and antiracist policy discourse because both are predicated on a discrete

set of experiences that often does not accurately reflect the interaction of race and gender. . . . Because the intersectional experience is greater than the sum of racism and sexism, any analysis that does not take intersectionality into account cannot sufficiently address the particular manner in which Black women are subordinated. (p. 24)

Therefore, intersectionality destabilizes conceptions of feminism that emphasize White women's issues and challenges the notion that racial solidarity requires women of color to be silent about experiences that are distinct from their male counterparts (Crenshaw, 2003; King, 1995). King (1995) elaborates:

A Black feminist ideology, first and foremost, thus declares the visibility of Black women. It acknowledges the fact that two innate and inerasable traits, Black and female, constitute our special status in American society. Second, Black feminism asserts self-determination as essential. Black women are empowered with the right to interpret our reality and define our objectives. While drawing on a rich tradition of struggle as Blacks and as women, we continually establish and reestablish our own priorities. (p. 312)

Ultimately, BFT is a means to move subjugated knowledge from the margins to the center of discourses about the state of being (Collins, 2000). Employing BFT to analyze Black female engagement in higher education institutions places Black women's interpretation of their experience in the forefront. It provides an interpretive tool that draws upon marginalized identities as a means to understand person-in-environment experiences.

Although Collins (2000) speaks about the totality of the Black woman's experience, she reminds us that an archetypal Black woman does not exist. Rather, there is a *collective* Black female standpoint arising from the aggregate of responses to common themes that Black women encounter because of their race and gender identity (Collins, 1998). Therefore, this study is designed to provide BFF with a forum to discuss their experiences as a means to determine how they are able to contribute to intellectual discourse and knowledge production in spaces where they, along with similarly situated women, may encounter resistance because of their identity.

DATA COLLECTION

This paper is part of a larger study that looks at how the opportunity structure and agency influence how underrepresented women engage higher education settings.[3] Given that the study explores how Black females experience and respond to professional socialization, qualitative methods were employed. Qualitative methods are most suited for this study because they are the best way to glean information about what experiences mean to individuals (Creswell, 1998; Patton, 2001). Furthermore, the philosophical assumptions of qualitative research are aligned with assumptions within BFT. For instance, the ontological assumption is that reality is subjective and the multiple realities can exist. The axiological assumption is that research is steeped in values based on the researchers' and participants' lived experiences. Finally, there is the belief that meaning is discovered through interaction with participants (Creswell, 1998). For these reasons, qualitative methods appropriately support the overarching theoretical assumptions of this study.

To identify participants, criterion sampling was employed. Such sampling allows for the selection of information-rich cases in order to answer orienting questions and contribute to emergent theory (Creswell, 1998). Because the larger study required that participants be able to reflect upon their career trajectory from graduate school to associate professor in PWIs, tenured Black women working at predominately White Carnegie Classified doctorate-granting institutions were sought. Also, to target disciplines with a relatively longer history of race and gender inclusion when compared to the STEM fields, only faculty in social sciences and humanities were recruited. Focusing on social sciences and humanities provided insight into the experiences of an underrepresented group in disciplines that have been historically, albeit limited, more accessible. Finally, social science and humanities were targeted because they have a stated purpose of studying human behavior and/or improving the social condition. Hence, the study contributes to our understanding of how socially marginalized groups perceive the conditions within departments that theoretically should be more attuned to issues related to social equity.

Targeting research institutions in the northern region of the United States, potential participants were identified through a faculty list forwarded by diversity officers, school Web sites, and participant referrals. Black female associate professors who met the aforementioned criteria were contacted via e-mail. Given that representation of BFF is still sparse at most PWIs, the length of tenured period was not a criteria. The main goal was to recruit faculty who could discuss their career progression from doctoral student to associate professor.

Interviews were the primary form of data collection. Interviews fostered the collection of in-depth information about how people make meaning of their experiences (Seidman, 1998). The emphasis is on depth rather than on breadth because the goal is to explore experiences and the meanings applied to those experiences (Marshall & Rossman, 1999). Another benefit of using interviews is that one is able to capture a great deal of information in a relatively short period of time.

Using open-ended questions, participants were interviewed in-person for approximately 2 hours. Questions were constructed to elicit information about (a) graduate school experiences, (b) experiences with colleagues and work role, and (c) navigational strategies (see appendix). According to the tenets of BFT, Black women create and assess knowledge through dialogue because it reflects the cultural tradition of connectedness—interaction that affirms the consciousness of speakers and listeners (Collins, 2000; hooks, 1989). Therefore, each interview session included probes to clarify meaning and foster dialogue. After the interview, I recorded my thoughts and observations of the participants. My journal notes were incorporated into the analysis of the data. Finally, all of the interviews were audio-recorded and transcribed verbatim. After coding the data, follow-up interviews were conducted to clarify information.

In addition to interviews, I collected demographic and academic career information through a short questionnaire. Furthermore, I reviewed the curriculum vitae or online biography of each participant. I also reviewed at least one course syllabi or one publication from each participant. These data allowed further insight into how participants functioned within their institutions and disciplines.

Data Analysis

To determine how the participants define their role and contribute to their institutions, I began by coding the transcripts. Next, I used local integration—summarizing interviews by focusing on the meaning of what was discussed (Weiss, 1994). Then, using Atlas TI, a software program that allows code-based theory building, I created open codes focusing on description and interpretation of what was expressed. To generate meaning, I compared and contrasted codes within and across cases to bring forth more inclusive categories. To do this, I employed I matrices to help me see patterns and develop thematic groups within and across cases

(Miles & Huberman, 1994). Specifically, I used descriptive, checklist, and conceptually ordered matrices.

The descriptive matrix was used to catalog and compare background information acquired through the questionnaire. The checklist matrix was employed within and across cases to categorize codes identified as elements of emergent themes such as service-oriented definitions of career success and social justice advocacy. Conceptually ordered matrices allowed for the clustering of a priori concepts to generate meaning. For instance, structural constraints, structural opportunities and navigational strategies were analyzed across cases, providing a way to test the relationship of responses to concepts.

I further tested my emergent understanding through follow-up interviews, examination of other data sources, and self-reflexivity. All of these verification approaches facilitated the consideration of alternative explanations for the ways in which the participants enact their professional role and alter their institutions. First, follow-up interviews were employed to clarify data and determine the credibility of interpretations. The process entailed reviewing each transcript and devising questions based on what needed clarification. I also shared my interpretation with participants to elicit feedback. Many of these discussions encouraged me to think deeply about how structure and agency combine to influence career trajectory. For instance, I acquired an appreciation for how agency mitigates structural constraints.[4] Follow-up interviews served as a form of triangulation—using different ways of corroborating findings—by providing another source of data verification (Patton, 2001). Reviewing professional documents served as another form of triangulation. As mentioned, I examined course syllabi, curriculum vitae, and publications. These data enhanced my understanding of how participants define career success and how they perform their role in the academy.

Lastly, the analysis subscribes to the belief that meaning is coconstructed. Coconstruction of meaning is essentially the coauthoring of meaning through human interaction (Heyl, 2001; Taylor, 2001). The notion of coconstruction is assumed within the principle of reflexivity, which asserts that it is impossible for researchers to be objective and separate from the research. Everything from the selection of research topic to the way in which the researcher analyzes data is a product of the researcher's experiences (Taylor, 2001). Hence, being self-reflexive helps researchers avoid making unsupported assumptions (Heyl, 2001). For this reason, I engaged in self-reflection through journaling during the data collection and analysis phases as a means to identify biases, orientations, and unexamined assumptions. Although reflexivity is useful for identifying biases, this study does not assume that bias (unlike unexamined assumptions) is detrimental. What is important is that the theoretical orientation and methodological approach are transparent (Creswell, 1998).

FINDINGS

PARTICIPANTS

The study is comprised of fourteen associate professors from four top-tier universities. Ten are in the social sciences and four are in humanities. The participants ranged in age from 35 to 56 years old, and the median age was 41 years old. All of the participants self-identified as Black or African American. However, three participants also noted that they are biracial or bicultural. In regard to education, the participants received their doctorate degrees between 1986 and 2001. However, eleven participants received their doctorates between 1990 and 1998. Lastly, at the time of the interview, the participants were tenured 1 to 13 years. One participant was tenured for 1 year, and one participant was tenured for 13 years, while the median number of years tenured was 5.5 years.

CRITICAL ENACTMENTS

In determining how the participants define their professional role and contribute to the academy, I focused on narratives that addressed how they measured career success. Additionally, the analysis was informed by how participants explained their scholarship (teaching, research, and service). I employ the term *critical enactment* to emphasize agency that advances social equity. These enactments are critical because they are concerned with naming and subverting social injustice (Collins, 2000; Lather, 1991). The term *enactment* is used to capture a sense of movement or creation in the way that the participants function within their institutions. As with the notion of multiple juxtapositions, enactments signify the ability to intentionally move through academe while critiquing it for its hegemonic qualities. According to Collins (1998), the notion of movement captures the way that Black women challenge injustices because it is by moving through spaces of unequal power *and* being moved by social inequities that people acquire the ability to critically assess their experiences. Furthermore, enactments indicate generative properties as there is an assumption of change occurring when one is moved to take action and when one is moving through multiple spaces. In this way, the emphasis remains on participant agency and intentionality. Hence, critical enactments highlight the complexities of Black women negotiating PWRIs through transformative endeavors. This study highlights three key critical enactments: (1) bringing race and gender issues to the forefront, (2) lifting as we climb (service to empower the community), and (3) upsetting orthodoxy through research.

Enactment I: Bringing Race and Gender Issues to the Forefront

What underlies how the women define and enact their role in the academy is that they are cognizant of ever-present identity-based inequities, particularly those rooted in racism and sexism. This knowledge has fostered a commitment to bringing race and gender into various conversations. They use their ability to access diverse communities within and outside of their institutions to spread the word about diversity and social justice. In this way, they serve as mechanisms or conduits for raising awareness about these issues. For instance, Tracee discussed how she deals with colleagues who advocate hiring people of color out of guilt rather than a commitment to educational diversity.

> The biggest challenges . . . are making it clear that we should be thinking about race and diversity in particular types of ways. And so sometimes I have very well-intended colleagues, you know, the well-intended liberal type, who will say something that might be kind of offensive, kind of like, oh, hiring a minority person is the right thing to do. . . . Talking about the White candidate in terms of the rigor of their scholarship, saying things like, if we're concerned with quality, we should hire this person. If we're concerned about diversity, then we should hire this person, saying that straight out. So, and then of course, I have to address it. So, that's been the type of challenges.

Jamila and Carmen talked about how they act as mouthpieces for equity issues. Jamila's actions sometimes make her disfavored by colleagues.

> So it was a little bit of adjustment having to go on and then you know, the truth is if you fuss about African minority and racism and justice issues you're not going to be that popular. You know, people don't want to hear that, and you know what, that's who I am . . . I'm going to talk about it until I'm tired of talking about it.

Carmen believes that her presence encourages her colleagues to think critically about diversity issues. However, she is dismayed by their lack of forethought about diversity.

> I think that I'm always pushing them. I'm the diversity coordinator now and I've been for a few years, so I think that it's one of those situations where if I'm not in the room, certain things may not come up. People may not think about it because diversity isn't the number one issue on their mind. When I say diversity, I mean across all the isms and diversity of thought as well. . . . I was on the Scholarship Committee . . . and people were talking about issues of diversity in terms of the students and they were all White, and it was for this particular pot of money. I said, "But this woman here is a single parent that is not a protected class, but it comes with a particular set of real issues that I think are diverse. . . . So it bothers me that nobody else in the room even thinks about it.

Nia talked about the sexism in her first department and how she had to advocate for female students.

> They weren't given candidacy. Or very occasionally were they advanced. It was very subtle and complicated. It was, well, she's just not a go-getter in my class. She's not assertive enough. She's not a leader in the class . . . She doesn't have what it takes . . . they'd use this vague terminology. And meanwhile, here they are, these old intimidating . . . they can't intimidate me, but they would intimidate these young students coming in. And the men would be seen as being more competent than the women even though I would get these same students in my classes, and I'd say, well, she's doing really well in my class.

Later she talked about using her membership on various university committees to introduce equity issues.

> I try not just to sit there, but try to articulate something, a viewpoint that other people might not see, or other people aren't talking about and say, you know, this is really a dire issue, when we have people of color at [the University] who are getting weeded out of the university, whether it's at the third-year review, the tenure review, or whether they're unhappy here . . . they feel their research . . . isn't being taken seriously, or there are problems with the people in their department. . . .

Similarly, the participants stated that they attempted to alter the assumption held by their colleges that diversity weakens academic excellence. Here she talks about how she defends students who attended historically Black institutions.

> In admissions every year . . . I always have to gear myself up to get ready for the fight because I have to be the one who deals with the test scores discussion that will come up. People who have never heard of an HBCU [historically Black college or university] are saying, oh that's not a good institution, that person coming from that school, that's not a good school. Well, you don't know about the school, so this person has done research with this person who is a good scholar. You just don't know that scholar because they don't do work in your area. The way that we talk…we're admitting students kind of out of the goodness of our hearts. Versus, like, you know, it's the right thing to do. Versus like, they're actually bringing in something unique.

Layla also defended the worthiness of the Black experience. Like Tracee, she felt compelled to advocate for Black people and defend the work of those who do research on Black people.

> Actually it came up when I was chairing the search committee and I was going to hire this Black woman who does research on Black people. Ooh, imagine that, and . . . I got several comments now that I think about it in a faculty meeting. One was 'isn't it limiting that she doesn't do comparative'. Can you believe that that is coming up in 2007? . . . I said some people find that thinking quite racist, there is so much heterogeneity within groups. There were like three or four comments that come up . . . I just shouted back my response and didn't let it grow into one of these academic things where everyone starts to blah, blah, blah and the next thing you know, your candidate is shot down.

Dziko, another participant, also talked about resisting standards for student and faculty recruitment.

> I was on a graduate committee, and there were three of us . . . I had to fight for GRE scores as not indicative of a person's capabilities. And it's something else that I was resistant to giving in to, particularly searches, you know documenting your information . . . and speaking out and standing up for those particular individuals. . . . I think that there are just different struggles . . . ideologies that I'm not willing to give up that I want to continue to represent . . . Black people. And so that enters into different kinds of ways in being a faculty member . . .

And so those are things that I'm not willing to change because of raw social political dynamics.

These experiences are also about legitimacy. Because Blackness is viewed with suspicion, participants take a defensive position in order to challenge logic that implies that Blackness undermines excellence. In essence, the narratives show that participants often take the lead in advocating for a broader view of scholarship and merit. In doing so, they act as an element of the institution's social conscience. In essence, they help transform institutional ethos to one that is more aligned with social justice.

Enactment II: Lifting As We Climb

The participants' personal definitions of career success were based on their ability to provide service to students, particularly students of color. They also talked about serving communities of color outside of their institutions. Almost universally, the women discussed giving back to communities that supported them. Their attitudes about and enactments of service are reflected in Dziko's comment.

> I think a number of people in terms of research or at the university don't necessarily see themselves giving of their time without being compensated . . . And I know that's part of the territory for me. We know it's an unwritten rule within the African American community . . . that we're supposed to give back from the community. It's a given for me. It's an unwritten rule for me that I have to go back and to disseminate information and to help somebody else because I'm standing on others' shoulders. But that's a whole particular cultural ideological stance that I would say that a number of my colleagues don't have.

Similarly, Carmen talked about why she gives back.

> Lifting as I climb. I feel like much has been given to me, so much is being asked . . . so I'm on committees where I know they need a representative to think like I do, so I volunteer for those things. I'm very interested in university and faculty governance and so I've been on those councils and those committees. . . . And then there are lots of community boards that I'm also on.

Notably, "lifting as I climb" is a Black American idiom. The saying comes from "lifting as we climb," which is NACW's motto. NACW was one of the most powerful Black organizations in the first half of the 20th century (Giddings, 1984; White, 1999). Its motto derives from the belief that the fate of Black individuals is tied to the condition of the Black community as a whole. This perception that one is only as successful as the community from which one emanates is reflected in the narratives of the participants. For instance, Dziko elaborated on her definition of success.

> I think success for me . . . has to be in terms of teaching and impacting other people's lives and success has to be reaching back to the community . . . so we have research, teaching, and outreach in terms of community. But you know as a Black woman scholar, I do have to continue to go back and give to the community. I'm committed to that . . . I have to be able to reach, especially students of color, especially Black students in my teaching. And my teaching cannot be just vacuous; I have to help them understand. I want them to reach new levels of cognizance . . . so that they can excel and we continue . . . going higher and higher in our accomplishments. I am so happy that my research focuses on Black women . . . So I think that's success for me.

In essence, she makes sure that her duties, teaching, research and service, are enacted to reinforce her commitment to helping Black people. Tracee also talked about helping Blacks.

> Success to me is being in a position where you can bring in others, so I'd go, I've said it many times already, that I feel very fortunate in the support that I was given both as a graduate student and as a young scholar before tenure. So being in a position where I can affect those same things and bring more people into the field—bring more Black folks.

As an example of her commitment to assisting Black scholars, she discussed her influence on the faculty search committee as a newly tenured professor.

> You do have a stronger voice in terms of leadership, so right after I became tenured, I became cochair of my area, which wouldn't have happened as a junior person and even that leadership role gives me some different kinds of forums in terms of talking to people, or bringing in faculty of color, so, this year, we hired a faculty, a Black faculty person and I don't think that's an accident that there were two tenured Black people on the committee who were willing to, who had some insights into certain areas of work, but also who were willing to fight certain types of perceptions about what's valuable research.

Similarly, Tamika spoke about her commitment to helping students of color.

> I feel so obligated to mentor students of color so that someone shows them in a way that people didn't show me. . . . I really try to reach out to students of color in my classes . . . and if someone shows an interest, I am very happy to take them to lunch and talk about what grad school would be like for them. And until this day, I've been here for 10 years, all of my students of color that have graduated and gone on to grad school continue to write me and thank me. So at that level I feel like I am doing something I've always wanted in terms of teaching. That's the main reason why I am still in this game because of those kinds of students.

The practice of *lifting as we climb* was not limited to the boundaries of the university. The participants were also active in facilitating collaborative relationships with external communities. For instance, Jaha discussed the work she does in her local community that is imbued with the spirit of giving back.

> I try and do things that make a difference. I've done things outside of the university that I feel pretty good about as well. I play for a church and encouraged them to purchase a piano lab, to give piano lessons to Black kids in the community, and adults . . . I assist in bringing in choirs, HBCU choirs, once a year to do concerts. . . . I established a connection with our office of minority affairs so that they can come here on campus while they're in town. And maybe some of them will consider [University] for graduate school. So you know, those little things where I see that someone else benefits.

Although service was a value upheld by the participants, they also indicated that their service load made them vulnerable; their services were in demand yet their work was not rewarded by their institutions. For instance, Layla talked about feeling conflicted because she believes service hinders promotion for women of color.

> On the other hand, they will pile service on you. It seems like the same people do all of the service. The same five percent do like 50% of the service and the other 50% are publishing (chuckle), you know. So it's hard not to get caught up in that, you know, 'Oh I need to lend my voice here and there and then you end up on 50,000 committees lending my voice and not getting any work done. I think I feel that

> especially now, pretenure I don't know if I felt that.... How can you... have tenure [and] still be a voice for women of color on this campus, but yet not get so slammed that you get kind of stuck there and don't ever make it to full? I mean it's ridiculous. It's a teeny, tiny percentage of women of color who are full professors.

Tamika described how her race and gender status make her a walking advertisement for service.

> Well, as you are going to find out (chuckle), every committee will want you either because you offer them person-of-color perspective that they need or you are representing Black women. So my service work within the department is pretty heavy. Students think they are doing you a favor. I have a lot of students who have worked with me and recommend me. So it's like 'you are not doing me a favor.' But they don't understand. At the university level, I have a lot of obligations because they want a reasonable voice that represents people of color, women, whatever.

Jamila explained that she had a difficult time meeting her pretenure research requirements because of her commitment to Black students.

> One thing that I found as a minority faculty person, you do have that burden of mentoring every face that comes and looks like yours. So I spent a lot of time in my opinion mentoring and advising, spending time with minority students. In fact, I guess . . . this was done in the spirit of kindness . . . but the advisors routinely assign all Black students to me whenever they're admitted . . . I automatically get them all. And so that does mean, and sometimes those come from . . . out of state, they're lonely, they're sick, you know I may spend more time talking with them, eating with them or even if I had to take them shopping, cause they didn't have clothing, not enough clothing that is, or couldn't buy the books for the course. So I spent an inordinate amount of time, I would have to say, up until about last year . . . doing lots of advising.

Even though there is a commitment to service work, Layla, Tamika, and Jamila's comments demonstrate that the workload can be overwhelming. Also, the women imply that their institutions expect them to represent diversity issues and act as a form of support for students of color. This practice has been called *cultural taxation* (Padilla, 1994). It occurs when faculty of color are expected to implement diversity work through service, teaching, and research. However, the extra work (i.e., cultural tax) they are expected to contribute is not rewarded by their institutions. On the other hand, majority faculty can claim to support diversity yet not be expected to do the work (Brayboy, 2003; Padilla, 1994).

In spite of the service pressures, the participants affirmed their commitment to enacting service that promotes social justice. For example, Halima described how her heavy service load was counterbalanced by the fulfillment she derives from service that advances equity.

> It's been, it was a lot of work . . . I think part of it, I just assumed so much responsibility. It's like chairing, division chair, doing that, associate editor, then editorial board for five things, and then on five search committees, and then having your students, and teaching two new course preps, and it just kept on and on, it was like a lot. But then there's some service things that I really, really like. So for example, this past year the president has this committee called the Diversity . . . and so he appointed me and another person as cochairs . . . we were involved in there to make a . . . strategic plan for the campus to implement diversity. And that was a ton of work . . . on average, 10 plus hours a week, it was a lot of work. But it was a really, I found it was rewarding, I felt it was something important to do.

She shared that she no longer wants to participate in generic service appointments. She stated, "I'll just lend all my stuff to primarily focus on ways that I can help improve the educational experiences of students of color." Sekai shares Halima's commitment to service that benefits diversity.

> Because I do believe I have to serve in the institution for example, I've got to serve on tenure and promotion. . . . I have to. Otherwise, some people might not be in that game very long, because folks can't understand their academic credentials, or understand the work that they've done. I have to be on things that have to do with diversity. So there's just some stuff I have to be on, but, other stuff I ignore. And then I have my own sort of projects.

So, regardless of the value that institutions place on service, the participants view it as part of their role and an aspect of their job that they value. In spite of the demands on them to publish, they have been able to create a space that allows them to address the needs of communities they care about.

Enactment III: Upsetting Orthodoxy

Although the women had to follow some protocols in order to achieve traditional forms of success, they also indicated that they were able to carve out a niche that allowed them to function in ways that reinforced nontraditional values. In essence, they were able to simultaneously work within and expand conventional parameters. For instance, the women accept the research, funding, and fund development markers of career success. However, what they value most is their ability to act as change agents by (1) mentoring students of color, (2) including social justice issues in various discourses, and (3) expanding knowledge about the lives of people of color and women. This section is designed to show how nonnormative attitudes and behaviors contribute to the teaching and learning environment. In going against the grain, the participants create alternative models of success and alternative ways of being in the academy.

All the participants focus on communities where people of color or women predominate. Most of the participants only study race and/or gender issues. The narratives that follow are indicative of the scholarship of the participants. For instance, Mesi's body of work reflects her interest in African American civic engagement and Black female empowerment. She talked about how she challenges her discipline through her research: "I'm trying to upset orthodoxy. I'm deeply committed to insisting on the central relevance of the people I study to grander narratives, right? It's that Black people matter."

Dziko, too, introduced the race and gender dynamic to her discipline. In doing so, she adopted an alternate epistemology.

> I believe as Patricia Hill-Collins and others, particularly her, she has written about this idea of getting away from Eurocentric masculinist validation tradition. . . . I've also been asking other community members, what I call insiders and outsiders . . . to assess this idea of . . . practices. To include community member's voices, their contributions in that whole research and not just based on my perspective and my analysis of it.

By viewing her participants as active contributors to the research process, she challenges paradigms that do not consider research subjects, particularly Black women, as engaged participants with the ability to be analysts of their realities. Dziko has also resisted convention through her methodology. She was adamant about not following the traditional path.

> You know . . . there's a lot of people that believe in quantitative. . . . I'm not there, sorry. I'm not going to do that kind of work. I don't think that that's the most valid or the most important kind of work. And so there are some changes that I've been resistant to.

Jamila has done a lot of research on various vulnerable populations, which is not unusual for her field. Her new line of research, however, focuses on conceptual and empirical analysis of a very marginal community of women, most of whom are women of color. She stressed the significance of her scholarship, "I'm the only one doing it. I think . . . it's filling a very needed gap in terms of what we have to offer here." She also gave an example of how her mode of scholarship compliments her interest in social injustice.

> I do . . . face-to-face interviews, surveys, and I do a lot of conceptual work as well . . . because in my opinion, we don't do a lot of conceptual stuff . . . but I think there's a place for that too. Like for example, I'm talking to you about the need to always think about racism, sexism, and classism, and I [can] sit down in a minute and write a paper about how we can do this theoretically and how I have done it. I mean so that's very conceptual in nature but it's practical. So I think that I do a variety of methods of data collection or writing in general—conceptual, theoretical, and empirical.

Rather than stay within the methodological confines of her field, she chooses to employ multiple ways of knowledge production. Similarly, Tracee challenges convention by not upholding Black cultural deficit models popularized in her discipline. Additionally, she defies orthodoxy by looking at within group experiences of Blacks. She does not believe that interracial comparisons (i.e., Whites compared to non-Whites) are necessary to advance knowledge about social issues. Most of her publications deal with African Americans.

> Most of my work, I don't take a comparative approach, I study only African-American adolescents and young adults and so I have felt very comfortable not comparing African-Americans to others, because of what was modeled to me by my mentors. To my department, I want to contribute a personally valuable area of scholarship. So an area of scholarship that can help inform what we know about African-American students. . . . And there are lots of things that we can learn about from studying African-Americans that could be useful to other people as

well. In fact, one example of that is . . . more and more scholars are saying . . . thinking about yourself in relation to others that's kind of useful. White scholars are discovering this. Whereas people have been studying cultural processes among African-Americans for a long time, we've been saying that having a nonindividualistic orientation can actually be quite useful. . . . So, contributing scholarship that can be helpful to Black folks . . . is what I hope to contribute to the discipline.

Layla also takes a different approach in studying Blacks. Most of Layla's publications focus entirely on the state of Blacks and other people of color. Several of these publications deal with Black women. Here is how she explained her scholarly contribution.

I guess I think for a long time researchers who were interested in race and ethnicity were getting a lot of mileage out of "woe is me" research because you know things are bleak. There are health disparities . . . and just ways in which we are trying to show how disadvantaged we are. So, I think what is different about my work is that I'm trying to highlight the way in which we actually have a strength that other people can benefit from, if we can figure out what it is.

Most of Halima's publications are about race relations and Black perceptions of race. Some of her most recent work is on the development of theory to explain race awareness.

I've always been interested in racism and in different times looking at racial identity . . . And now I've been focused much more on this notion of racial color blind ideology and how people deny, distort, and minimize the existence of structural racism. . . . And what does it mean for Blacks, and other people of color.

Sekai's research challenges traditional data collection and validation processes. Her areas of interest include multicultural issues, Black feminism, pedagogy, and spirituality. She does not make efforts to perfectly fit into her department. Her resolve is rooted in her commitment to her service work and research. She explained, "I write about Black women. I care about Black women . . . does the academy reward it? Not to the degree they would reward something that was much more mainstream." She asserted,

I'm incredibly consistent. I mean, it really is about helping other people learn how to do their work, so if you look at my research, it has been about troubling the academy. About troubling the notion of methodology, about troubling the ideas of teaching, and what teaching is for. . . . Um, and if we're trying to get to a research that doesn't hurt people, and that doesn't villainize particular communities, and that doesn't pathologize particular groups of people, then you might need to rethink what methodology is.

Part of Mesi's agenda to upset orthodoxy is to infuse love into the academy. She believes that love is the key to creating nurturing learning environments for students and faculty. The following narrative shows both her frustration and optimism about instilling love in the academy.

The disappointment of academia, of course, is that I have not found a way to mobilize the power of love with my colleagues, right? Which is to say, I came in here believing not only that I could teach with love, but that love could be the ethic for everything I did. And I have been so disabused of that. And it's very hurtful. Can I find my way back to that? I don't know. Perhaps. Can I learn more sophisticated ways to manifest love? Perhaps. Would I like to be a full professor, so that I can insist on love? Absolutely. Will anybody go along with me? No. But it's really what I believe. I really believe in the communion of human beings and the capacity of that communion that universities are just full of opportunities to experience in ways that so many others aren't. So these days I love my students.

Mesi's efforts to infuse love into the academy are reminiscent of the tenets of critical pedagogy. Within critical pedagogy, love is the prerequisite for teaching that values what students bring to the classroom. It is a means to validate the whole person (hooks, 2003). In practicing love, teachers reject the notion that they must disconnect from the lives of their students. Mesi's desire for love to be practiced in all facets of the academy interrogates the discourse about institutional access and engagement. It is a call for institutional actors to interface in ways that consider emotional and physical well-being.

SUMMARY

The "work" for the participants is transformative. They are concerned about transforming their institutions and larger communities so that they are responsive to need, reflective of diversity and embodiments of reciprocity.

According to the participants, these goals are not always celebrated within their institutions. Nevertheless, they remained steadfast in their enactment of transformative values.

The women realized that they did not perfectly fit into academe because of their identity and their values, yet they were not apologetic. These spaces inspired them to critically assess their institutional norms and propose alternative ways of being. Thus, for them, the *work* is not a job at a particular institution. The *work* is about one's passion. The job itself is a springboard for larger work such as improving the lives of poor children, unearthing Black female theories, studying communication patterns of people of color, analyzing gender in the arts, demystifying the academy, or exploring racial identity. They were able to negotiate the academy on their own terms. They stayed true to their passion, and their passion helped to make the challenges surmountable. So, going against the norm was about self-affirmation.

The participants are upsetting traditional paradigms through service and research. They have asserted the women and people of color are worthy topics of study. Their interest in marginalized groups has broadened the intellectual boundaries within their fields. By doing the work, they have validated other standpoints, thereby invalidating claims of universal truths that are devoid of diversity considerations.

The participants' research challenges orthodoxy not only through their choice of subject but also in their epistemological claims. For instance, they do not approach communities of color with an assumption of deficiency or ignorance. They believe that their subjects have ways of being, knowing, and validating truth that can advance knowledge about phenomena. Furthermore, racism, classism, sexism, and other inequities are considered in their work. Hence, the questions they ask and their analytical frameworks further interrogate dominant paradigms.

If I had to pick one word that encapsulates how the women talked about their role in the academy, it would be *service*. Not the kind of service associated with selflessness and suffering. Not the service on behalf of one's discipline or institution. It is service rooted in the idea of liberation. Bell hooks (2003) explains ,

> Service as a form of political resistance is vital because it is the practice of giving that eschews the notion of reward. Satisfaction is in the act of giving itself, of creating the context where students can learn freely. When as teachers we commit to service, we are able to resist participation in forms of domination that reinforce autocratic rule (p. 91).

This emphasis on service is not unusual. Historically, Black female educators have always "assumed that education should be fundamentally intertwined with moral responsibility and social justice" (Evans, 2007, p. 6). Also, commitment to service may stem from collective remembrance of struggle and awareness of inequities. According to Collins (2000), Black women may be in a better position to recognize interconnections of oppression because they comprise a group that is adversely affected by multiple oppressions. Thus, they may feel more compelled to alter interdependent practices that hinder inclusiveness in the academy. It has been argued that a key way to destabilize institutional discrimination (normalized practices that disadvantage targeted social groups yet give other groups an advantage) is through agency that challenges domination (Baez, 2000). Baez asserts that a conception of social structure that is too rigid "prevents understanding how human agency can subvert the power of structures" (p. 385). In essence, social-justice oriented agency manifested through service can whittle away structural barriers.

Whether it is through research, teaching, mentoring, or volunteering— the underlying theme is that their work is enacted to advance intercultural competence, empowerment, and social equity. The participants serve by making their institutions more accessible for students and other faculty. Furthermore, the participants' work compliments their institutions' stated missions of creating an inclusive environment.

So, professional role definition was about their ability to interrogate normative practices in academe. Whether it was through a need to challenge hiring processes or to decenter traditional epistemological frameworks, the women expressed a desire to act as change agents. It is their passion for discussing the complexity of the Black experience or for facilitating access to higher education that fuels their work—their service. Despite the rigors of the tenure process, participants held strong to their passion. Thus, their efforts to acquire tenure were a means to an end. Tenure ensured longevity so that they could engage in transformative work.

IMPLICATIONS AND SIGNIFICANCE

The participants demonstrate that it is indeed possible to create a space for insurgency within research institutions. Also, they serve to remind colleagues and students that higher education is a means to advance the public good through commitment to social equity. All of the institutions have a stated commitment to diversity, yet the narratives show that there is still is a lot of work to be done. It is these insurgent academics that not only remind institutions of their stated goals, but also have taken the lead to help institutions meet those goals.

One might ask how this study pertains to Black women who may not exemplify oppositional position, an awareness of being a part of a socially marginalized group combined with resistance against individual and collective marginalization. What contributions do these women make and what benefits can they derive from this study? In response, I contend that Black women are inherently oppositional within PWRIs because they represent the antithesis of a legitimate scholar. Their mere presence contributes to PWRIs because it decenters the idea that only White males can occupy that realm. Nevertheless, being oppositional does not mean that all Black women maintain an oppositional position. In other words, though Black women encounter common racialized and gendered themes, the degree of dissonance created by these themes may differ. Consequently, their agency may reflect different choices—such as choices that only reproduce rather than reform or work outside of dominant paradigms. Nevertheless, choosing not to enact and define one's professional role in a way that conveys awareness of oppression does not negate that oppression exists. Black women who chose not to address power hierarchies still benefit from transformative work because it is that work that broadens the discourse around Black female legitimacy within all predominately White institutions.

Most importantly, this study is instructive for Black women and other members of the academy who are committed to critiquing and transforming dominant social structures. This study shows how one can thrive within an institution while working to transform it. Multiple juxtapositions foster the ability to employ critical enactments. By operating within normative structures of academe, the participants could maintain a position of conformity while agitating for change within and outside of the boundaries of their institutions. With access to legitimatized knowledge centers, social networks and resources, internal agitation at once allowed the participants to comply with established patterns of discourse and expand the discourse on educational access and merit. However, participants took their cues for agitation from the racialized and gendered imbalance of power that transcended their institutions. Thus, the efficacy of their work derived from their ability to understand and rearticulate concerns of their communities of interest. Therefore, their enactments were informed by intellectual and physical movement between internal and external contexts.

Again, this mode of operation is useful for anyone (Black, White, male, or female) interested in challenging norms that foster inequitable distribution of resources. However, it is particularly valuable to those who may raise suspicion because of socially inscribed beliefs about their inherent value and legitimacy in resource-rich institutions.

With the erosion of affirmative action programs and the lower rates of tenure for women and people of color (Aguirre, 2000; Allen et al., 2002; Cooper & Stevens, 2002; Trower, 2002; Trower & Chait, 2002), this study responds to the need to pay attention to institutional climate.

It is important for institutional members to recognize that there are embedded practices that marginalize certain groups and to provide a space for people to enact scholarship that challenges institutions to live up to and broaden their missions. Hence, the culture and practices of higher education institutions must be accessible for diverse students, faculty, and staff. This study is important because it captures perceptions of how faculty members are able to fit into and manipulate spaces where they were historically barred from entering. With this knowledge, institutions can better identify norms that undermine or support the professional development of underrepresented groups.

REFERENCES

Aguirre, A. (2000). *Women and minority faculty in the academic workplace: Recruitment, retention, and academic culture, ASHE-ERIC Higher Education Report, 27*. Washington, DC: George Washington University, Graduate School of Education and Human Development.

Allen, W., Epps, E., Guillory, E., Suh, S., Bonous-Hammarth, M., & Stassen, M. (2002). Outsiders Within. In W. Smith, P. Altbach & K. Lomotey (Eds.), *The racial crisis in American higher education*. Albany: State University of New York Press.

Baez, B. (2000). Race-related service and faculty of color: Conceptualizing critical agency in academe. *Higher Education, 39*, 363–391.

Bell, L. A. (1997). Theoretical foundation for social justice education. In M. Adams, L. A. Bell, & P. Griffin (Eds.), *Teaching for diversity and social justice*. New York: Routledge.

Benjamin, L. (Ed.). (1997). *Black women in the academy*. Gainesville: University Press of Florida.

Berry, T. R., & Mizelle, N. D. (Eds.). (2006). *From oppression to grace*. Sterling, VA: Stylus.

Brayboy, B. M. J. (2003). Implementation of diversity in predominately White colleges and universities. *Journal of Black Studies, 34*(1), 72–86.

Collins, P. H. (1998). *Fighting words*. Minneapolis: University of Minnesota Press.

Collins, P. H. (2000). *Black feminist thought*. New York: Routledge.

Cooper, J., & Stevens, D. (Eds.). (2002). *Tenure in the sacred grove*. Albany: State University of New York Press.

Crenshaw, K. (2003). Demarginalizing the intersections of race and sex: A Black feminist critique of antidiscrimination doctrine, feminist theory, and antiracist politics. In K. Wing (Ed.), *Critical race feminism*. New York: New York University Press.

Creswell, J. (1998). *Qualitative inquiry and research design*. Thousand Oaks: Sage.

Evans, S. Y. (2007). *Black women in the ivory tower, 1850–1954*. Gainesville, FL: University Press of Florida.

Giddings, P. (1984). *When and where I enter*. New York: William Morrow and Company.

Gregory, S. T. (1999). *Black women in the academy: The secrets to success and achievement*. Lanham, MD: University Press of America.

Gurin, P. (1999). Expert Report of Patricia Gurin. In *The compelling need for diversity in higher education* (pp. 99–234). Ann Arbor, MI: University of Michigan.

Gurin, P., Dey, E. L., Hurtado, S., &Gurin, G. (2002). Diversity and higher education: Theory and impact on educational outcomes. Harvard Educational Review, *72*(3), 330.

Heyl, B. S. (2001). Ethnographic interviewing. In P. Atkinson, A. Coffey, S. Delamont, J. Lofland, & L. Lofland (Eds.), *Handbook of ethnography*. London: Sage.

Hine, D. C. (1994). *Hine sight: Black women and the reconstruction of American history*. Bloomington, IN: Indiana University Press.

Hine, D. C. (1995). Race and the inner lives of Black women in the west: Preliminary thoughts on the culture of dissemblance. In B. Guy-Sheftall (Ed.), *Words of fire*. New York: The New Press.

Hine, D. C., Brown, E. B., Patterson, T., & Williams, L. (Eds.). (1990). *Black Women in United States History: From Colonial Times to the Present*. New York: Carlson Publishing.

Hine, D. C., & Thompson, K. (1998). *A shining thread of hope*. New York: Broadway Books.

hooks, b. (1989). *Talking back.* Boston: South End Press.

hooks, b. (2003). *Teaching community, A pedagogy of hope.* New York: Routledge.

John, B. M. (1997). The African American female ontology: Implications for academe. In L. Benjamin (Ed.), *Black women in the academy* (pp. 53–63). Gainesville, FL: University of Florida Press.

King, D. (1995). Multiple jeopardy, multiple consciousness: The context of Black feminist ideology. In B. Guy-Sheftall (Ed.), *Words of Fire* (pp. 294–318). New York: The New Press.

Lather, P. (1991). *Getting Smart: Feminist research and pedagogy with/in the postmodern.* New York: Routledge.

Marshall, C., & Rossman, G. B. (1999). *Designing qualitative research.* Thousand Oaks: Sage.

Milem, J., & Hakuta, K. (2002). The benefits of racial and ethnic diversity in higher education. In C. Turner, A. L. Antonio, M. Garcia, B. Laden, A. Nora, & C. Presley (Eds.), *Racial and ethnic diversity in higher education.* Santa Barbara, CA: Pearson Custom Publishing.

Miles, M. B., & Huberman, A. M. (1994). *Qualitative data analysis.* Thousand Oaks: Sage.

Moses, Y. T. (1997). Black women in academe. In L. Benjamin (Ed.), *Black women in the academy* (pp. 23–38). Gainesville: University of Florida Press.

Myers, L. W. (2002). *A broken silence: Voices of African American women in the academy.* Westport, CT: Bergin & Garvey.

Padilla, A. (1994). Ethnic, minority scholars, research, and mentoring: Current and future issues. *Educational Researcher, 23*(4), 24–27.

Patton, M. Q. (2001). *Qualitative research and evaluation methods.* Thousand Oaks, CA: Sage.

Perkins, L. M. (1990). The Black female American missionary association teacher in the south, 1861–1870. In D. C. Hine, E. B. Brown, T. Patterson, & L. Williams (Eds.), *Black Women in United States History: From Colonial Times to the Present* (Vol. 3). New York: Carlson Publishing.

Seidman, I. (1998). *Interviewing as qualitative research.* New York: Teachers College Press.

Sulé, V. T. (2008). *Black female faculty and professional socialization: Constraints, enablements and enactments.* Unpublished doctoral dissertation: University of Michigan, Ann Arbor.

Taylor, S. (2001). Locating and conducting discourse analytic research. In M. Wetherell, S. Taylor, & S. Yates (Eds.), *Discourse as data: A guide for analysis* (pp. 5–48). Thousand Oaks: Sage.

Trower, C. (2002). *Women without tenure, part two: The gender sieve.* Retrieved October 2, 2005, from http://nextwave.sciencemag.org/cgi/content/full/2002/01/24/7

Trower, C., & Chait, R. (2002, March-April). Faculty diversity. *Harvard Magazine,* 23–28.

Turner, C. S., Antonio, A. L., Garcia, M., Laden, B., Nora, A., & Presley, C. (Eds.). (2002). *Racial and ethnic diversity in higher education.* Boston: Pearson Custom Publishing.

Weiss, R. (1994). *Learning from strangers: The art and method of qualitative interview studies.* New York: Free Press.

White, D. G. (1999). *Too heavy a load.* New York: W.W. Norton & Company.

ENDNOTES

1. Social equity refers to social justice or a society in which the distribution of resources is based on need and where all groups have an opportunity for full participation (Bell, 1997).

2. In recent years, affirmative action programs have been abolished in several states, most notably in Florida, California, Washington, Texas, Michigan, and Nebraska.

3. In the larger study, the interplay between opportunity structure and human agency as factors in the professional socialization of tenured Black female faculty was analyzed. Opportunity structure refers to constraining and enabling aspects of higher education institutions that influence one's work role, access to resources, and status. Agency denotes the ability of individuals to identify and implement alternatives (Sulé, 2008).

4. Structural constraints are social policy and practices that limit opportunities and life chances.

APPENDIX

Excerpt of Interview Schedule

Graduate School
- How did you decide to get your doctorate?
- Tell me about your graduate school experience.
- If you could change anything about your graduate school experience, what would it be?

Faculty Experiences with Colleagues and Work Role
- Can you describe your relationship with your colleagues in your department?
- Can you describe your sources and types of career support?
- What factors help and hinder your career development?
- If you could change anything about your work environment, what would it be?
- How do you define career success in academe?
- What have you done to be successful?

Navigational Strategies
- How would you describe your teaching practice?
- How would you describe your research?
- How would you describe your service work?
- Did you have to change anything about yourself to fit into your department?
- What do you ultimately want to contribute to your department? Discipline?

Childcare Options in South Korea: Experiences and Perceptions of Female College Faculty

Hae Ja Shin*
Director General of BIS-WIST
Professor
Dongseo University, South Korea

This study investigates the perceptions of 203 female college/university faculty members about childcare policies in South Korea. All of the respondents had experience with childcare; most were aware of the option of maternity leave (89.7%), and many had taken such leave (43.3%). Regarding postchildbirth leave for childcare purposes (parental leave), 39.4% were aware of the option and only 6.9% had used such leave. The childcare needs of most respondents were met by relatives and private-hire services (e.g., nannies), whereas daycare facilities were considered unreliable. Most of the women reported that their spouses considered childcare the woman's responsibility; this low paternal childcare involvement was attributed to husbands having high workloads, low degrees of childcare knowledge, unsupportive workplace cultures, and increased financial pressures. Societal and workplace cultures had great impact on the use of childcare policies. These findings provide insight into the current childcare status in South Korea and could support development of new family-friendly workplace initiatives.

South Korea is experiencing very dramatic economic and social changes as it becomes the first country since World War II to transition from a developing to developed country. The contributions of Korean women are recognized as indispensable to this process (Kim & Na, 2003), as women seek to move from the traditional passive roles to having more active functional roles in society. As such, an increasing number of women are

---

**Acknowledgements:* This work was supported by a grant from the Korea Ministry of Science and Technology and partially by a grant from the Metropolitan City of Busan. The author would like to thank these two organizations for their support.

entering the workforce, the number of dual-income parents is rising, the number of single-parent families is rising, more men are becoming primary caregivers, and the overall population is aging (Korea National Statistics Office, 2002; The Federation of Korean Industries, 2002).

Currently about half of the college students in Korea are female, and this population is demonstrating better academic achievement overall compared to male students (Korea Ministry of Education and Human Resources Development, 2006). The proportion of employed females has increased dramatically in many fields. However, 50.1% of the economically active women in South Korea were in the workforce in 2005 (Korea National Statistics Office, 2002), compared to 60.2% in the United States in 2000 (Timmermann, 2005). This number is the lowest among countries in the OECD (Organisation for Economic Co-operation and Development). Furthermore, the economic participation rate of Korean women drops suddenly between the ages of 25–34, returning to higher levels thereafter (Korea Ministry of Labor, 2008). Childbearing and childrearing are believed to be major reasons for this trend (Evans & Kelly, 2002; Liddicoat, 2003; Na, Yoo, & Moon, 2003; Thornthwaite, 2004), due to the traditional societal context that imposes family responsibilities primarily on women in South Korea (Na et al., 2003; Sung, 2003; Won & Pascall, 2004). A substantial proportion of South Korean women with children are urged to quit their jobs. For most working Korean women, childbirth becomes a dilemma (Na et al., 2003; Won & Pascall, 2004): should they quit their job and just be a mother; or try to be a career woman and remain childless, knowing that it will be a struggle?

Thus, it is necessary for working women in Korea to maintain a balance between work and family responsibilities. Numerous organizations in South Korea have sought to offer family-friendly initiatives (Kim & Na, 2003; Won & Pascall, 2004). These policies, in general, have yielded company benefits such as reduced staff turnover, reduced absenteeism, increased productivity, and improved employee morale (Liddicoat, 2003). According to Kamerman (1991, 2000), Sweden, Norway, and Canada have the most beneficial policies with 1 year of paid leave. In contrast, the European Union has mandated a shorter 14-week paid maternity leave and the United States provides 12 weeks, which is unpaid. In Korea companies must provide 90 days of paid maternity leave. However, in practice, these family-friendly policies have proven to be more symbolic than substantive, and are often either not communicated, or used only infrequently due to risks to career advancement and job security (Blair-Loy & Wharton,

2002; Kim & Na, 2003; Sung, 2003; Waters & Bardoel, 2006; Won & Pascall, 2004). Several factors are believed to account for the gap between the provision and utilization of work-family policies, including a lack of communication about the policies, high workloads, poor management attitudes, negative career repercussions, negative peer influence, daunting administration processes (Waters & Bardoel, 2006), organizational time expectations, and gender equity (McDonald, Brown, & Bradley, 2005). Korea is especially influenced by philosophies that encourage societal collectivism, whereas the United States is considered one of the most strongly individualistic countries (McMullen, 2005). Thus, a common concern in Korea is that child-centered philosophy and methods are often in conflict with the ideas of parents and communities about how best to care and educate the children (Hsieh, 2004; Lee, 1992). This is similar to the controversy seen in the United States about the best way to care and educate ethnic, minority, and urban children (Stipek & Ryan, 1997).

The jobs perceived as being most favorable toward women in Korea are governmental and teaching positions (DongA News, 2007), which typically offer flexible work schedules and allow women to take advantage of childcare policies without fear of adverse effects on their careers. In this regard, female faculty members at the university and college level are presumed to have even less burden in childcare due to long vacations, flexible work schedules, the availability of yearlong sabbaticals, and the high incomes associated with these positions.

Currently, one out of every three doctoral-level graduates in Korea is female (Korea Ministry of Education and Human Resources Development, 2006). The quota system enacted by the Korean government in 2003, which requires universities to hire more female faculty members, has contributed to the increased number of female faculty members hired by colleges as adjunct, visiting and research professors, and full- and part-time lecturers. However, although the number of female faculty members has increased over time, relatively few studies have investigated their perceptions on the use of available childcare policies to mitigate work-family conflicts. This present survey of female faculty members seeks to take advantage of the respondents' insights regarding childcare policies, in the hopes of identifying critical elements that are less likely to be identified by members of other groups. First, the reported perceptions of female faculty members regarding childcare policies in Korea are outlined. Next, these findings are placed within the context of Korean views towards the use of childcare policies, and policy implications for better family-friendly workplace initiatives are discussed.

METHODS AND ANALYSIS

Two-hundred-three mothers were randomly selected from the adjunct, visiting and research professors, and full- and part-time lecturers at 16 4-year universities and 30 2-year colleges in the Busan, Ulsan, and Gyeongnam regions of South Korea. The relevant area statistics and childcare policies were obtained from various sources, including Web pages and rulebooks of 30 2-year colleges and 16 4-year universities. Related articles, research papers, and policy reports were included in order to improve the quality of research.

A structured interview format was chosen as the method of data collection for this study to minimize nonsampling errors and standardize survey process. Although questionnaires were generally used to collect data, direct-interview questioning was also employed to obtain more in-depth information. The interviews were conducted between May 1–28 of 2007. The majority of questions were given a tick-the-box or rating-scale style, with space provided for respondents to write comments. The questions covered the following issues: recognition and use of childcare policies, obstacles in taking the policy-mandated leaves, difficulties with returning to job after maternity/parental leave, current childcare situation, spousal participation in childcare, and perceptions regarding the future of family-friendly workplaces. The questions also included demographic items, such as the respondent's current age, ages at each childbirth, number of children, educational level, major field, length of service, position at college/university, and salary scale (Appendix A). Two-hundred-fifty questionnaires were distributed and two-hundred-three were returned and finally analyzed. The raw data were coded and entered into a Statistical Package for the Social Sciences data file.

RESULTS AND DISCUSSION

MATERNITY AND PARENTAL LEAVE POLICIES IN SOUTH KOREA

A previous study showed that work-family conflict is one of the major obstacles limiting the employment and successful career development of women in Korea (Shin, 2008a, 2008b). Among the work-family policies available in South Korea, this paper focuses on the perceptions toward usage of maternity and parental leave. According to the Labor Standard Act and the Equal Employment Opportunity Law, companies must provide 90 days of paid maternity leave for female workers experiencing childbirth; the first 2 months are paid for by the company, while the last month is funded by the employer's insurance company. This law is applicable to both full- and part-time workers. Current maternity leave is legislated only for women, but spousal leave is occasionally allowed at the workplace's discretion. When the revised Equal Employment Opportunity Law became effective on June 2008, male workers were granted 3 days of paternity leave (Korea Ministry of Labor, 2008). The concept of parental leave has gained ground in recent years due to the needs of employees attempting to balance the demands of work and family (Newman & Mathews, 1999; Thornthwaite, 2004; Won & Pascall, 2004). This policy, which is based on the thought that male workers have the same responsibility and right for childcare as female workers, was introduced in 1987 in Korea. The current parental leave policy (revised in December 30, 2005) enforces the right in such a way that a maximum 1-year parental leave is available to workers with a child less than 3 years old. During parental leave, allowances of about $400 USD per month are paid from an employment insurance fund (Korea Ministry of Labor, 2008).

College and university faculties are further governed by the Rules for Public Educational Personnel and Staff. The current act (amended in Jan. 28, 2000) grants parental/maternity leave to parents who have a child less than one year old, or female workers who are expecting or give birth. An initial 1-year leave may be given to female employees upon request, and an additional extension of up to 2 years total is recommended. Adopted children are also included under this act.

First, an assessment was made concerning whether the surveyed universities/colleges in the Busan, Ulsan, and Gyeongnam districts of South Korea followed the relevant maternity and parental leave policies (Appendix B). Findings showed that most of the universities/colleges obeyed the policies fairly well, although a few of the colleges still maintained older version of acts that allowed only maternity leave. In contrast, some of the universities offered better parental leave than required, allowing parental leave to be extended for up to 3 years, or allowing parental leave for husbands with children under 3 years old. Clearly these universities are supportive of parental leave.

GENERAL STATUS OF FEMALE FACULTY MEMBERS

Just as the proportion of female faculty members has increased worldwide since 1969 (Bentley & Blackburn, 1992; Macrae, 2005), the proportion of female faculty members across South Korea increased from 15.6% in 2000 to 18.7% in 2006. Similarly, this proportion is increased in the districts relevant to the present study: Busan (13.7% to 17.1%), Ulsan (11.8% to 14.7%), and Gyeongnam (10.8% to 16.2%) (Korea Ministry of Education and Human Resources Development, 2006). In Busan, the most common fields of female faculty employment were the arts (35.4%) and education (35.3%), followed by liberal arts (23.3%) and engineering (3.4%). In Ulsan, these included education (60.0%), natural science (25.3%), the arts (20.3%), and engineering (1.6%); while female faculty members in Gyeongnam were found in medicine (38.4%), education (32.5%), the arts (31.9%), and engineering (3.2%). The distribution of major field varied markedly by district, which may be partially due to regional characteristics. It is worth noting that few female faculty members were employed in engineering regardless of district, confirming the previous report (Bentley & Blackburn, 1992) that women face serious difficulty entering the field of engineering. This is believed to add to problems of "fixing the leaky pipeline" that exist throughout this field.

The demographic characteristics of the study respondents are shown in Appendix A. The respondents included female faculty members in their 30s (24.1%), 40s (41.4%), 50s (31.0%), and 60-plus (3.4%). Most of them had doctorate degrees (74.9%), and the positions they held included full professor (43.8%), associate professor (14.8%), assistant professor (18.2%), full-time lecturer (12.3%), and part-time lecturer (10.8%). Most of the respondents (53.2%) had been in their current job for more than 10 years, routinely working 8–10 hours per day; this indicates that respondents, except for part-time lecturers, had relatively secure jobs with comparably lower workloads compared with female workers in other occupations in Korea. Most respondents had one (35.5%) or two children (58.1%) and reported an annual income of $30,000–60,000 (USD). Half of the respondents reported an annual family income over $120,000, meaning that they are economically well off in Korean society.

In sum, the respondents were overall well-educated women with relatively flexible schedules that would seem to allow for childcare involvement, high incomes that would support the financing of childcare, working in organizations that offer relatively good childcare policies. It can be speculated that female faculty members are better able to choose strategies for managing work-family conflicts, such as role elimination, role reduction, and role sharing, as previously demonstrated in high-growth female entrepreneurs (Shelton, 2006). Therefore, it is expected that this group of Korean women could provide insight into the awareness and use of childcare policies.

Recognition and Use of Maternity and Parental Leave

Women tend to juggle many roles and typically have a more diffuse distribution of work across paid work, childcare, and housework (Macrae, 2005; Shelton, 2006). A substantial proportion of female workers with children prefer not to have paid employment. Even so, paid employment is important to most mothers who are active in the labor market: almost two-thirds (64%) of women with children would still want employment even if their household did not need the income (Glezer & Wolcott, 2000). According to Shelton (2006), role sharing might be the preferable method for mitigating work-family conflict, since women experience enhancement in their jobs by participating in both family and work roles. Here, I assessed Korean female faculty members' perceptions of their work-family situations and role conflicts. Most of the respondents gave birth to their first child in their 20s and the second in their 30s; this relatively late childbirth was generally due to their longer doctoral education periods. Many of the respondents were holding somewhat insecure positions (e.g., graduate student, researcher, or adjunct professor) at the time of their first childbirth, but held more secure positions (e.g., full-time lecturer or assistant/associate professor) at the time of their second childbirth. Approximately 43% of the respondents reported using maternity leave for their childbirth (Table 1).

Table 1. Period of maternity leave used.

Categories	Numbers	Percentage
Less than 30 days	3	3.4
30–59 days	44	50.0
60–89 days	27	30.6
90–180 days	14	15.9
Total	88	100

*Among 203 respondents, 88 persons (43.3%) had used maternity leave.

Approximately 84% of them took less than the 90-day legal period for maternity leave. Only 15.9% of them used 90–180 days of maternity leave. There might be several reasons for this relatively short maternity leave, including an unsupportive workplace culture or the woman's fear of peer or career repercussions, as discussed in other reports (Kim & Na, 2003; McDonald et al., 2005; Thompson, Beauvais, & Lyness, 1999; Waters & Bardoel, 2006; Won & Pascall, 2004).

About half (53.4%) of the respondents reported that their workplaces showed positive attitudes toward maternity leave, while 45.5% reported negative or neutral attitudes. Only one person responded that she had to fight for her maternity leave, which her workplace didn't plan to allow. These results indicate that maternity leave policy has not yet been fully accepted as a natural and expected benefit, even among faculty groups in Korean society. Examining this in more detail revealed that most of the respondents (89.8%) reported receiving their normal salaries during their maternity leave, while 10.2% did not. During their maternity leave, about half of the respondents (47.7%) had their classes covered by substitute lecturers. The substitutes were hired either by school (64.3%) or by the female faculty members themselves (35.7%), and were paid either by the school (78.6%) or by the female faculty members (21.5%). These results, which are in good accord with those in previous reports (Kim & Na, 2003; Sung, 2003; Won & Pascall, 2004), indicate that the actual use of maternity leave is fairly constrained among the faculty group in Korea.

Prince (2000) states that "even the best programs won't succeed if employees aren't aware of them," indicating that recognition is critical in policy implementation. Accordingly, an assessment was made concerning whether respondents were aware of the childcare policies in place (Table 2).

The respondents reported varied degrees of awareness regarding the details of the available childcare policies. Most of the respondents (89.7%) were aware of maternity leave, but fewer of them (39.4%) knew that parental leave was permitted to women with children less than 1 year old. Only 35% of them knew that parental leave also applied to men. Thirty percent knew that pregnant women were exempt from holiday shifts, while only 16.7% knew that pregnant women were exempt from more than 2 hours of extra work per day. Recognition of nonharmful duty benefits was fairly low, with less than a quarter of respondents knowing that policy mandated nonharmful duty for pregnant women (24.6%), nonharmful duty for women with children less than one year old (17.2%), and mandatory switching of pregnant women to nonharmful duty (18.2%).

TABLE 2. Awareness and experience of childcare policies.

Categories	Awareness N (%)	Previous experience N (%)	Agreement on indispensability N (%)
Pregnant women provided with maternity leave	182 (89.7)	88 (43.3)	127 (62.6)
Pregnant women exempted from night shifts	70 (34.5)	6 (3.0)	136 (67.0)
Pregnant women exempted from holiday shifts	61 (30.0)	6 (3.0)	129 (63.5)
Pregnant women exempted from more than 2 hours extra work per day	34 (16.7)	2 (1.0)	131 (64.5)
Nonharmful duty given to pregnant women	50 (24.6)	4 (2.0)	149 (73.4)
Nonharmful duty given to women with childbirth of < 1 yr	35 (17.2)	4 (2.0)	144 (70.9)
Pregnant women switched to nonharmful duty	37 (18.2)	4 (2.0)	143 (70.4)
On-site childcare center required at organization with >300 workers	69 (34.0)	2 (1.0)	157 (77.3)
Nursing time provided to women with < 1-yr-old child	61 (30.0)	3 (1.5)	145 (71.4)
Parental leave provided to women with < 1-yr-old child	80 (39.4)	11 (5.4)	154 (75.9)
Parental leave provided to men with < 1-yr-old child	71 (35.0)	3 (1.5)	146 (71.9)

About 30% knew that organizations with more than 300 workers should establish on-site childcare facilities and provide nursing time to women with children less than 1 year-old.

Although 43% of respondents had used maternity leave, they showed almost no usage of other childcare policies (all below 3.0%) beside maternity/parental leave. This is consistent with a previous report (Gerson & Jacobs, 2001) showing that even when work-family policies are formally available, workers may conclude that taking advantage of them entails unspoken but very real costs to their careers. In contrast, a majority of respondents (>62%) acknowledged that all of these policy items could be indispensable. Most (77.3%) respondents cited establishment of an on-site daycare facility as their first choice for a new family-friendly workplace initiative.

Only 6.9% of the respondents or their spouses had used parental leave (Table 2). This is consistent with research by Drago, Crouter, Wardell, and Willits (2001) showing that the most progressive work-family policies are likely to be ignored by academic faculty. The workplace attitude for parental leave was reportedly less positive (35.7%) than that for maternity leave (53.4%), although only one person reported having received direct objection from the workplace. These data suggest that the respondents generally believed the use of childcare policies would have a negative impact on their careers. This is in accord with a previous suggestion that employees believe the use of any work-family policies might be interpreted

Childcare Options

as a lack of commitment, negatively influencing promotions or contract renewals (Waters & Bardoel, 2006). The major reason respondents gave for using parental leave was that they were willing to take care of the child by themselves, and that there was no family member or reliable daycare center available to do so. Most reported that they would have used helpers or reliable daycare facilities if available. Similar to the case of maternity leave, some of the respondents hired substitute lecturers out of their own pockets during their parental leave. However, the female faculty members did not report having difficulties when returning from maternity/parental leave. This may be ascribed to their professional job position.

In several western countries, parental leave aims to provide an appropriate amount of economic support to the family (Clancy & Tata, 2005). In Norway, for example, parental leave is allowed with 80% payment for 1-year leave or 100% for 9 months, until the child is one year old (Bø, 2006). Similarly, in New Zealand, parental leave was made a paid position as of 2002 (Liddicoat, 2003). Recent legislation in Britain also provides a good example: Under the Employment Act 2002, parents of children under 6 and disabled children under 18 have the right to apply to work flexible hours, and their employers must seriously consider their requests (Thornthwaite, 2004). In other words, parental leave is designed to protect deterioration of the family's economic situation due to childbirth and childcare. From a national perspective, this policy can prevent birthrate decline due to monetary troubles, improving labor resources for the next generation. Korea has experienced a birthrate decline due to the overwhelming burden of childcare: The total fertility rate was at the desired population replacement level of 2.1 in 1983, but fell to 1.7 in the late 1990s and hit a record low of 1.17 in 2002 (Korea Ministry of Health and Welfare, 2005; Na et al., 2003). Thus, current childcare policies should be reinforced in terms of economic support and process streamlining, in order to encourage childbirth in South Korea.

CURRENT CHILDCARE SITUATION

To assess the current childcare situation of each respondent, I asked who cared for their children during weekdays, weekends, and in emergency situations; and whether the respondents had access to reliable daycare centers. Table 3 reveals that weekday childcare came from maternal family members (26.6%), nannies (26.1%), paternal family members (23.2%), daycares (14.3%), the respondents themselves (8.4%), and other (1.5%).

Table 3. Current weekday and weekend childcare.

Categories	Weekday Numbers	Weekday Percentage	Weekend Numbers	Weekend Percentage
Respondent	17	8.4	182	89.7
Spouse	0	0	4	2.0
Maternal relative	54	26.6	8	3.9
Paternal relative	47	23.2	6	3.0
Nanny or home care	53	26.1	3	1.5
Daycare center	29	14.3	0	0
Other	3	1.5	0	0
Total	203	100.0	203	100.0

Most of the respondents were involved in weekend childcare (89.7%). In-home childcare was most common regardless of who was in charge of childcare (53.7% weekdays, 93.6% weekends). In the case of emergencies (data not shown), childcare responsibilities went to the maternal grandparents (41.9%), paternal grandparents (28.6%), babysitters (9.4%), brothers and sisters (8.9%), nobody (6.4%), daycares (3.0%), and neighbors (2.0%).

These findings are similar to those of previous studies showing that informal care arrangements, such as having relatives as caretakers, were the most utilized means of care for dependents (Fuller-Thomson & Minkler, 2001; Lee, Chang, Chung, & Um, 2002; Liang, Fuller, & Singer, 2000; Liddicoat, 2003).

Daycare facilities were used at a fairly low frequency (14.3% on weekdays, 3% in case of emergency), even though 54% of the respondents reported having accessible childcare nearby. Therefore, it is postulated that the lack of reliable childcare facilities may be a constraint preventing their regular use. An initial step for improved maternal protection policies could be supplementation of reliable daycare facilities nearby. The types of daycare facilities used included nurseries (large daycare, 57.2%), playrooms (small daycare, 26.4%), infant facilities (8.2%), workplace daycares (5.0%), and other (3.1%).

There might be several reasons why daycare facilities are not popular in Korea. In general, there are too few accessible and reliable childcare facilities, meaning that the handful of reliable daycare facilities known to offer high-quality services in a given area will tend to have very high levels of competition for admission. Furthermore, parents may lack confidence in public daycare services, including having concerns regarding whether their children will get sufficient individual attention, or whether they will be victimized by peer bullying (Kim & Na, 2003). Women pointed out inaccessible and unreliable daycare facilities in Korea, as is clear from the following statements:

> With my first child, I had a difficult time with daycare facilities. My baby was ill all the time and I really wanted to quit my job, wondered what on earth I was doing. . . .

> Since I had been busy finishing my dissertation, I had no time to pay attention to my child in daycare facilities. Occasionally my child came home hurt and bruised in his face or leg. The teachers did not pay individual attention to my child, which made me upset.

> All of my family members took a turn standing in the long line during a cold winter night, in order to get my son enrolled in a famous private daycare/kindergarten. We were lucky but unhappy with the high cost.

A report by Evans and Kelley (2002) found that approval or disapproval of institutional care for children was driven by perceptions about whether such facilities can provide sufficient individual attention to facilitate children's learning and meet their needs for nurturance and affection. In addition, the Korean societal context may mean that parents tend to prefer using blood kin for childcare (Kim & Na, 2003; Lee et al., 2002). There is a general bias toward trusting family members in Korea, which is thought to be one reason for the low adoption rate in this country. In the present study, I found that the respondents preferred to care for the children themselves (89.7%, weekends) or leave them with family members (49.8%, weekdays), versus trusting their children with strangers (Table 3). Finally, family income might also be a factor in the low utilization of daycares, which tend to be relatively expensive, as discussed previously (Kim & Na, 2003). Taken together, the findings suggest that the establishment of more reliable, affordable daycare facilities could help complement the childcare system in Korea.

PARTICIPATION OF SPOUSES

According to respondents, only 2% of their spouses participated in weekend childcare (Table 3). Gender equity in childcare is a major issue in Korea (Won & Pascall, 2004), whereas it is less so in most developed countries. In Sweden, where most mothers have jobs, fathers with children of 3 years old or less work the shortest hours outside the home and largely contribute to childcare (Bjornberg, 2000; Burgress, 1997). Liddicoat (2003) states that in New Zealand, family-friendly initiatives should be available to all employees since husbands have the highest level of family responsibility.

As described earlier, the current maternity leave policy in Korea was intended only for women. However, even though paternity leave is not mandated, some workplaces have been providing a few days of spousal leave at the time of childbirth. In the present study, 91% of respondents did not answer the question of how long their spouse took leave after they gave birth, and 6.4% responded "0 days." This may be seen as indicating that spouses generally did not take leave for childbirth. Table 4 shows the various reasons why the spouses did not use maternity leave (Table 4), including the spouse's high workload (37.4%), ignorant attitude toward childcare (25.1%), unsupportive workplace culture (21.2%), economic situation, and other (15.3%). However, if paternity leave had been a granted provision in the spouses' workplace, approximately 70% of respondents said that their spouses would have used the policy. This suggests that societal recognition or approval of paternity leave might be necessary for utilization of the policy. Prior studies have indicated that younger men are more likely to hold the intention of being actively involved fathers (Burgress, 1977; Hand & Lewis, 2002; Hogarth, Hassluck, & Pierre, 2000). Role-sharing strategies with active participation of both spouses is likely to be the preferred scenario, because it allows both parents to enjoy work and family life (Shelton, 2006). Thus, paternity leave should be encouraged.

Table 4. Reasons for spouse not using maternity leave.

Categories	Numbers	Percentage
Unsupportive workplace culture	43	21.2
High workload	76	37.4
Ignorant attitude to childcare	51	25.1
Economic reason	2	1.0
Other	14	6.9
No response	17	8.4
Total	203	100.0

Next, the respondents' perceptions regarding their spouses' awareness and usage of parental leave were examined. Most respondents (88.2%) answered that there was no parental leave available at their spouses' workplace, while only 11.8% responded that such leave was available. When asked about the duration of available parental leave, 70.8% had no response, while others reported 90 days (12.5%), 1 year (12.5%), and 180 days (4.2%). The reasons given as to why spouses had not used parental leave included unsupportive workplace culture (48%), difficulties with handling the child (32%), and other (20%).

TABLE 5. Solutions to improve spousal participation in parental leave.

Categories	Numbers	Percentage
Supportive social culture	113	55.7
Flexible work hours and duties	51	25.1
Spouse's volunteerism	38	18.7
Wife's demand	1	0.5
Total	203	100.0

The focus then shifted to examining what might prompt Korean fathers to participate more in parental leave (Table 5). The answers given by respondents included supportive societal and workplace cultures (55.7%), flexible work hours and duties (25.1%), improvements in their spouses' attitudes toward childcare (18.7%), and demands by wives (0.5%). However, temporary participation of the spouse in childcare was below 20% across all of the examined items, which included playing, exercising, bathing, holding, and so forth, demonstrating that Korean men typically prioritize their work and life over family. Working women still assume a majority of household responsibilities (Friedman & Greenhaus, 2000; Macrae, 2005; Noor, 2004; Ozgun & Honig, 2005; Won & Pascall, 2004). Women's responsibilities in the household might be universal, as discussed in an Australian report indicating that 68% of fathers feel that they have too little involvement with their children (Russell & Bowman, 2000). Thornthwaite (2004) also states that for women, working hour preference is clearly linked with work-family balance issues; whereas for men, broader work-life balance issues are more important. It seems likely that household labor, including childcare, is generally perceived as being the woman's responsibility; whereas income earning is considered the man's responsibility, even though it falls on the shoulders of working women.

CONCLUSION

Overall, the survey results confirm the notion that societal context affects the use of childcare policies in Korea. The Korean female faculty members surveyed herein tended to use maternity leave, but preferred informal childcare arrangements, most often involving the child's grandparents. Parental leave for parents of children less than 1 year old was cited by respondents as their first choice among possible workplace initiatives. Parental leave was not widely recognized by respondents and was rarely used due to social bias. Unsupportive workplace cultures, biased views on childcare, and high workloads were perceived as limiting husbands' uses of childcare policies and their participation in childcare. Thus, it seems as though the environment and culture in which the childcare policies are implemented is even more important than the policy itself. In order to improve childcare use and applicability in Korea, both parents must take responsibility in childcare, and more reliable and accredited daycare facilities should be made available. Korean society faces many problems due to the relatively low fertility rate in this country, making childcare an enormously important part of reducing looming human resource shortages in Korea.

OPTIONS FOR IMPROVING CURRENT CHILDCARE POLICIES

There are several options for improving the current childcare policies in South Korea. First, recognition and acceptance of parental leave must be enhanced through publicity. (Note: That is a suggestion for future research, not an option for improving policies.) It might be important to actively educate workers on parental leave, using written means of information dissemination, organization policies, staff handbooks, and company newsletters. Workplaces should guarantee that employees will not suffer any negative consequences of using parental leave. Third, an organizational system must be put in place to promote husbands' use of parental leave and their participation in childcare. A paradigm shift in the traditional Korean societal context will be required to create a more family-friendly culture in which men have an equal right to use childcare policies and an equal responsibility to participate in childcare. Fourth, reliable childcare facilities should be expanded. Although childcare facilities have been expanded to provide various nursing and education services in recent years, their quality apparently did not meet consumer demand, meaning that additional expansion and improvement is necessary. Lastly, financial assistance for childcare and household should be made available for part-time lecturers in the form of government seed grants or loans that will decrease an employer's potential financial burden when hiring a woman of childrearing age.

FUTURE RESEARCH

Considering the social status of faculty members in Korea, my findings might overestimate the recognition and use of childcare policies overall. Workers in other occupations might face situations that are not dealt with here. For example, after-school care and free childcare institutions might be very important in some cases. More broad investigation including a greater range of stakeholders will be required before comprehensive conclusions can be drawn. It would be interesting to assess whether the themes discussed in this study are applicable to higher education institutions where female faculties work and to focus more on part-time lecturers. Future research could replicate this study for other sectors of female workers and compare academia's perception about childcare compared to that of other sectors.

REFERENCES

Bentley, R. J., & Blackburn, R. T. (1992). Two decades of gains for female faculty? *Teachers college record, 93,* 697–709.

Bjornberg, U. (2000). Equality and backlash: Family, gender and social policy in Sweden. In L. Haas, P. Hwang, & G. Russell (Eds.), *Organizational change and gender equity: International perspectives on fathers and mothers at the workplace* (pp. 55–75). Thousand Oaks, CA: Sage.

Blair-Loy, M., & Wharton, A. S. (2002). Employees' use of work-family policies and the workplace social context. *Social Forces, 80*(3), 813–845.

Bø, I. (2006). Working life and family life: Ambiguous communication at work. *Community, Work and Family, 9*(2), 123–141.

Burgess, A. (1997). *Fatherhood reclaimed: The making of the modern father.* London: Random House.

Clancy, M., & Tata, J. (2005). A global perspective on balancing work and family. *International Journal of Management, 22*(2), 234–241.

DongA News. (2007). News on society. Retrieved October 8, 2007 from http://www.DongA.com

Drago, R., Crouter, A., C., Wardell, M., & Willits, B. S. (2001). Final report to the Alfred P. Sloan Foundation for the Faculty and Families Project. Retrieved from http://lsir.la.psu.edu/workfam/faculty&families.htm

Evans, M. D., & Kelley, J. (2002). Attitudes towards childcare in Australia. *The Australian Economic Review, 35*(2), 188–96.

Friedman, S., & Greenhaus, J. (2000). *Allies or enemies? What happens when business professionals confront life choices?* New York: Oxford University Press.

Fuller-Thomson, E., & Minkler, M. (2001). American grandparents providing extensive child care to their grandchildren. *Gerontologist, 41,* 201–9.

Gerson, K., & Jacobs, J. A. (2001). Changing the structure and culture of work. In R. Hertz & N. Marshall (Eds.), *Working families: The transformation of the American home* (pp. 207–26). Berkeley, CA: University of California Press.

Glezer, H., & Wolcott, I. (2000). Conflicting commitments: working mothers and fathers in Australia. In L. Haas, P. Hwang, & G. Russell (Eds.), *Organizational change and gender equity: International perspectives on fathers and mothers at the workplace* (pp. 23–56). Thousand Oaks, CA: Sage.

Hand, K., & Lewis, V. (2002). Fathers' views on family life and paid work. *Family Matters, 61,* 266–29.

Hogarth, T., Hasluck, C., & Pierre, G. (2000). *Work-life balance 2000: Summary report,* Warwick, UK: Institute for Employment Research.

Hsieh, M. F. (2004). Teaching practices in Taiwan's education for young children: complexity and ambiguity of developmentally appropriate practices and/or developmentally inappropriate practices. *Contemporary Issues in Early Childhood, 5*(3), 309–329.

Kamerman, S. B. (1991). Child care policies and programs: An international overview. *Journal of Social Issues, 47,* 179–196.

Kamerman, S. B. (2000). Early childhood education and care: An overview of developments in the OECD countries. *International Journal of Educational Research, 33,* 7–29.

Kim, M., & Na, J. (2003). *Early childhood care and education in Korea: National policies and practices. Joint Training Programme on Early Childhood Care and Education.* Beijing: UNESCO.

Korea Ministry of Education and Human Resources Development. (2006). Statistics System on National Human Resources. Retrieved from http://www.moe.go.kr

Korea Ministry of Health and Welfare. (2005). The Reformed Law of the Equal Opportunity Legislation, from http://www.mohw.go.kr

Korea Ministry of Labor. (2008). Changes of labor policies in 2008. Retrieved from http://www.molab.go.kr

Korea National Statistics Office. (2002). National statistics database (in Korean).

Lee, K. Y. (1992). *Early childhood education curriculum*. Seoul, Korea: Kyo Moon Sa.

Lee, K. S., Chang, Y., Chung, M., & Um, J. (2002). *Introduction to Early Childhood Education*. Seoul, Korea: Yang-Seo-Won (in Korean).

Liang, X.Y., Fuller, B., & Singer, J.D. (2000). Ethnic differences in child care selection. *Early Childhood Research Quarterly, 15*, 357–84.

Liddicoat, L. (2003). Stakeholder perceptions of family-friendly workplaces: An examination of six New Zealand organizations. *Asia Pacific Journal of Human Resources, 41*(3), 354–70.

Macrae, N. (2005). Women and work: A ten year retrospective. *Work, 24*, 331–9.

McDonald, P., Brown, K., & Bradley, L. (2005). Explanations of the provision-utilization gap in work-life policy. *Women in Management Review, 20*(1), 37–55.

McMullen, M., Elicker, J., Wang, J., Erdiller, Z., Lee, S., Lin, C., & Sun, P. (2005). Comparing beliefs about appropriate practice among early childhood education and care professionals from the US, China, Taiwan, Korea and Turkey. *Early Childhood Research Quarterly, 20*(4), 451–464.

Na, J., Yoo, H.J., & Moon, M. (2003). Early childhood education and care policies in the Republic of Korea. OECD Thematic Review of Early Childhood Education and Care Policy: Background Report. Seoul: Korean Educational Development Institute CR 2003–4 (in Korean).

Newman, M., & Mathews, K. (1999). Federal family-friendly workplace polices. *Review of Public Personnel Administration, 19*(3), 34–58.

Noor, N. (2004). Work-family conflict, work- and family-role salience, and women's well-being. *Journal of Social Psychology, 144*(3), 389–405.

Ozgun, O., & Honig, A. S. (2005). Parental involvement and spousal satisfaction with division of early childcare in Turkish families with normal children and children with special needs. *Early Child Development and Care, 175*(3), 259–70.

Prince, M. (2000). Practices worth copying: Keys to successful work/life programs. *Business Insurance, 34*, 33–5.

Russell, G., & Bowman, L. (2000). *Work and family: Current thinking, research and practice.* Canberra, Australia: Department of Family and Community Services.

Shelton, L. M. (2006). Female entrepreneurs, work-family conflict, and venture performance. *New insights into the work-family interface, 44*(2), 285–97.

Shin, H. J. (2008a). Employee and employer perceptions of the entry of female scientists and engineers into industry. Manuscript submitted for publication.

Shin, H. J. (2008b). Career development of female scientists and engineers in industry: the views of employees and employer. Manuscript submitted for publication.

Stipeck, D., & Ryan, R. H. (1997). Economically disadvantaged preschoolers: Ready to learn but further to go. *Developmental Psychology, 33*(4), 711–723.

Sung, S. (2003). Women reconciling paid and unpaid work in a Confucian welfare state: The case of South Korea. *Social Policy & Administration, 37*(4), 342–60.

The Federation of Korean Industries. (2002). *Effects of increase in elderly population on economy and society and future policies.* CER-2002-29 (in Korean).

Thompson, C. A., Beauvais, L. L., & Lyness, K. S. (1999). When work-family benefits are not enough: The influence of work-family culture on benefit utilization, organizational attachment, and work-family conflict. *Journal of Vocational Behavior, 54*, 392–415.

Thornthwaite, L. (2004). Working time and work-family balance: A review of employees' preferences. *Asia Pacific Journal of Human resources, 42*(2), 166–84.

Timmermann, S. (2005). What working women want: crossing the gender gap to a secure retirement. *Journal of Financial Service Professionals*, 29–32.

Waters, M. A., & Bardoel, E. A. (2006). Work-family policies in the context of higher education: useful or symbolic? *Asia Pacific Journal of Human resources, 44*(1), 67–82.

Won, S., & Pascall, G. (2004). A Confucian war over childcare? Practice and policy in childcare and their implications for understanding the Korean gender regime. *Social Policy and Administration, 38*(3), 270–289.

APPENDIX A

General Characteristics of Respondents

Categories	Divisions	%	Categories	Divisions	%
Age	30s	24.1	Job duration	1–5 yrs	12.8
	40s	41.5		5–10	13.3
	50s	31.0		10–15	16.3
	60s	3.4		15–20	16.7
				20–25	18.7
				>25	22.2
Academic degree held	BA	0.5	Working hours per day	7 hrs	11.8
	MA	12.8		8	30.6
	PhD	86.7		9	17.7
				10	27.6
				>11	12.3
Major	Liberal arts	24.6	Annual income	10,000$	4.4
	Arts	7.4		30,000	10.3
	Science/engineering	24.6		60,000	47.8
	Business	0.5		80,000	28.1
	Pedagogy	9.4		>80,000	8.4
	Medicine	14.8		No response	1.0
	Domestic science	17.7			
	No response	1.0	Annual family income	30,000	2.5
				60,000	12.3
				80,000	11.3
				100,000	24.1
				120,000	21.7
				>120,000	26.6
				No response	1.5
Position	Full professor	43.8	Number of children	1	35.5
	Associate professor	14.8		2	58.1
	Assistant professor	18.2		3	6.4
	Full-time lecturer	12.4			
	Contract professor[1]	10.8			

[1.] Contract professor includes adjunct, visiting and research professors as well as part-time lecturers.

APPENDIX B

Various Childcare Policies of Institutions in Busan, Ulsan, and Gyeongnam Districts of South Korea

Institutions	Policy contents	Policy level
Fourteen 4-year universities and twenty-nine 2-year colleges	90 days paid parental leave Maximum 1-year parental leave available to workers with a child less than 3 years old	Complying with state's policy
One 2-year college	Allowing temporary rest from work upon request to female faculty expecting or giving childbirth	Needing amendment for parental leave
One 4-year university	Allowing parental leave twice, with each for 3 years, during period of work	Exceeding state's policy
One 4-year university	Allowing parental leave to faculty with a child less than 3 years old	Exceeding state's policy

Crossing Boundaries: Understanding Women's Advancement from Clerical to Professional Positions

Susan V. Iverson*
Assistant Professor of Higher Education
  Administration and Student Personnel
Kent State University

> *This article describes findings from a qualitative study designed to understand how women in clerical roles cross the real and perceived boundaries of their rank and advance into professional positions. Informed by phenomenology, this inquiry employed interviews with 22 women from one public research university in New England. Findings illuminate the significance of (1) instrumental individuals in women's advancement, (2) organizational processes that served as barriers, (3) "advanced knowledge," and (4) how being a woman shapes the career journey. Following discussion of the ways that existing practices may unwittingly limit women's advancement, the author articulates implications for practice.*

As the numbers of women in U.S. higher education grow, so does the body of scholarship documenting their experiences on campus. Research continues to reveal a chilly climate for women in a discriminatory and masculinist organizational culture (Currie, Thiele, & Harris, 2002; Hagedorn & Laden, 2002; Tierney & Bensimon, 1996); and scholars conclude that the organizational culture, practices, structure, and policies too often work against women (Armenti, 2004; Benschop & Brouns, 2003; Glazer-Raymo, 1999; Townsend, 1998). One consequence of this organizational culture is continued under-representation of women in senior

---

*Acknowledgements: Dr. Iverson expresses appreciation to Sharon McDade for her valuable feedback on an earlier iteration of this manuscript.

administrative ranks and the real and perceived failure of organizations to support women's advancement (Jawahar & Hemmasi, 2006).

An ever-growing body of research exists on women and advancement in higher education, articulating challenges and delineating strategies for women as they seek promotion and enter leadership roles (e.g., professional development, leadership training, mentoring). However, as Harlan and Berheide (1994) observe in their analysis of the advancement of women who work in low-paying jobs, the vast majority of employed women will never advance high enough to encounter the "glass ceiling"—the invisible barrier that keeps women from advancing because they are women. Rather, they are trapped on what Berheide termed the "sticky floor"—low-wage, low-mobility jobs (Noble, 1992). Further, as some scholars observe, certain jobs, such as clerical positions, may actually constrain advancement (Gale & Cartwright, 1995; Johnsrud, 1991). This study is designed to understand the experiences of those women who occupied clerical positions and then advanced into professional positions.

SIGNIFICANCE

The concerns of professional women—those occupying faculty, administrative, and managerial ranks—remain the focus of most scholarship on women's employment experiences in higher education. Little scholarly attention has been given to women in classified and clerical roles (Bonk, Crouch, Kilian, & Lowell, 2006; Johnsrud & Banaria, 2005), and in particular there is a dearth of information on the experiences of women in such roles who move into professional positions, and much of that is focused on library personnel (Hite & McDonald, 2003; Pilgrim, 1997; Ransel, Fitzpatrick, & Hinds, 2001). This study of women's advancement from clerical to professional positions intends to bridge that gap.

In addition to making a contribution to the literature on women and advancement, findings from this investigation of how women cross the boundary between clerical and professional ranks can expand understanding of the effect of organizational decision making on the careers of women and the ways in which existing practices may unwittingly limit women's advancement by failing to connect clerical women with "pipelines" in the organization (Harlan & Berheide, 1994). Finally, these findings can provide useful insight for university personnel charged with executing organizational practices and employment policies, and hopefully will inform revisions to such policies and practices.

PURPOSE AND QUESTIONS

The purpose of this descriptive and interpretive qualitative study is to understand and describe the experiences of 22 women at one university who moved from classified (clerical) roles into professional positions. In seeking to understand their experiences, I explored:

- What personal and professional needs and interests motivated one's move into a new position?

- What institutional factors enhanced or impeded each woman's job transition?

- What level of educational attainment preceded a woman's advancement?

- What formal and informal systems of support do women take advantage of?

Key Terms

This study strives to describe women's experiences moving from classified to professional ranks. To discern the boundaries between these two groups, definitional distinctions were sought. A query posed to the director of human resources (HR) at the university in this study illuminated one difference—professionals are exempt from both minimum wage and overtime pay, whereas classified employees are not exempt. Professional employees, thus, are typically paid on a salaried basis and classified employees are generally paid hourly wages,[1] and separate collective bargaining units represent each group.

For the purpose of this paper, the following definitions give further meaning to these two groups. Professionals (salaried employees, in other words) are distinguished by a key qualification: advanced knowledge, "customarily acquired by a prolonged course of specialized intellectual instruction."[2] The U.S. Fair Labor Standards Act elaborates on the significance of advanced knowledge to the identification of a professional (a point to which I will return later in this paper).

> "Work requiring advanced knowledge" means work which is predominantly intellectual in character, and which includes work requiring the consistent exercise of discretion and judgment. *Professional work is therefore distinguished from work involving routine mental, manual, mechanical or physical work. . . . . Advanced knowledge cannot be attained at the high school level.*[3] (italics added)

Classified employees as a category is often without definition, or rather it is defined by that which it is not. The labor relations act in the home state of the institution in this study defines "classified" as "any employee not engaged in professional work."[4] Thus, if professional work is "distinguished from work involving routine mental, manual, mechanical or physical work," then one can infer that the work of a classified employee involves "routine mental, manual, mechanical or physical work"—what Rasmussen (2001) referred to as "dirty work" and what Berheide (Noble, 1992) observed as less valued and less rewarded. All the participants in this study started their university employment as "classified" employees (more specifically, for all but one, they held clerical positions), and they all later advanced into positions that were designated "professional."

REVIEW OF RELEVANT LITERATURE

Explanations for the problem of limited advancement of women continue to be a focus of much research. Many studies examine the impact of very specific factors on women's advancement, such as the role of mentoring (Anderson, 2005). For instance, Mattis (2004), in her analysis of women entrepreneurs who left corporate careers to start their own businesses, illuminates the lack of role models and mentoring as one of several factors associated with corporate "glass ceilings." Others' studies have investigated a range of variables that may serve as determinants of advancement (Giscombe & Mattis, 2002; Ivarsson & Ekehammar, 2001; Tharenou, Latimer, & Conroy, 1994). For example, Marongiu and Ekehammar (1999), in their study of the influence of individual and situational factors on the career advancement of women and men, found that instrumentality/masculinity is positively linked (and the major predictive factor) to managerial advancement. Finally, still other analyses have advanced theoretical conceptions of the barriers and challenges for women—notably, feminist critiques of masculinist organizational culture (Acker, 1990; Britton, 2000).

This review of literature is organized into three explanatory categories shaping women's advancement: (1) individual factors, such as skill, aspirations, or difficulty balancing work and family; (2) interpersonal factors, such as networks and mentors; and (3) organizational influences, such as selection and training.

INDIVIDUAL FACTORS

One explanation for women's advancement (or lack thereof) in the workforce is related to individual factors. Scholars have sought to understand what personal characteristics influence advancement, including investigations of personality traits (Metz, 2004), aspirations (Hite & McDonald, 2003), skill and knowledge (Ohlott, Ruderman, & McCauley, 1994). For instance, some studies of women's advancement report that "personality or perceptions of women's personality traits can assist or derail their careers" (Metz, 2004, p. 695; also Brescoll & Uhlmann, 2008; Seibert & Kraimer, 2001). For example, Metz (2004), in her study of whether personality traits of ambition, masculinity, and adaptability are related to women's managerial advancement, observes that "ambitious women managers may be willing to work longer hours than their less ambitious colleagues to signal their commitment to their organization" (p. 697). Others, such as Eccles (1994) in her research on women's under-representation in high-status occupations (i.e., science, math, engineering), note that "occupational choices are not made in isolation of other life choices, such as the decision to marry and have children" (p. 605). Family issues, observe Hite and McDonald (2003), influence women's career aspirations and attainment. These researchers, employing a focus group methodology, conducted four focus groups with 26 women employed in nonmanagerial positions; their findings indicate that career goals are often adapted to meet life circumstances, such as increased family responsibilities (Hite & McDonald, 2003). Other individual factors that hinder women's advancement are gaps in skill or knowledge (Ohlott et al., 1994) and a lack of understanding of the political climate of an organization (Wentling, 1996).

INTERPERSONAL FACTORS

Some scholars suggest that interpersonal factors (or social capital) are more important than human capital (ability, traits, skills) for women to advance within the organization (Metz & Tharenou, 2001; Tharenou, 1999). Examples of interpersonal factors (or social capital) are support networks, mentoring, and role modeling. Burt (1998) distinguishes that human capital reflects individual ability and social capital reflects opportunity. For instance, Jawahar and Hemmasi (2006), in their survey of 518 female executives, managers, and professionals in the national women executive association, observe a relationship between organizational support and women's advancement, and note even further that perceptions of organizational support of women's advancement are negatively related to turnover of qualified professional women (also Kottke & Agars, 2005). Thus, many organizations implement mentoring programs and support networks to compensate for real and perceived barriers to women's advancement, and scholars attest to the efficacy of such interpersonal influences (Anderson, 2005; Evans & Cokley, 2008). For instance, Singh, Vinnicombe, and James (2006) revealed from their in-depth interviews with ten professional women that young career-minded women use role models to construct a professional identity. Giscombe and Mattis (2002), in their multiphase study of women of color in business careers, found that retention of women of color was positively correlated with supportive behaviors of supervisors. Similarly, Anderson (2005) attests to the importance of mentoring to career advancement; however, she observes that "women's exclusion from informal networks may limit their visibility and, in turn, their chances of finding a mentor" (p. 70). Thus, factors within an organization influence women's advancement.

ORGANIZATIONAL INFLUENCES

As Myerson and Fletcher (2000) stated, "it's not the glass ceiling that's holding women back; it's the whole structure of the organizations in which we work" (p. 136). From an organizational perspective, "the occupational behavior and status of women and men is determined not so much by the characteristics they bring with them into the workplace, but by the structures they encounter there" (McIlwee & Robinson, 1992, p. 14). Numerous researchers agree that structural barriers are pervasive and women (and racial minorities) have less opportunity to advance and less access to power than men do (Anderson, 2005; Gale & Cartwright, 1995; Newman, 1993; Rasmussen, 2001; Worts, Fox, & McDonough, 2007). Badjo and Dickson (2001), in their cross-cultural examination of the relationship between organizational culture and women's advancement, note that the potential influence of gender on organizational culture is often overlooked. Bonk et al. (2006) analyzed data collected from a personal economies survey distributed to support staff in 2002 and again in 2005. Their goal was to gain insight into the economic conditions of these educational support personnel (who are 86 percent female), and to accurately state the impact of one university system's compensation practices on its employees. Their findings reveal an employee group that is grossly underpaid and illuminates organizational practices that undervalue this, largely female, support staff unit. The consequence is the university "closes an avenue of professional success . . . by basing the clerical way scale on throwback discriminatory attitudes toward women's work" (Bonk et al., 2006, p. 114).

Organizations tend to reinforce the value system of the dominant gender, meaning organizational cultures shaped predominantly by men generally emphasize hierarchy, independence, and top-down communication (Badjo & Dickson, 2001; Duerst-Lahti & Kelly, 1995; Johnsrud, 1991; Tharenou, 1999). The implications of a masculinist organizational culture are often most directly felt by women (and racial minorities), since the dominant culture determines the criteria for distribution of rewards and availability of advancement opportunities (Johnsrud, 1991). For instance, women tend to be clustered in entry-level positions and are rewarded for "long-term loyalty and single-job stability," whereas men tend to enter positions that "foster opportunity because they provide incumbents with exposure, visibility, information, and connections" (Johnsrud, 1991, p. 130). Nearly 15 years later, Johnsrud and Banaria (2005) document the same gendered distribution in occupations, with women vastly outnumbering men in the clerical and secretarial groups, and men vastly outnumbering women in the skilled crafts (p. 88). These authors suggest the need for assessments of employee perceptions of their jobs, benefits, and working conditions (Johnsrud & Banaria, 2005, p. 105).

METHODS

This qualitative study of women's experiences moving from classified to professional positions is informed by phenomenology. According to Patton (2002), phenomenology serves "to describe one or more individuals' experiences of a phenomenon" (p. 40). The phenomenological approach "seeks to make explicit the implicit structure and meaning of human experience" (Sanders, 1982, p. 354), and "focuses on people living experiences" (Davis, 1991, p. 9); through rich and descriptive data, it elicits how people "construct the world through descriptions of perceptions" (p. 11). Perceptions constitute the primary source of knowledge in phenomenological studies, affixing textural descriptions explaining "what" was experienced and structural descriptions explaining "how" it was experienced (Creswell, 2007, p. 227). Through the conscious act of describing perceptions, reflective judgments are made revealing previously undisclosed meaning concerning life's experiences (Kockelmans, in Moustakas, 1994).

Central to this approach is the "temporary suspension of all existing personal biases, beliefs, preconceptions, or assumptions" in order to be more open to the phenomenon (Sanders, p. 355); this suspension process is called *bracketing*. As a university employee, committed to women's equity within higher education, it was necessary for me to acknowledge and attempt to bracket those experiences. This bracketed matter does not cease to exist; rather it is "temporarily put out of action" (Sanders, 1982, p. 355) enabling the researcher to take a fresh perspective and to "perceive freshly" (Moustakas, 1994, p. 34).[5]

The success of phenomenological research, according to Colaizzi (1978), depends upon the extent to which the research questions touch lived experiences. Since the purpose of this study is to understand women's experiences, motivations, and assumptions concerning their career transition and advancement, a research design informed by phenomenology is appropriate and will provide rich, in-depth insight concerning the everyday, taken-for-granted experiences of women negotiating job transitions and their perceptions of the experience (Creswell, 2007).

Participant Selection: The sample for this study consisted of 22 women from one public research university in New England. This comprehensive institution has a student enrollment of nearly 12,000, with 83% of the students from in-state, and only 5% of undergraduates are racial minorities.[6]

The only criterion for participation required that each woman had advanced from classified to professional ranks at the university. Initial subjects were identified using both personal and professional contacts, and these included the HR director and the assistant director of equal opportunity who served as "key informants" (Marshall, 1996). These subjects, with special expertise, quickly illuminated limitations to identifying potential participants through HR data. Recognizing that peers would be better able to identify potential respondents, snowball sampling served as an instrumental strategy for identifying participants. Snowball sampling relies on referrals from initial respondents to generate additional participants (Patton, 2002). Each subsequent contact was asked for recommendations for additional subjects matching the research criterion. Of more than 40 contacts, 22 women agreed to participate in an interview. While this approach risks being biased toward highly connected actors, it is an advantageous strategy for identifying hidden populations (Marshall, 1996; Semaan, Lauby, & Liebman, 2002; Tsvetovat & Carley, 2007).

The 22 women who comprised the sample for this investigation were employed at the university from 7–45 years; they had entered the university workforce from 1961–99. The women ranged in ages from early 30s to mid-60s. All but two women spoke of marriages, divorces, and/or remarriages; and rearing one to four children. All participants are White, and two self-identified as Franco-American. This racial profile is reflective of the university's predominantly White demographic; of the 580 female classified employees and 290 female professional employees, nearly 98% are Caucasian (per 2007 institutional data).

At the time of their interviews the women in this sample held a variety of professional positions with the university, such as HR director, assistant director for equal opportunity and diversity, assistant director for financial aid, computer and network specialist, and senior assistant to the provost. Yet, all started their career at the university in a classified role. They entered the university in both part-time and full-time positions, such as secretaries, stenographers, receptionists, clerk typists, and records technicians.

Data Collection: Data gathering was through in-depth, semi-structured interviews (Fontana & Frey, 1994; Sanders, 1982), with an interview protocol set in advance to garner a greater depth of information regarding the careers and lives of the participants. All participants were encouraged to speak from their own personal experiences in order to add to the richness of the data collection. Interview questions covered the following: description of current position, first position, and career trajectory; what personal and organizational factors contributed to advancement (i.e., length of service, skill development, further education); what are differences in perceptions (by self and others) of roles as "classified" and "professional"; what systems of support (i.e., professional organizations, unions, mentoring) were sought or used; what was significant to the career journey about being a woman.

Data Analysis: Each audiotaped interview was transcribed and the transcripts were imported into NVivo, computer software designed for qualitative data analysis. Summarized by Sanders (1982), there are four levels of phenomenological analysis: description of phenomena, identification of themes that emerge from description, subjective reflections of the emergent themes, and explication of essences present in these themes and subjective reflections. This analysis began by reading all transcripts several times to obtain an overall feeling for them and highlighting 'significant statements' that provide an understanding of the experience of women advancing from classified to professional positions. During this step in the analytic process, the subjective reflections of the emergent themes were sought. Consider the following example: one participant recalls "the response came back from [HRs] that . . . I did not qualify as a professional . . . and that I [should] be demoted. . . . I was really angry. I had worked very hard and I felt pretty demoralized." Reference to the decision by HR is an objective statement of a decision or action taken; however, stating that it makes this participant feel "angry" and "demoralized" is a subjective reflection on the objective statement. This represents the individual's perception of the reality of the phenomena under investigation. Meanings were then formulated from significant statements and phrases; these were clustered, allowing for the emergence of an "essential structure" common to all the participants' transcripts (Polkinghorne, 1989; also Giorgi, 1994; Sanders, 1982). The results were then integrated into an in-depth description of the phenomenon. Methodological rigor, contributing to the trustworthiness and soundness of the findings, was achieved through bracketing past experiences, using an adequate sample, maintenance of an audit trail, and keeping field notes.

FINDINGS

Several key findings were identified in women's descriptions of their experiences moving from classified to professional ranks. Namely, participants[7] identified the following factors influencing their advancement: (1) organizational processes that posed challenges along the way, (2) individuals who were instrumental in their career development, (3) the necessity for "advanced knowledge" and the parameters defining this, (4) what changed (or didn't) when one advanced from classified to professional ranks, and (5) the significance of being a woman on their career journey. After providing an overview of their entrée to and early years in their employment with the university, I will describe their experiences illuminating the five factors influencing advancement delineated above.

Early Career

The participants' reasons for entering the university workforce varied. Foremost, a lack of intentionality along the career path was evident. Only one participant in this study, Clara, started her employment with a clear goal in mind: "I got my [bachelor] degree [in food and nutrition], and I went looking for work within the food industry, with the intent of someday working my way up to a manager's position." For all other participants, they accepted their first positions as a job to pay the bills, or it was a position for which they were trained or socialized for while in high school, or they may have come to the university following and/or supporting a husband. They generally did not have a career in mind. As Janet notes, "I worked [at the university] initially when my husband was going to college. That is one of the reasons why I ended up going back to school later. I worked [as a department secretary] to help him." When her husband finished school, "I kind of followed the traditional line of having children and following his career." She changed positions over the years, and ultimately "the Dean promoted me to administrative associate, which was the highest level you could be at in the classified ranks."

Another respondent, Kate, commented: "I started as a classified employee right out of high school.... They used to have [in the 1970s] some sort of internship program where they would place classified employees while they were in high school, sort of on-the-job training." Entering the university a decade later, Karen tells almost the same story: "in high school one either took college courses, business courses or voc tech courses, and I took business program and was placed [in a job] in my senior year, . . . where instead of going to school, I would go and work, and I worked for a bank for 2 years." She then began working for the university as a clerk typist: "I was hired was to process transcript requests."

THE PATH TO ADVANCEMENT

The path to advancement varied: for some women, they applied for positions that would offer them increased responsibility, more money and better benefits, or both; others were promoted by a supervisor; for a few, their positions were reclassified to a higher rank.

Reclassification occurred in several ways. Some positions were reclassified as part of changes in positions types. For instance, Jamie explains that in the mid-1980s, "Administrative assistants [AA] became either AA1, AA2, or administrative associates, with administrative associate being the highest clerical support position still that the University has. It requires that you supervise other employees." Karen adds: "a study was done that evaluated or looked at job descriptions and titles for classified employees. . . . My job was reevaluated. I was, at the time, supervising someone. So I was made an administrative associate."

Desk Audit

Typically, reclassification involved a "desk audit"—when someone from HR evaluates the existing job duties to discern if a change in title, and pay, is warranted. As Mimi notes "it's really difficult to get raises. . . . The only way to make significant increases in your salary is to do some kind of desk audit." This process can be initiated by a supervisor or by the employee; if the latter, the supervisor must still endorse the request.

Generally, women described the desk audit process as Shannon does: "Grueling, it's awful." Shannon elaborates on the process: "Someone from HR comes over and watches you and grills you. . . . they sit and pass judgment on whether or not you should be promoted." Mimi described her two desk audits as "long and painstaking . . . It's a chore. It's not fun. . . . When I had to have someone from HR come in and sit down with me—that was humiliating. It was just one of the most uncomfortable processes I've ever gone through. And it was a successful audit"—meaning, Mimi received her promotion.

Not everyone has a successful audit. Jamie "was hired [in the 1970s] as a stenographer, a title that doesn't even exist any more. . . ."; she changed departments and positions over the next 20 years, until "I requested to be reclassified as a professional." Jamie also described a burdensome and demoralizing process: "There was absolutely no value given to what I was doing." However, Jamie felt confident and hopeful throughout the process. Her request for a desk audit was preceded by the elimination of several professional positions in her department. "Every time that happened, if it was something I was interested in assisting with, I volunteered to take it on. By [the time of the desk audit], I had absorbed pieces and parts of at least three professional positions. I felt like I had a pretty good handle on it." Finally, "over a year after I had started this process, the response came back from [HR] that not only was I not qualified as a professional, . . . I shouldn't even be an Administrative Associate, and she [HR representative] recommended that I be demoted to AA2 immediately with a cut in pay. . . . I was really angry. I had worked very hard, and I felt pretty demoralized." With advocacy from a new supervisor, Jamie continued to fight for recognition as a professional, and ultimately won her battle, earning a new title and rank, but her pay raise was not retroactive to the date of request (which is typically the procedure). Her job responsibilities continued to change over the subsequent years; and at the time of our interview, she was again waiting (for nearly 15 months) for another change in title and rank.

An Instrumental Individual

Most participants acknowledged an instrumental individual who told them they were capable and worthy of more. For instance, Serena observed "When I was a secretary, [the director] was one of those people that really values your service to the university, your experience to the university, and really gives people opportunity. . . . she [was] always gently pushing, . . . [expecting me] to step forth and represent the [department]." Many women cited their supervisor as the key support who coached them to take on new endeavors. Stacy recalled, "When it comes to my promotion a lot of the information and the guidance I got were just from . . . two older supervisors who had been here many years who were still in the classified unit saying, 'you need to work towards becoming a professional'." Mimi also reflected: "My immediate supervisor and the director were very supportive and very encouraging, a moving force in getting it [promotion] done."

Advanced Knowledge

The women in this sample had varied educational backgrounds: 3 women held a high school diploma, 2 women held associate degrees, 3 women had completed 30+ credit hours toward their bachelor degrees, 9 women held bachelor degrees in subjects ranging from microbiology to Spanish, from human development to food and nutrition, 1 woman was pursuing and 3 had completed master degrees, and 1 woman had earned her PhD. For those who were pursuing or had recently earned their degrees, their educational pursuits were spurred by their interest in a professional position.

As noted previously, the U.S. Department of Labor defines professional (among other things) as "work requiring advanced knowledge," and further elaborates that this "advanced knowledge cannot be attained at the high school level."[8] Thus, promotion and (re)classification of a professional position centers on having a college degree. As Dorian explains, "The deal [was] that we would have to have a degree or be working towards a degree if we were going to [be promoted]." Those few who advanced with less than a 4-year degree struggled with how this was perceived in their current roles. For instance, Jill says, "I know that I have worked harder because I don't have that degree. . . . I had to prove to them that I could do it without a degree." Corrin, who had not yet earned a 4-year degree, stated "I feel like there is a glass ceiling above my head. . . . Whenever raises are talked about, it comes up. [My supervisor will say] 'It's hard to justify it when you don't have a degree'."

Crossing Boundaries

Many women felt that "advanced knowledge" could or should be defined as work experience. For instance, Dena, who has a 2-year degree, reflects: "Our Dean has always had the mindset that if you don't have a 4-year degree, you can't be a professional. Well, I don't, I have a 2-year degree. But . . . I had been doing the job for a few years now and the experience was more important than the two letters behind your name. . . . I was probably the first professional he had appointed without a 4-year degree." Colleen considered:

> A professional position probably should have the 4-year degree, but . . . you might have the experience required for that position and, lots of times in life, common sense prevails over all education. Yes, technically the professional world signifies a degree, but is it really necessary? I think some people could do the professional work without the degree, but the degree is what typecasts them as a professional.

When asked what barriers prevent their pursuit of education, Corrin, like others, notes the stress of juggling work and family. She states "I've chosen to wait until after the kids get out of school. . . . My life took a different path; that is the bottom line. I got married young and had two kids young." A few participants identified challenges getting release time from their offices to take classes, but the primary conflict when trying to take classes is balancing the demands of coursework with work and family. However, it is notable that an inflexibility of work schedules requires an employee to take classes at night, when the scheduling conflicts with home life would be greatest. Serena illustrates:

> It was frustrating. . . . My supervisor put a lot of emphasis on the degree. . . . The last leg of my bachelor's degree was when [I had to take a required course] that met once a week at 2 p.m. . . . I had to write a letter to the dean, and I had to get permission to take it; and it was this big deal and I had to account for every second, and how I was going to make up the time and post my schedule; and I had a child in school. . . . I had to jump through a lot of hoops.

Next, I will turn to the participants' experiences after their advancement from classified to professional positions.

What changed, or didn't?

I asked each woman "what changed?" once she entered professional ranks. Several articulated how they are still trying to make sense of what it means to be a professional, and how and why that is different from being a classified employee. Perhaps obvious, changing jobs from classified to professional results in a jump in wages and benefits (e.g., vacation time, retirement packages). However, several women noted other differences they experienced once they advanced from classified to professional positions.

Parking. Several women observed a parking policy that has since changed. For instance, Carey shares, "Back then, the parking lots were green for classified staff and blue for professional. The blue were closer [to one's building], the green were further out, and then the students were way out. . . . When [promoted to professional], I went to get my blue decal, [thinking] 'Oh boy, big classist distinction'!"

Meetings. Many observed that campus meetings are organized based upon one's employee classification. Jamie remarks:

> General information meetings about things that affect all of us are split up. . . . For example, if there is a candidate for president, classified employees have to come at one time and professionals at another. Why? Are they afraid that somebody is going to ask a stupid question? Anybody can ask a stupid question!

Library. One respondent, Brenda, noted a library policy that distinguishes employee type:

> If you go to the library and you take out a book as a graduate student, you get it for the semester. If I go to the library . . . I can have it for the semester because I am a professional. If you are hourly-paid, . . . you can have it for 2 weeks. I asked why and they told me, because the library wanted to promote the academic pursuit of professionals and graduate students. Are we saying that hourly-paid have no academic pursuits? They said, 'It's not really that, it's about circulation.' I see it as a class issue.

Professional Development. Several expressed concern about distinctions in professional development offerings based upon rank, meaning classified employees attend 1 day of workshops designed to meet their needs, and professional employees attend another day with a slate of different topics. Serena recalls,

Even the professional development days that we do [during the semester], are separate . . . I mean, you could [offer workshops] regardless of whether you were professional or classified. But most of the time, oh my gosh, keep them separate. Don't let them all in the same room.

Perceptions. The biggest distinction participants observed regarding what it means to be a classified versus a professional employee was perceptions. "Unfortunately," Stacy remarks, "there's a huge line between classified and how they perceive professionals and vice versa. . . . I didn't run out and tell anybody [when I was promoted to professional] because I was afraid they would treat me differently." Similarly, Mimi ponders "How do you let people know that you're now a professional and not a classified because you do get treated a little bit differently. . . . It's not something you go about and shout, 'Oh now I'm a professional', because now, you're one of 'them'." This sentiment resounds in Serena's reflection "I think once you've been in the classified staff, that is how it is always viewed . . . I have been on search committees and as you are walking into a room with faculty or deans or whoever, they expect that you are going to be there to take the minutes." Wendy echoes this observation when she shares, "The hardest part, even today, is getting people to take you seriously and not see you as just a secretary...I'm a member of the [senior administrator's] executive council . . . and I can't tell you how many times people have said to me, 'Well, where are the notes?' Take your own, I don't do it."

SIGNIFICANCE OF BEING FEMALE

Finally, informed by the scholarship on gendered organizational culture and women's work experiences (Badjo & Dickson, 2001; Johnsrud, 1991), I entered this investigation seeking to understand how *women* in classified roles advance into professional positions. During the interviews, I asked each woman "What, if anything, do you think is significant to your journey about being a woman?" Karen summarized what most participants noted: "It's about office work, and I think the majority of people who are in support positions are women. . . . [Men] usually are either in a more blue-collared-type job or management." Serena also remarked on the gendered nature of work: "Men have more of a trade. . . . I got married young . . . I was 18 when I had my daughter and, you know, it wasn't until I got to this environment [the university] that I guess I thought about what I could do as a woman. . . . I just didn't really see the alternatives until I came to the university and began to take classes and meet people."

Foremost, participants observed a wage gap.[9] Clara recalled that she and her husband started working for the university at the same time, and she, in her classified position, was getting paid more than he was, as a patrol officer. "He remained a patrol officer all of his 26 years on campus. . . . [and at the time of his retirement] his straight pay was higher than mine. He never took a promotion. I did. I went from classified to professional, and yet, okay?" She paused and added, "There's a slight resentment." When asked to what she attributed the difference in wages, she observed that police carry firearms; "Other than that, I have no idea." Similarly, Jamie remarked, "After all these years and all of the changes, my current salary is less than other [male] directors. But as a woman and as a [former] classified employee, I guess it [change] just happens extremely slowly."

Finally, several women noted that their experience would have been different if they were men. For instance, Paula stated "I cannot help but think they [men] would be treated completely differently. I notice it—I see other male professionals, and they aren't treated the same way." Carey also remarked that she and a colleague who were promoted to professional positions had "two desks facing each other behind a partition, cubicle, little half-walls . . . I just always felt that if we'd been men, we would not be in this kind of office space." Sarah, who worked in Athletics, observed "I was a woman coming in and changing things . . . I was a threat to the good old boys. . . . I think if this position had a man in it, there probably wouldn't have been the same issues."

DISCUSSION

The participants in this study identified several factors that were significant to their advancement. Specifically, the findings illuminate the significance of (1) individual factors that served as barriers, (2) instrumental individuals for women's advancement, (3) organizational processes that erect structural barriers, and (4) how being a woman shapes the career journey. Here, I extend an interpretive discussion of the findings, drawing upon existing literature.

Women in this investigation amplified how individual factors, such as knowledge or difficulty balancing work and family, served as real or perceived barriers to advancement. These women made choices that were similar to Eccles' (1994) description of factors that contribute to gendered patterns occupational planning, including the impact of rigid gender-role socialization on the determinants of vocational and achievement choices (also Hite & McDonald, 2003). For example, the career choices of the participants in this study were greatly influenced by other life choices, such as one participant's deferral of her continued education until her children are grown, even if this means compromising further career advancement.

Second, participants illustrated the importance of relational and interpersonal influences to one's career choices and advancement (Crozier & Dorval, 2002). Most notably, the women in this study attested to the significance of an instrumental individual—family, friends, colleagues, supervisors—who mentored, coached, and guided their career journey, and in particular their advancement from classified to professional ranks. Findings from this study seem to resonate with Lalande, Crozier, and Davey (2000), who found that relationships play a key role in understanding the career development of women (also Bolton, 1980; Ragins & Cotton, 1999). Identifying mechanisms to amplify the importance of mentors and support systems (e.g., training for supervisors, developing formal mentoring programs) is an important strategy for supporting women's advancement.

Third, women illuminated the organizational factors that continue to erect structural barriers for women seeking opportunities to advance. For instance, most women had stories of how organizational policies and procedures left them frustrated, demoralized, and isolated (e.g., desk audit process), as well as how organizational practices created exclusive boundaries between classified and professional positions (i.e., separate meetings and professional development, different benefits). As Jamie reflects with frustration, "I think HR and Equal Opportunity *are* the glass ceiling on this campus." Moreover, several women noted that once they assumed their role as a professional employee they were typically required to supervise other employees; yet, nothing had prepared them for this responsibility. Further, most women identified educational credentials as critical to advancement (consistent with findings by Martins & Pereira, 2004). Yet, even with university benefits enabling employees to take classes for free, for most it was a challenge, a constant negotiation, to take classes. In an institutional culture that does not assume hourly employees desire further education, organizational practices fail to support flexible scheduling and release time; and, as Rhoades, Hendrickson, and Maitland (2003) illuminate, increasingly difficult fiscal times may further erode an institutional commitment to employees' professional development. Many of these policies and practices could be easily changed, and such alterations hold the potential to transform organizational climate and culture. As Ashenfelter and Rouse (2000) assert, "educational policies have the potential to decrease existing, and growing, inequalities in income" (p. 111). Findings from this study can inform procedural changes within HR (and other relevant areas), as well as inspire ideas for employee training and professional development.

Finally, in terms of the range of factors that influence advancement, what is significant about being a woman? The answers to this question have been implicit in several points described and discussed above (i.e., gender socialization to prioritize family obligations over occupational aspirations). The significance of gender is also prominent in organizational practices and is most evident in participants' descriptions of the wage gap. Participants' experiences echo the findings of studies of the wage gap: a marked gender pay gap remains; and females, especially in public sector, are relatively worse off (Miller, 2008; also Blau & Khan, 2006). Further, the findings of this study resonate with Miller's (2008) conclusion that a "sticky floor"[10] is a feature of the wage distribution, notably in the government sector, where, among low-wage earners, male employees have a greater advantage over their female counterparts. Finally, participants amplified differences in their experiences then they perceived would have been the case for their male counterparts (i.e., office space, support by immediate bosses). One view of this, consistent with attribution theory, suggests that women may attribute problems of their advancement to others and their successes to themselves. However, Metz and Tharenou (2001) posit that women's advancement is "partly beyond their control because it can depend on decisions made by men, who may be influenced by nonwork factors such as stereotypes" (p. 334). Thus, universities need to be aware of possible gender discrimination, negative attitudes, and bosses who do not employ an egalitarian approach to staff development.

IMPLICATIONS FOR PRACTICE

The results of this study have implications for organizational change efforts focused on improving advancement opportunities for women. In this section, I offer a few recommendations for improving practice.

1. *Design "chaotic" mentoring programs.* The participants in this study attribute much to the support and guidance of an instrumental individual mentoring their career. Research attests to the benefits of such relationships (Boyle & Boice, 1998; Chesler, Single, & Mikic, 2003). However, in addition to "top down" mentoring (meaning a more

senior or seasoned person mentors junior personnel), I recommend the establishment of mentoring relationships that are lateral (peer-to-peer), bottom up (meaning the knowledge of junior persons is valued equally or more than senior persons' knowledge), and "irregular," meaning design and choice are open. As Stacey (1992) observes, such "chaotic interactions" and the creative tensions they inspire may facilitate empowering conversations and relationships within and among individuals and groups.

2. *Break ranks.* Many women in this study shared frustration about the strict boundaries that demarcate classified and professional personnel. These boundaries contributed to their feelings as outsiders of both categories after they advanced from classified to professional and were maintained by policies and practices that addressed classified and professional groups differently (i.e., separate professional development opportunities or meetings). Administrators can draw upon these findings to inform changes in policies and practices that will address and engage staff as a collective.

3. *A role for unions.* Notably, in participants' identification of systems of support, no one suggested the potential of unions to support one's aspirations for advancement or to advocate for increases in wages or improved benefits, even though a few participants noted that unions were instrumental in negotiating changes from which they are now benefiting (e.g., improved retirement packages for classified employees). When asked directly about the role or potential of unions, only one participant indicated she was actively involved with unions; all others expressed either indifference or aversion to unions. However, it is important to note that unionized women earn a wage much closer to that of their male counterparts than do nonunionized women, and unionized women are more likely to have pension and health benefits than nonunionized women (*Union members*, 2001). Arulampalam, Booth, and Bryan (2007), in particular, note a positive association between the magnitude of the sticky floor and the extent of collective bargaining. Thus, educating women about the role and purpose of unions could benefit their current and future employment. Moreover, union officials might benefit from these findings, namely regarding the implications of providing representation solely based on job classification, which may unwittingly disadvantage women who seek advancement to a position in another rank.

CONCLUSION

While some of the findings from this investigation resonate with explanations found in previous research, the participants' experiences make a unique contribution as they are expressed through the women's lens as classified employees, more likely to be trapped on the "sticky floor" of their low-mobility jobs; yet, they advanced into professional roles. Moreover, while they share many of the challenges faced by professional women navigating a male-dominated organizational culture, these women also negotiated the positional boundaries that define (and can constrain) what it means to be classified or professional. Consequently, most of the women in this study felt as if they occupy neither category once promoted—no longer a member of the classified ranks, and never feeling fully admitted or welcomed into the professional ranks. Further, many of the participants offered insight into the significance of social class on their experiences, amplifying the ways in which assumptions about classified workers as "less than" professionals and responsible for the "dirty work" had implications for each individual's worth and potential within the organization. More research is warranted to investigate the real and perceived effect of social class on women's advancement.

In sum, this study sought to understand how women navigate and negotiate advancement from classified roles into professional positions in higher education. These findings illuminate the ways in which socio-political-cultural contexts surrounding "classified" and "professional" statuses produce constraining categories and demarcate real and perceived boundaries that women must cross. The stories of the participants in this study provide further evidence of the ways in which organizational practices, institutional cultural structure, and employment policies can work against women in higher education. I hope this inquiry inspires new questions and further research about the unique challenges faced by women in classified positions seeking to enter professional ranks, and how certain jobs, such as clerical positions, may actually constrain advancement.

REFERENCES

Acker, J. (1990). Hierarchies, jobs, bodies: A theory of gendered organizations. *Gender & Society, 4*(2), 139–158.

Anderson, D. R. (2005). The importance of mentoring programs to women's career advancement in biotechnology. *Journal of Career Advancement,*

32(1), 60–73.

Armenti, C. (2004). May babies and post-tenure babies: Maternal decisions of women professors. *Review of Higher Education, 27*(2), 211–231.

Arulampalam, W., Booth, A., & Bryan, M. (2007). Is there a glass ceiling over Europe? Exploring the gender pay gap across the wages distribution. *Industrial and Labor Relations Review, 60,* 163–186.

Ashenfelter, O., & Rouse, C. (2000). Schooling, intelligence and income in America. In Arrow, Bowles, & Durlauf (Eds.), *Meritocracy and economic inequality.* Princeton, NJ: Princeton University Press.

Badjo, L. M., & Dickson, M. W. (2001). Perceptions of organizational culture and women's advancement in organizations: A cross-cultural examination. *Sex Roles, 45*(5–6), 399–414.

Benschop, Y., & M. Brouns. (2003). Crumbling ivory towers: Academic organizing and its gender effects. *Gender, Work, and Organization, 10*(2), 194–212.

Blau, F. D., & Kahn, L. M. (2006). The U.S. gender pay gap in the 1990s: slowing convergence. *Industrial and Labor Relations Review, 60,* 45–66.

Bolton, E. B. (1980). A conceptual analysis of the mentor relationship in the career development of women. *Adult Education, 30*(4), 195–207.

Bonk, J., Crouch, J., Kilian, M., & Lowell, L. (2006, Fall). Higher ed staff personal economies: We can't eat prestige. *Thought & Action, 22,* 111–120.

Booth, A. L., Francesconi, M., & Frank, J. (2003). A sticky floors model of promotion, pay, and gender. *European Economic Review, 47,* 295–322.

Boyle, P., & Boice, R. (1998). Systematic mentoring for new faculty teachers and graduate teaching assistants. *Innovative Higher Education, 22(3),* 157–179. Retrieved November 15, 2005 from http://www.uvm.edu/~pbsingle/pdf/1998Boyle.pdf

Brescoll, V. L., & Uhlmann, E. L. (2008). Can an angry woman get ahead? Status conferral, gender, and expression of emotion in the workplace. *Psychological Science, 19*(3), 268–275.

Britton, D. M. (2000). The epistemology of the gendered organization. *Gender & Society, 14*(3), 418–434.

Burt, R. S. (1998). The gender of social capital. *Rationality and Society, 10*(1), 5–46.

Chesler, N., Single, P. B., & Mikic, B. (2003). On belay: Adventure education and peer-mentoring as a scaffolding technique for women junior faculty in engineering. *Journal of Engineering Education, 92,* 257–262. Retrieved November 15, 2005 from http://www.uvm.edu/~pbsingle/pdf/2003Single2.pdf

Colaizzi, P. F. (1978). Psychological research as the phenomenologist views it. In Valle & King (Eds.), *Existential phenomenological alternatives in psychology* (pp. 48–71). New York: Oxford University Press.

Creswell, J. W. (2007). *Qualitative inquiry and research design: Choosing among five approaches* (2nd ed.). Thousand Oaks, CA: Sage Publications.

Crozier, S., & Dorval, C. (2002). The relational career values of post-secondary women students. Canadian Journal of Career Development, *1*(1). Retrieved July 15, 2008 from http://www.contactpoint.ca/cjcd/v1-n1/article1.pdf

Currie, J., Thiele, B., & Harris, P. (2002). *Gendered universities in globalized economies: Power, careers, and sacrifices.* Lanham, MD: Lexington Books.

Davis, K. (1991). *The phenomenology of research: The construction of meaning in data analysis.* Paper presented at the Annual Meeting of the Conference on College Composition and Communication, Boston, MA.

Duerst-Lahti, G., & Kelly, R. M. (Eds.). (1995). *Gender power, leadership, and governance.* Ann Arbor, MI: The University of Michigan Press.

Eccles, J. S. (1994). Understanding women's educational and occupational choices. *Psychology of Women Quarterly, 18,* 585–609.

Evans, G. L., & Cokley, K. O. (2008). African American Women and the Academy: Using Career Mentoring to Increase Research Productivity. *Training and Education in Professional Psychology, 2*(1), 50–57.

Fontana, A., & Frey, J. H. (1994). Interviewing: The art of science. In N. K. Denzin & Y. S. Lincoln (Eds.), *Handbook of qualitative research.* Thousand Oaks: Sage Publication.

Gale, A., & Cartwright, S. (1995). Women in project management: Entry into a male domain? A discussion on gender and organizational culture. *Leadership & Organization Development Journal, 16*(2), 3–8.

Giorgi, A. (1994). A phenomenological perspective on certain qualitative research methods. *Journal of Phenomenological Psychology, 25*(2), 190–220.

Giscombe, K., & Mattis, M. C. (2002). Leveling the playing field for women of color in corporate management: Is the business case enough? *Journal of Business Ethics, 37*(1), 103–119.

Glazer-Raymo, J. (1999). *Shattering the myths: Women in academe.* Baltimore: The John Hopkins University Press.

Hagedorn, L. S., & Laden, B. V. (2002). Exploring the climate for women as community college faculty. *New Directions in Community Colleges, 8,* 69–78.

Harlan, S. L., & Berheide, C. W. (1994). *Barriers to work place advancement experienced by women in low-paying occupations.* Cornell University. Retrieved March 16, 2006 from http://digitalcommons.ilr.cornell.edu/cgi/viewcontent.cgi?article=1123&context=key_workplace

Hite, L. M., & McDonald, K. S. (2003). Career aspirations of non-managerial women: Adjustment and adaptation. *Journal of Career Development, 29*(4), 221–235.

Ivarsson, S. M., & Ekehammar, B. (2001). Women's entry into management: Comparing women managers and non-managers. *Journal of Managerial Psychology, 16*(4), 301–314.

Jawahar, I. M., & Hammasi, P. (2006). Perceived organizational support for women's advancement and turnover intentions. *Women in Management Review, 21*(8), 643–661.

Johnsrud, L. K. (1991). Administrative promotion: The power of gender. *Journal of Higher Education, 62*(2), 119–149.

Johnsrud, L. K., & Banaria, J. S. (2005). Higher education support personnel: Trends in demographics and worklife perceptions. *The NEA 2005 almanac of higher education* (pp. 85–105). Washington, DC: National Education Association.

Kottke, J. L., & Agars, M. D. (2005). Understanding the processes that facilitate and hinder efforts to advance women in organizations. *Career Development International, 10*(3), 190–202.

Lalande, V. M., Crozier, S. D., & Davey, H. (2000). Women's career development and relationships: A qualitative inquiry. *Canadian Journal of Counseling, 34*(3), 193–203.

Marshall, M. N. (1996). Sampling for qualitative research. *Family Practice, 13*(6), 522–525.

Marongiu, S., & Ekehammar, B. (1999). Internal and external influences on women's and men's entry into management. *Journal of Managerial Psychology, 14*(5), 421–433.

Martins, P. S., & Pereira, P. T. (2004). Does education reduce wage inequality? Quantile regression evidence from 16 countries. *Labour Economics, 11,* 355–371.

Mattis, M. C. (2004). Women entrepreneurs: Out from under the glass ceiling. *Women in Management Review, 19*(3), 154–163.

McIlwee, J. S., & Robinson, J. G. (1992). *Women in engineering: Gender, power, and workplace culture*. Albany: State University of New York Press.

Metz, I. (2004). Do personality traits indirectly affect women's advancement? *Journal of Managerial Psychology, 19*(7), 695–707.

Metz, I., & Tharenou, P. (2001). Women's career advancement: The relative contribution of human and social capital. *Group & Organization Management, 25*(3), 312–342.

Miller, P. W. (2008). The gender pay gap in the U.S.: Does sector make a difference? *Journal of Labor Research, 29*(2). Retrieved July 15, 2008 from http://www.springerlink.com/content/p14j9k12n77mq524/fulltext.pdf

Moustakas, C. (1994). *Phenomenological research methods*. Thousand Oaks, CA: Sage.

Myerson, D. E., & Fletcher, J. K. (2000). A modest manifesto for shattering the glass ceiling. *Harvard Business Review, 78*(1), 127–136.

Newman, M. A. (1993). Career advancement: Does gender make a difference? *American Review of Public Administration, 23*(4), 361–384.

Noble, B. P. (1992, November 22). And now the 'sticky floor'. *The New York Times*.

Ohlott, R. J., Ruderman, M. N., & McCauley, C. D. (1994). Gender differences in managers' developmental job experiences. *Academy of Management Journal, 37*(1), 46–67.

Patton, M. Q. (2002). *Qualitative research and evaluation methods* (3rd ed.). Newbury Park, CA: Sage.

Pilgrim, J. (1997). Secretarial and clerical staff career progression: Some organizational perspectives. *Librarian Career Development, 5*(3), 105–112.

Polkinghorne, D. E. (1989). Phenomenological research methods. In R. S. Valle & S. Halling (Eds.), *Existential-phenomenological perspectives in psychology* (pp. 3–16). New York: Plenum.

Ragins, B. R., & Cotton, J. L. (1999). Mentor functions and outcomes: A comparison of men and women in formal and informal mentoring relationships. *Journal of Applied Psychology, 84*(4), 529–550.

Ransel, K. A., Fitzpatrick, J. D., & Hinds, S. L. (2001). Advancement at last: Career-ladder opportunities for library support staff. *Technical Services Quarterly, 19*(2), 17–26.

Rasmussen, B. (2001). Corporate strategy and gendered professional identities: Reorganization and the struggle for recognition and positions. *Gender, Work and Organization, 8*(3), 291–310.

Rhoades, G., Hendrickson, R., & Maitland, C. (2003). Bargaining professional development. *The NEA 2003 almanac of higher education* (pp. 67–74). Washington, DC: National Education Association.

Sanders, P. (1982). Phenomenology: A new way of viewing organizational research. *Academy of Management Review, 7*(3), 353–360.

Seibert, S. E., & Kraimer, M. L. (2001). The five-factor model of personality and career success. *Journal of Vocational Behavior, 58*, 1–21.

Semaan, S., Lauby, J., & Liebman, J. (2002). Street and network sampling in evaluation studies of HIV risk-reduction interventions. *AIDS Reviews, 4*, 213–223.

Singh, V., Vinnicombe, S., & James, K. (2006). Constructing a professional identity: How young female managers use role models. *Women in Management Review, 21*(1), 67–81.

Stacey, R. D. (1992). *Managing the unknowable: Strategic boundaries between order and chaos in organizations.* San Francisco: Jossey-Bass.

Tharenou, P. (1999). Gender differences in advancing to the top. *International Journal of Management Review, 1*(2), 111–132.

Tharenou, P., Latimer, S., & Conroy, D. (1994). How do you make it to the top? An examination of influences on women's and men's managerial advancement. *Academy of Management Journal, 37*(4), 899–931.

Tierney, W. G., & Bensimon, E. M. (1996). *Promotion and tenure: Community and socialization in academe.* Albany, NY: State University of New York Press.

Townsend, B. K. (1998). Women faculty: Satisfaction with employment in the community college. *Community College Journal of Research and Practice, 22*(7), 655–661.

Tsvetovat, M., & Carley, K. M. (2007). On effectiveness of wiretap programs in mapping social networks. *Computational and Mathematical Organizational Theory, 13*(1), 63–87.

Union members in 2000. (2001). U.S. Department of Labor's Bureau of Labor Statistics. Retrieved March 28, 2007 from ftp://ftp.bls.gov/pub/news.release/History/union2.01182001.news

Weinberg, D. H. (2004). *Evidence from Census 2000 about earnings by detailed occupation for men and women: Census 2000 Special Report.* U.S. Census Bureau. Retrieved March 28, 2007 from http://www.census.gov/prod/2004pubs/censr-15.pdf

Wentling, R. M. (1996). A study of the career development and aspirations of women in middle management. *Human Resource Development Quarterly, 7*(3), 235–270.

Worts, D., Fox, B., & McDonough, P. (2007). 'Doing something meaningful': Gender and public service during municipal government restructuring. *Gender, Work and Organization, 14*(2), 162–184.

ENDNOTES

1. More detailed definitions are set forth by the U.S. Department of Labor. Others have been instructive in my understanding the differences in these two staff groups, including Harlan and Berheide's (1994) discussion of low-paying jobs and Rasmussen's (2001) distinctions between professional tasks and "dirty work."

2. See the U.S. Department of Labor's definition of a professional. Retrieved March 24, 2007 from http://www.dol.gov/esa/regs/compliance/whd/fairpay/fs17a_overview.htm

3. Retrieved March 24, 2007 from http://www.dol.gov/esa/regs/compliance/whd/fairpay/fs17d_professional.htm

4. The state to which this passage refers is not cited in order to protect the identity of the home campus at which participants are employed.

5. Moustakas (1994) admits that this is seldom perfectly achieved; however, I embraced this idea when beginning this project by bracketing out my experience and assumptions before proceeding to hear the experiences of others.

6. Minorities are defined by this institution as Blacks, Native Americans, Asian Americans, and Hispanic.

7. The participants' names are pseudonyms.

8. Retrieved March 24, 2007 from http://www.dol.gov/esa/regs/compliance/whd/fairpay/fs17d_professional.htm

9. U.S. Census data documents a continuous earnings gap between men and women; women earn 77 cents to the dollar compared with men (Weinberg, 2004).

10. Miller is drawing upon a sticky floor model of pay and promotion explicated by Booth, Francesconi, and Frank (2003). In their analysis, women may advance at the same rates as men, but they find themselves stuck at the bottom of the wage scale for the new grade.

If You Don't Ask, You'll Never Earn What You Deserve: Salary Negotiation Issues Among Female Administrators in Higher Education

Suzette Compton
Account Manager
SunGard Higher Education

Louann Bierlein Palmer
Associate Professor, Department of Educational
　Leadership, Research and Technology
Western Michigan University

> *The salary equity gap continues to exist, with men earning more on average for every dollar a woman makes. Research suggests that women's underdeveloped negotiation skills play a role, yet limited research on this issue exists for women in higher education. To this end, the negotiation strategies and gendered communication traits of 22 female administrators across four higher education institutions were studied. Findings indicated that these women tended not to consciously negotiate, given socialization and other issues. Many place a lower priority on salary and often perceive negotiating in a negative manner. When they did negotiate, participants used both masculine and feminine communication traits. Based on data from this study, ideas on how women in higher education can more fully use negotiation to address the gender equity salary gap were offered.*

Despite the many gains women have made to chip the glass ceiling, they continue to experience serious salary inequities. Recent statistics show that the earning gap between college-educated men and women working full-time, yearlong, is 74% (American Association of University Women, 2007). Data also show that such inequities grow over time, with men earning an even higher percentage over women at 10 years or more of experience (Goldberg Dey & Hill, 2007). Such salary gaps remain a pressing gender equity issue, and some suggest that one potential solution is for women to improve their *salary negotiating skills* (Barron, 2003; Swiss, 1996). If women became better at negotiating higher salaries upfront and/or as part of career advancements, this might significantly impact salary inequities.

The concept of women negotiating for higher salaries sounds simple, but there are many complicating issues, and limited research could be found on this issue within the higher education arena. To that end, we conducted a study to examine the extent women leaders in higher education negotiated for their compensation and, if so, what strategies and gendered communication traits they used.

Before we examine the specifics of our study and its findings, we must first review the concept of negotiation, which is a special type of communication and form of exchange. Fisher, Ury, and Patton (1991) describe negotiation as follows:

> Negotiation is a basic means of getting what you want from others. It is back-and-forth communication designed to reach an agreement when you and the other side have some interests that are shared and others that are opposed. (p. xvii)

Putman and Kolb (2000) claim that exchange is a gendered activity in traditional negotiation models. This means that the attributes of a given activity are more closely related to one gender than the other, whereby the attributes of the other gender are less valued. For example, qualities of effective bargaining that are valued in negotiation include independence, competition, forcefulness, analytic rationality, and aggressiveness (Arliss, 1991; Wood, 1997). Yet these qualities are linked to masculinity. Feminine qualities such as sense of community, intuition, emotionality, sympathy, and compassion are less valued as effective negotiation qualities (Kray, Thompson, & Galinsky, 2001).

Some contend that lessons learned in childhood regarding socialization carry over to adulthood and into the workplace, including negotiation strategies (Kolb, 1992; Tannen, 1995). Because most men have learned to be independent and strive for status, while many women have learned to connect and build relationships, their communication styles are developed from very different perspectives. Men are more likely to behave in ways to get themselves recognized by those in power, while women often take a low-key approach. Because of childhood socialization, most men learn early on that their peers reward them for speaking about their accomplishments. Women often learn they must downplay their accomplishments in order to be rewarded by their peers.

A number of previous studies have focused specifically on negotiation issues among women, with nearly all focused on corporate settings. A sampling of these studies follows, and unfortunately, does not paint a pretty picture regarding this issue.

First, women are *less likely than men to negotiate for what they want.* As one example, Babcock and Laschever (2003) examined salaries of students graduating from Carnegie Mellon University with their master's degrees and found that the starting salaries of men were 7.6% higher on average than those of women, representing almost a $4,000 difference. The research also showed that only 7% of the female students had negotiated for their beginning salary, whereas 57% of men had asked for more money. Additional findings revealed that those who did negotiate, mostly men, increased their starting salary by an average of 7.4%, about the same difference in starting pay between men and women.

Within higher education, Thompson-Stacey (1996) found gender gaps in salary and the lack of career advancement opportunities to be top equity issues among 20 community college-level female deans, vice presidents, and presidents. A key finding related to negotiation was that these women indicated they felt uncomfortable in asking for something for themselves. While women are able to effectively advocate for others, they are constrained by gender-linked stereotypes, roles, and norms when it comes to advocating for themselves (Wade, 2001).

A second major previous research finding is that *women lack aggressive salary goals, and are willing to accept lower offers.* For example, Stevens, Bavetta and Gist (1993) studied this issue within full-time Masters in Business Administration students, and they found women set lower goals than men and as a result negotiated significantly lower salaries than men. The men in this study negotiated beginning salaries that were on average $1,349 more than those negotiated by women. This study also revealed that women used significantly fewer tactics during negotiation.

In a similar vein, Barron (2003) found a significant correlation between pay expectations and negotiation strategies when studying masters-level students' requests for salary, whereby the men's initial requests were significantly higher than women's. She also found that initial salary requests were significantly correlated with final negotiated salaries and that women were often uncertain how to evaluate the value they brought to the organization and left it to the organization to decide their worth.

Overall, previous research documents salary inequities and gender differences regarding negotiation strategies, comfort, and outcomes. Numerous studies have been undertaken on these issues within the corporate world, to the point where researchers are now extracting data from what they refer to as a second generation of research on gender and negotiation within business settings (Bowles, Babcock, & Lai, 2007). Yet, very little research exists on these issues within higher education settings. To this end, we explored whether women leaders in higher education negotiated for their compensation and, if so, what strategies and gendered communication traits they used.

RESEARCH METHODS

We used a qualitative design for this research, involving interviews with 22 female executive and mid-level administrators across four public universities, asking them to share their experiences and advice for future higher education female administrators. Specifically, we used a narrative inquiry approach to examine the perceptions and understanding of female higher education administrators regarding their use (or nonuse) of negotiation as part of their current and previous positions.

We defined female administrators to include those at the director level or above, excluding the positions of president and chancellor. The specific population we targeted included executive-level positions such as vice president, associate and assistant vice president, and deans, as well as mid-level administrators such as directors and department chairs. These positions were chosen since they are at a level in which salary negotiation could more likely be attempted.

We targeted female administrators at four public universities within one region of a Midwest state. These four institutions have similar regional characteristics, including comparable salary levels and standards of living. These institutions are also within a few hours drive of the researchers, allowing all interviews to be held face-to-face with the female administrators.

Purposeful and snowball sampling techniques were undertaken with the goal of identifying at least ten female administrators within each of the executive and mid-career levels across various university departments. Efforts were made to find participants across a range of ages and to have minority representation. Ultimately, our study included a total of 22 female administrators who agreed to participate in this study, including 12 executive-level and ten mid-level administrative participants. Table 1 (located within the next section on "Key Findings") offers a demographic summary of the 22 participants. Specific position titles are not included in order to protect the identity of the participants.

Within the executive level, four participants were 65 years of age or older and 8 were in the middle-age range (40 or over, but less than 65 years of age). Seven of these women were married and five of them were either single or widowed, with one being African American and the rest Caucasian. Within the mid-level administrative participants, eight were in the middle-age range, with two in the 30s-age range. Seven of these mid-level participants were married and three were single, with four being African American and six Caucasian. It should be noted that extensive snowballing efforts occurred to locate minority female higher education administrators within these four universities, and five were ultimately identified (which is not as many as we had hoped, but at 23% this sample is actually an overrepresentation of such individuals in these four universities).

Individual interviews were held with each participant during which time questions regarding the following topics were explored: experiences with negotiating for salary and additional compensation, communication traits and styles used when they negotiated (or those they recommended should be used), reasons for not negotiating, perceptions regarding stereotypes of men's and women's negotiation strategies, and perceptions of most and least effective negotiation strategies.

Audiotapes of the interviews were transcribed and analyzed using a qualitative data reduction methodology, which included locating key phrases, searching for meaning, and offering tentative statements about the phenomenon. Experiences and the voices of individual members were examined to identify commonalities or themes across participants as a group. We used member checks whereby participants reviewed the themes extracted from their interviews. We also had an external individual, well versed in gender communication theory and feminist research, review our data and conclusions.

KEY FINDINGS

The experiences of these 22 female administrators in higher education regarding salary issues resulted in findings that allowed for thick, rich descriptions. Analysis of the data revealed a number of themes and subthemes (Compton, 2005), of which two main themes are summarized in this article. We found that within this sample of female higher education administrators,

(1) Most initially voiced that they, as women, tend *not* to negotiate because:

   (a) they are socialized not to,
   (b) their jobs are more important than their compensation, and/or
   (c) their salary expectations were met or exceeded.

(2) Upon reflection, however, most realized that they do actually negotiate to some degree, growing more confident with experience and positions of power, and using a combination of masculine and feminine communication traits.

Table 1 summarizes the demographics of the 22 participants (using fictitious names) and indicates to what extent they offered data leading to a given theme. We did not find any differences within these themes when broken down by positional level, age groups, racial groups (which in this case included only Caucasian and African American), marital, status and whether they were geographically mobile or not. This may have been true since there were only two participants in their 30s and four aged 65 or older, eight participants who were single, five minority participants, and five who were geographically mobile. Or it may be that these themes transcend these demographic categories. Following Table 1, select quotes are offered that bring to life the essence of these themes.

Theme 1a: Most of these female higher education administrators voiced they tend not to negotiate because they were socialized not to.

When asked the extent to which they had negotiated throughout their careers, every participant noted that they, like other woman, generally did not negotiate. When asked to explain their reasons for not negotiating, gender socialization issues were nearly always the response. For example, Darcy, a mid-aged married Caucasian executive-level administrator within Student Affairs, spoke about the patriarchal nature of society, specifically of White society, and points out such gendered traits as compliance and being quiet.

> It [patriarchy] manifests itself differently in the way women are socialized, but in general, I think White women are socialized to be

Table 1. Participant summary: Demographics and themes.

	Level	Department	Age	Race	Marital Status	(1) Tend Not to Negotiate Because: (a) Socialization Issues	(b) Job More Import. than $	(c) Salary Expect. Met	(2) Negotiation Traits
Melissa	Exec	Mult Cult Affairs	65+	AA	M	X		X	Fem
Jill	Exec	Health Professions	65+	C	M*	X		X	Fem
Lea	Exec	Academic Affairs	65+	C	S	X	X	X	Mas
Jackie	Exec	Health & Hum Srvs	65+	C	S	X	X	X	Mas
Rose	Exec	Academic Affairs	Mid	C	M	X	X	X	Mas
Millie	Exec	Human Resources	Mid	C	M	X	X	X	Mas
Marge	Exec	Development	Mid	C	M	X	X	X	Mas
Ginny	Exec	Academic Affairs	Mid	C	M	X	X	X	Mas & Fem
Darcy	Exec	Student Affairs	Mid	C	M	X		X	Fem
Monica	Exec	Educ & Hum Srvs	Mid	C	S	X	X	X	Mas
Kendra	Exec	Educ & Hum Srvs	Mid	C	S*	X	X	X	Mas
Suzie	Exec	Univ Adv & Mktg	Mid	C	S*	X	X	X	Mas & Fem
Denise	Mid	Mult Cult Affairs	Mid	AA	S*	X	X		Mas
Debbie	Mid	Educ & Hum Srvs	Mid	AA	M*	X	X		Mas
Tina	Mid	Student Affairs	Mid	AA	M	X	X	X	Mas
Lisa	Mid	Dining Srvs	Mid	C	M	X	X	X	Mas
Mandy	Mid	Alumni	Mid	C	M	X	X	X	Mas
Sandy	Mid	Health Srvs	Mid	C	M	X	X	X	Mas & Fem
Megan	Mid	Human Resources	Mid	C	M	X	X	X	Mas & Fem
Kay	Mid	Academic Affairs	Mid	C	M	X	X	X	Mas
Terry	Mid	Minority Stud Srvs	30s	AA	S	X	X	X	Mas & Fem
Kim	Mid	Enrollment Srvs	30s	C	S	X	X	X	Mas

Note. For Race/Ethnicity, AA = African American; C = Caucasian. For Marital Status, M = Married; S = Single; and those with a "*" indicated they were geographically mobile. For Negotiation Traits, Mas = Masculine; Fem = Feminine negotiation/communication traits used and/or recommended to be used by participants.

quiet, be nice and say thank you, yes ma'am, no sir and I'll take what I can get and walk away and do my work.

Ginny, a mid-aged married Caucasian executive-level administrator in Academic Affairs, believes that gender socialization impacts negotiation, indicating, "Well, nice girls don't talk about money . . . I think we are all told not to be too much of a bother." She also believes that men tend to overvalue themselves, while women tend to undervalue themselves. She also feels that women tend to be apologetic, in reference to explaining their position on issues, for example:

> I feel like I have to explain, not to you exactly, but to other people. I have to say, "Well it wasn't fair the way it was." I usually [feel defensive] or guilty or like I'm selfish.... I don't think all women do but I think if you have any leftovers of traditional gender role conditioning, you probably do.

Kim, who is Caucasian, in her 30s, single and serves in a mid-level administrative position within Enrollment Services, indicates that men have been socialized to be more confident in their negotiating.

> I also think that just in terms of their [men's] gender roles that they're taught to be more confident and they're taught to ask for things, and they expect other people to take them seriously and to consider what they have to say.

Terry, who is in her 30s, single, African American and a mid-level administrator in Minority Student Services, has impressions similar to Kim's. Within this quote, she points out gendered traits exhibited in women when negotiating, such as being passive and accommodating while men are direct.

> I think men are expected to be more open and direct about their desires, wants, needs, and expectations as far as salaries and negotiation might be concerned.... I think women are expected to be more docile, passive, and accepting of what is offered to them because this should be good enough for you.

Sandy, a mid-aged, married Caucasian mid-level administrator in Health Services, also shares her perception that men are more direct and women are somewhat timid when it comes to negotiating.

> I think maybe, my personal opinion, and that's all it is, is that men, it's easier for them or they're more likely just to put the facts on the table and say this is it. I need this much and take it or leave it or whatever, where a woman is more reluctant for whatever reason to do that. It's harder for her to do that.

Embedded within this socialization theme is that being aggressive as part of negotiation has a negative connotation for women, but not for men. For example, Darcy, a mid-aged married Caucasian executive-level administrator in Student Affairs, notes:

> I don't think they [men] would hesitate to, excuse my language, 'play

hard ball.' I think women are not nearly as adept at this. . . . I think women hesitate because we don't want to come across demanding/bitchy/unappreciative. Men [say] pay me what I'm worth and if you're not going to pay me what I think I'm worth, I'm moving on to somewhere else.

In a similar vein, Mandy, a mid-level, mid-aged married Caucasian administrator in Alumni Services, discussed a negative connotation for women, stating, "I do believe that there is that philosophy that women who are assertive are considered aggressive and a 'bitch.' I think that exists. And I think men who are assertive are just assertive."

The interviews also revealed that women are socialized not to "haggle." For example, Debbie, a married African American mid-aged mid-level administrator within Education and Human Services, notes:

I'm not a haggler and I think at that last negotiation, I think it may have been more haggling. I'm just not a haggler and I know. . . . And so when I think about negotiations, I think about it being about haggling.

Megan, a married Caucasian mid-level mid-aged administrator within Human Resources, also refers to negotiating as haggling, indicating: "I needed to be happier professionally, that was more important to me than haggling. . . . Of course I think back now and that was pretty silly of me." Inherent in this quote is the realization that she was hurting herself in reference to salary equity.

THEME 1B: MOST OF THESE FEMALE HIGHER EDUCATION ADMINISTRATORS VOICED THEY TEND NOT TO NEGOTIATE BECAUSE THEIR JOBS ARE MORE IMPORTANT THAN THEIR COMPENSATION.

This theme was very prominent throughout the study, with 19 of the 22 women specifically indicating that their jobs were more important to them than the compensation they received. Things of import are the challenge of the position; the individual they work for; the kind of duties they perform; security; and the responsibility, authority, and autonomy of their position.

For example, Suzie, a mid-aged, single Caucasian serving as an executive-level administrator within her university's Advertising and Marketing area, discussed desires to ensure her future and build her career so she could be independent: "And so it really wasn't just about money, it was really more about job security and building my future so that I could take care of myself and not have somebody else take care of me."

Rose, a mid-aged, married Caucasian working as an executive-level administrator within Academic Affairs, pointed out she chose to pursue her current position for the experience and fun.

> I read this dumb book and then I'm thinking you don't want to undersell yourself. And then I'm thinking okay, as far as I'm concerned, I wasn't going to ask [about the salary], cause to tell the truth of the matter, I'm not doing this for money. I did this for the fun—for the experience to do this.

Darcy, a mid-aged, married Caucasian executive-level administrator within Student Affairs, also said that salary was not the most important thing and shared her primary motivation, which was about taking the job for the experience.

> Salary was very secondary . . . I didn't go looking for a job for salary. If I was looking for a job based on salary, I wouldn't be in this field. That was never a primary motivator. . . . I was going for the experience.

Lisa, a mid-aged married Caucasian mid-level administrator within Dining Services, spoke about the importance of having a good relationship with her boss. She said, "Now one thing I'd like to share with you is that salary wasn't my primary criteria at all. To me it is so important to have a good working relationship and a good honest relationship with my boss."

As a mid-aged married Caucasian mid-level administrator within Health Services, Sandy was much more concerned about the service operation she was directing than the salary. Although salary was not totally unimportant to her, the operation took priority as she notes.

> The money really wasn't the issue at that point. I really believed in what we were doing here, and it was at a time when there were serious budget constraints in the State . . . there were real threats to these operations, and I wanted to do whatever I could to make sure that the services stayed here.

Lea, a single Caucasian aged 65 years or older serving as an executive-level administrator within Academic Affairs, was also very direct and confident about the insignificance salary held for her. Because of her years of experience and the fact that she believes this will most likely be her last position, she indicated:

I couldn't have cared less. I think it's an obligation to provide service to the institution at a critical time and as long as I was paid relatively adequately I wouldn't have cared what my salary was. I still probably don't.

Lea continued by discussing her beliefs about the importance of getting the job versus getting the salary:

I think you're always trying to make the judgment about whether you want to do the work versus get the salary. I think you often make that choice between arguing for another $2000 versus having a job. . . . Sometimes it's a question of getting the work and getting the opportunity to demonstrate what you can do versus worrying about the entry-level salary . . . I'm very practical.

Some realized that their lack of focus on salaries was not good for gender equity as a whole, as shown by Jill, a married Caucasian aged 65 years or older serving as an executive-level administrator within a Health Professions area, when she shared:

I probably should have negotiated for a higher salary but I didn't really care, which isn't doing a good service for whoever follows me. . . . I don't think it is [a fair salary] . . . I thought well, I'm not going to fight this. I don't care. I'm not jeopardizing being able to do what I want to do.

And as realized by Millie, a mid-aged married Caucasian executive-level administrator within Human Resources, when she notes:

I guess if we are ever going to get gender equity in salary, we need to make salary more important for females. And I don't know that I want to do that, because to me that seems, again, maybe the female's coming out in me, that's not the most important thing.

THEME 1C: MOST OF THESE FEMALE HIGHER EDUCATION ADMINISTRATORS VOICED THEY TENDED NOT TO NEGOTIATE BECAUSE THEIR SALARY EXPECTATIONS WERE MET OR EXCEEDED.

Nearly all (20 of 22 participants) voiced that for the most part their salary expectations were met or exceeded, and that they were being treated fairly. Many of these women indicated they felt fortunate to have the job or the salary. This reduced or eliminated the need to negotiate for salary.

Let us review a few examples. When Rose, a mid-aged married Caucasian executive-level administrator within Academic Affairs, was hired for her current position, she was prepared to discuss salary and ensure she would be paid a fair amount for the position. She shared, "But as it turned out, he had a letter all ready for me and he said [a certain amount of money] and I thought, well, that was more than I had wanted as a base and that was fine."

Monica, a mid-aged single Caucasian executive-level administrator within Education and Human Services, was also surprised by the amount she was offered and shared the experience when she received more than expected:

> And so when that happened, she wrote it down and I said oh, yea. I had in my mind what [co-worker] made, because I was thinking that she would take 10% off and I'd put the 10% back on and even a couple more thousand. She offered me a little bit more than the 10% and the couple thousand. So I didn't know what to say. So I said oh yes right away because it was more than I had planned.

Terry, a single African American in her 30s serving as a mid-level employee within Minority Student Services, was also offered more than she had expected when she accepted her first position at the university where she is currently employed. She had decided to accept the position if she was offered $5,000 more than she was currently making. She was offered considerable more than that, so she felt obligated to take it.

Ginny, a mid-aged married Caucasian executive-level administrator within Academic Affairs, also felt she had been offered a fair salary for her current position. She had done quite a bit of investigating to see what others in this type of position were making, so she was prepared when the salary was offered:

> When I came here, I had gone through the same thing, looking around at what I should expect for salary and so on. . . . I remember thinking, if I made [this much] . . . that was the right amount for me, which was still a nice raise from what I was making. And I was offered [substantially more]. So I went, thank you; that will be just fine.

Jill, an executive-level administrator within a Health Professions area who is a married Caucasian 65 years of age or older, spoke about how she never really developed negotiating skills because she was always offered what she thought was a fair salary for the field she works in, saying, "I never developed good negotiating skills because I never really needed to."

Embedded within the theme that many of these women didn't negotiate because they thought they were being offered a fair salary is the idea that many felt fortunate to have the job or the salary.

For example, Kay, a mid-aged married Caucasian mid-level administrator within Academic Affairs, spoke about her first full-time position, having been looking for a position for quite some time. She shared, "They offered me a job and I jumped at it. . . . The salary was fair." Rose, a mid-aged married Caucasian executive-level administrator within Academic affairs, was also happy to obtain her first position and spoke about the small amount of money she had been making in graduate school versus what she was offered for her first position. "That was the same thing my father was making as he was retiring from the public school. To me, that was a huge amount of money."

Marge, a mid-aged married Caucasian executive-level administrator within her university's Development Office, also discussed the fairness regarding the salary she received for her current position, saying, "I knew I wanted excellent health benefits, and I looked at what others [in this position] were making at that time . . . I was hired in at right about what they were doing, and I thought it was fair."

As a married African American aged 65 years or older in an executive-level position within Multi-Cultural Affairs, Melissa's comments echo the voices of many when she notes: "I was seasoned, and I never got to negotiate for salary. [I was told] this is the job and this is what it pays. But you know, once again I was just happy to be able to eat."

THEME 2: UPON REFLECTION, MANY OF THESE FEMALE HIGHER EDUCATION ADMINISTRATORS REALIZED THEY DO ACTUALLY NEGOTIATE, GROWING MORE CONFIDENT WITH EXPERIENCE AND POSITIONS OF POWER, AND USING A COMBINATION OF MASCULINE AND FEMININE COMMUNICATION TRAITS.

Although most participants expressly stated that they did not participate in negotiation, it became obvious during the interviews that these women did indeed directly or indirectly negotiate for some portion of their compensation at one time or another. As an example, Millie, a mid-aged married Caucasian executive-level administrator within Human Resources, shares, "Actually after talking to you on the phone and saying you know we don't really do that [negotiate]. But then I thought, yes we do." In a similar vein, Jill, a married Caucasian aged 65 years or older serving as an executive-level administrator within the Health Professions area, indicated that she didn't worry too much about salary and didn't negotiate. However, she did negotiate for a substantial amount of moving expenses when she moved from the east coast back to the Midwest: "When I came out here, I really negotiated for moving. They paid $14,000 to move me out here. We'd been married for several years and had all this stuff."

Once the participants began to realize that they have indeed participated in some forms of negotiation, many began to relate the conditions under which this existed, and what strategies they used. One subtheme was that as participants gained experience, both in their positions and in their negotiations, their confidence grew. For example, Tina, a mid-aged married African American mid-level administrator within Student Affairs, indicated:

> I've had a chance to do a little bit of reading, but I really think the other part of it is maturing. Just trying to look at it and saying what can I lose? If they really want me, I'm not demanding that they give me this, I'm asking for it . . . I really think for me it's just maturing and recognizing that people can do whatever they want to do within certain mild constraints . . . now I'm to the point where I am going to ask. I have asked. I'm more knowledgeable and aware.

Jackie, a single Caucasian aged 65 years or older within an executive-level position in Health and Human Services, confirmed that her confidence has grown through experience when she talks about her negotiations.

> I've gotten better. I do a lot of negotiating and not just about myself . . . and I think it's just been doing it. Although I have to say that there's been a couple of workshops that I have taken that have given me a few insights.

When Marge, a mid-aged married Caucasian executive-level administrator within the Development area, talks about how her skills have changed over the years she says, "I think I am more direct. I always come in with an agenda . . . what the points are going to be and go through it . . . I probably winged it when I first started." She also talks about taking courses in negotiation, which helped her with her skills in that area.

Positional power was identified as an important ingredient, whereby most participants talked about situations that placed them in positions of power when negotiating. Several of these women talked about not needing to have a position for which they were negotiating. Some discussed being solicited for a position and pursued by the employer. Others indicated that their expertise put them in a position where the employer was eager to employ them. These types of situations put these women in an enviable bargaining position.

For example, Kim, a single Caucasian in her 30's within a mid-level administrative position in Enrollment Services, indicated she was fortunate to never have needed a specific job. She notes:

> And I also think in line with the negotiation process, I think you're more apt to really express what you want in a salary capacity when there isn't that pressure that you have to take something. And I think that people perceive that in a positive and sort of strong way.

In a similar vein, Suzie, a mid-aged single Caucasian executive-level administrator within Advertising and Marketing, speaks of her confidence: "It wasn't a situation where I had to have a job. So I felt like what's the worst that can happen to me?" Kendra, a mid-aged single Caucasian executive-level administrator within Education and Human Services, also felt this confidence as she shared: "I didn't have to have the job. There were going to be other opportunities. He called back and he said, 'okay the president took a big gulp and he said that's fine.' So we didn't renegotiate. That was it."

The last aspect of this theme is that when the women did negotiate, they often described communication traits stereotypically masculine in nature such as being assertive, unemotional, and confident in presenting prior accomplishments (Kray, Thompson, & Galinsky, 2001). As shown in Table 1, 14 of the 22 participants described such masculine traits when sharing effective negotiation or other communication strategies. Five of the participants were balanced between masculine and feminine communication traits, and three of the participants described primarily feminine traits when referring to negotiation.

As an example of those expressed typically defined masculine traits, Rose, a mid-aged married Caucasian executive-level administrator within Academic Affairs, voices the traits of being decisive, strong, confident, tough, and independent when she indicates: "Well, I think rather than just making up my mind, once I decide I think something is fair, then I'm going to demand what's fair and if they're not going to be just about it, then you take the hit."

In a similar vein, Lea, a single Caucasian aged 65 years or older within an executive-level position in Academic Affairs voices the masculine traits of being tough, direct, and assertive as she states: "I think you have to be firm about what's reasonable and be specific about it and if you are serious, you have to be prepared for the consequences." She spoke of one incident where fairness was an issue. Using her direct approach, she addressed this:

> One of them . . . nickel and dimed me for a year and a half. So finally I threatened to quit. . . . then he finally said he'd take it under advisement. So 3 weeks later I went into his supervisor and told her I was going to quit and I wasn't going to work with him. My situation was obviously then corrected.

Other examples illustrate the use of communication traits and strategies stereotypically associated with being feminine, including a key focus on listening and relationship-building (Tannen, 1995). For example, Millie, a mid-aged married Caucasian executive-level administrator within Human Resources, notes: "I really need to listen to what the other person is saying. . . . I think that's why it's worked . . . because they feel like they're listened to and their issues are addressed." In a similar vein, Ginny, a mid-aged married Caucasian executive-level administrator within Academic Affairs, described a situation in which she was negotiating for a salary that was offered and was lower than she expected. In working through the negotiation, she indicated:

> I was very respectful but also just, I wasn't whiney and I wasn't leaning across the table or pounding my fists or anything. . . . My style is we are all in this together. . . . It's probably as simple as I know that people respond well to me when I behave in this way. . . . If you stop and think about it, it's negotiation for a continuing relationship.

Ginny, like a few others, also spoke of the need to use both feminine (e.g., gentle) and masculine (e.g., assertive) traits:

> It is interesting to find a balance with your comfort level with whatever femininity or masculinity roles are out there . . . people in my interview saying, you are such a nice person, are you sure you are going to be able to make the hard decisions? And now they're saying—it's the velvet hammer.

CONCLUSIONS AND RECOMMENDATIONS

One significant conclusion from the interviews of these 22 female administrators within higher education settings is that such women, as a whole, tend not to consciously participate in negotiations. When first asked about the use of negotiation, most participants initially expressed that they did not negotiate for compensation, nor did many other women. However, as the conversation continued, most realized that while they may not have negotiated specifically for their base salary, many did negotiate for other forms of compensation (e.g., moving expenses, professional development, travel). Yet most of these women had not really thought of these strategies as formal negotiations.

We were not too surprised to find that most of these women perceived they do not negotiate, since previous research had found this as well (e.g., Babcock & Laschever, 2003). But what was surprising is the extent to which they described how they had been socialized not to formally engage in this activity. The negative connotation of negotiation was voiced by several of the women, indicating they didn't like to "haggle." These participants voiced that gender socialization affects negotiation strategies by voicing that negotiating is easier for men, men are more confident and effective, men negotiate more, and men are expected to negotiate while women are not.

The literature review validates the perception by these women that men tend to negotiate, while many women do not. Liberal feminism concludes that gender behavior is mainly the result of childhood socialization (MacDonald, 2002). Lessons learned in childhood regarding socialization carry over into adulthood and into the workplace (Kolb, 1992; Tannen, 1995). Because men are more likely to behave in ways to get recognition while many women take a low-key approach, men are more likely to negotiate than women. This may be explained by women often downplaying their accomplishments due to their childhood gender socialization.

Another contributing factor to these women not consciously focusing on negotiation has to do with the gendered trait of compliance, whereby many women wait to be rewarded, not knowing if they deserve something unless someone else points this out for them (Babcock & Laschever, 2003). Women in our study exhibited such compliance on several occasions when they described situations when they did not negotiate for salary.

In addition, the women in this study spoke about relationships being more important than the money they earned. Given socialization issues this makes sense, since the feminine focus is often on lasting relationships while the masculine focus is frequently on individualization. Many women, therefore, will tend to avoid such masculine traits. Indeed, because relationships mean so much for many women, they may choose to be silent instead of damaging a relationship, leading them not to negotiate or haggle. This is supported by Tannen (1990), who indicates that men are often focused on status, whereas many women tend to downplay their work experience and attempt to build rapport by equalizing status through the creation of symmetry. This reluctance to negotiate ultimately has a chilling effect on a woman's ability to obtain equitable compensation over her career. This doesn't mean that women need to act like men in order to claim the same resources and privileges as men. Indeed, some researchers have warned against such attempts (e.g., Bowles, Babcock, & Lai, 2007). But it does mean doing your homework on the issues.

Despite initial responses of "we don't negotiate," nearly all participants offered ideas on effective negotiation skills, and many of them used at least some of these skills at one time or another to obtain either a higher salary or other forms of compensation. They used or recommended a number of negotiation strategies, and following is a recap of their advice.

1. Know your worth by inventorying your skills and expertise, and for once, overvalue yourself.
2. Set goals and be prepared to specifically request a desired salary.
3. Develop alternatives, which increase your flexibility through options.
4. Get fresh perspectives by consulting with others to obtain different views.
5. Use humor to strategically ease tension.
6. Be persuasive, using your personal, logical, and emotional skills.
7. Use interpersonal communication by listening, providing feedback, and speaking effectively.
8. Be persistent by sticking to the purpose and not conceding.
9. Avoid struggle and dispute by acknowledging differences of opinion.
10. Do not be apologetic in your requests.
11. Use a blend of feminine and masculine communication traits.
12. Learn to play the negotiation "game" by reading about the subject or attending specific training.

Embedded within this list of recommended strategies are several approaches through which women can give voice to negotiation, which in turn is supported by feminist theory (Kolb, 1992). One approach is through a relational view of others. While men may see negotiation as a contest or competition, women can instead see it as an opportunity to build relationships. Another approach is a contextual understanding of issues and interests. While men may focus on individual achievement, women can look at events in terms of their impact on relationships and a way to be more attentive to others' needs. A final approach is a communicative view of strategy. In the context of communication, men may see negotiation as a way to establish status and position, while women can see it as an opportunity to create community and connection.

Indeed, Laura Kray, an expert in the impact of gender on negotiations, recently shared with a group of higher education leaders that it is essential to "teach women that gender differences are a product of stereotypes and not innate" abilities and that women must "focus on the value of feminine traits" when negotiating (Women in Higher Education, n.d., pp. 3–4). Indeed, her research has shown that if women are explicitly told that stereotypically feminine traits are important determinants of negotiation success, such as expressing their thoughts verbally, having good listening skills, and possessing insight into the negotiator's feelings, then such women are more apt to consciously use such techniques. This in turn can actually lead to a female advantage at the bargaining table (Kray, Reb, Galinsky, & Thompson, 2004).

In closing, the result we find most troubling is that nearly all of the women in the study indicated that in at least one or more cases, their salary expectations were met or exceeded. Most did indicate they had done some homework regarding prevailing wages for various positions and had a mentor to advise them on such issues. Yet the salary equity gap still exists. Previous research has shown that women have lower pay expectations (e.g., Stevens, Bavetta, & Gist, 1993), and this certainly connects to our finding that salary is not the most important issue for most of these women. Unfortunately, a woman's own perceived value in the workplace may prevent her from being properly prepared to negotiate for salary and from using negotiation strategies.

In order to overcome issues such as salary equity and reduce the salary gap, women must consciously employ salary negotiation strategies. They possess the ability to negotiate but have not fully employed various strategies. Women's negative perception of negotiation and their lower priority on salary versus other facets of a position negatively affects their ability to obtain higher salaries. Because traditional negotiation models have historically been closely associated with masculine communication traits, women need to learn and use such traits *and add their own feminine style as well.* They need to set aside any preconceived ideas they have about "haggling," and create a negotiation voice that works for them: one that not only clearly communicates their value, but also maintains the relationships important to them. Indeed, the greatest lesson from this study is a simple one: "If you don't ask, you'll never earn what you deserve."

REFERENCES

American Association of University Women. (2007). *Gains in learning, gaps in earning.* Retrieved March 1, 2008, from http://www.aauw.org/research/statedata/index.cfm

Arliss, L. P. (1991). *Gender communication.* Englewood Cliffs, NJ: Prentice-Hall.

Babcock, L., & Laschever, S. (2003). *Women don't ask: Negotiation and the gender divide.* Princeton, NJ: Princeton University Press.

Barron, L. A. (2003). Ask and you shall receive? Gender differences in negotiators' beliefs about requests for a higher salary. *Human Relations, 56*(6), 635–662.

Bowles, H. R., Babcock, L., & Lai, L. (2007). Social incentives for gender differences in the propensity to initiate negotiations: Sometimes it does hurt to ask. *Organizational Behavior and Human Decision Processes, 103*(1), 84–103.

Compton, S. (2005). Salary negotiation strategies of female administrators in higher education (Doctoral dissertation, Western Michigan University, 2005). *Digital Dissertations,* AAT 3197559.

Fisher, R., Ury, W., & Patton, B. (1991). *Getting to yes: Negotiating agreement without giving in* (2nd ed.). New York: Penguin Books.

Goldberg Dey, J., & Hill C. (2007). *Behind the pay gap.* Washington, DC: American Association of University Women Educational Foundation.

Kolb, D. M. (1992). *Is it her voice or her place that makes a difference? A consideration of gender issues in negotiation.* Kingston, Ontario: Industrial Relations Centre Queen's University.

Kray, L. J., Reb, J., Galinsky, A. D., & Thompson, L. (2004). Stereotype reactance at the bargaining table: The effect of stereotype activation and power on claiming and creating value. *Personality and Social Psychology Bulletin, 30,* 399–411.

Kray, L. J., Thompson, L., & Galinsky, A. (2001). Battle of the sexes: Gender stereotype confirmation and reactance in negotiations. *Journal of Personality and Social Psychology, 80,* 942–958.

MacDonald, E. (2002). Gender theory and the academy overview. In A. M. Martinez Aleman & K. A. Renn, *Women in higher education: An encyclopedia* (pp. 71–76). Santa Barbara, CA: ABC-CLIO.

Putnam, L. L., & Kolb, D. M. (2000). Rethinking negotiation: Feminist views of communication and exchange. In P. M. Buzzanell, *Rethinking organizational & managerial communication from feminist perspectives.* Thousand Oaks, CA: Sage.

Stevens, C. K., Bavetta, A. G., & Gist, M. E. (1993). Gender differences in the acquisition of salary negotiation skills: The role of goals, self-efficacy, and perceived control. *Journal of Applied Psychology, 78*(5), 723–735.

Swiss, D. J. (1996). *Women breaking through: Overcoming the final 10 obstacles at work.* Princeton, NJ: Peterson's/Pacesetter Books.

Tannen, D. (1990). *You just don't understand: Women and men in conversation.* New York: HarperCollins Publishers.

Tannen, D. (1995). The power of talk: Who gets heard and why. *Harvard Business Review, 73,* 138–148.

Thompson-Stacy, C. (1996). In her own words: Overcome gender bias by developing negotiation skills. *Women in Higher Education, 5*(2), 5.

Wade, M. E. (2001). Women and salary negotiation: The costs of self-advocacy. *Psychology of Women Quarterly, 25*(1), 65–76.

Women in Higher Education. (n.d.). *Overcome gendered stereotypes on negotiating.* Retrieved July 18, 2008 from: http://www.wihe.com/printBlog.jsp?id=456

Wood, J. T. (1997). *Gendered lives: Communication, gender, and culture* (2nd ed.). Belmont, CA: Wadsworth Publishing Company.

Women Higher Education Administrators With Children: Negotiating Personal and Professional Lives

Sarah M. Marshall
Assistant Professor, Educational Leadership
Director of the Educational Leadership Doctoral Program
Central Michigan University

> *The purpose of this exploratory study was to understand how female higher education administrators with children made sense of and negotiated their multiple roles and commitments as professionals and parents. Women at the professional level of dean or higher, at a college or university, and who had school-aged children or younger were interviewed to determine how they negotiated their personal and professional lives. Findings detailed motivations to pursue advanced careers as well as advantages and disadvantages of managing career and family.*

Only recently—with women's increasing presence in the academy—have we begun to pay attention to how family affects faculty careers (Bassett, 2005; Colbeck & Drago, 2004; Marcus, 2007; Mason & Goulden, 2002; Perna, 2005; Sallee, 2008; Wolf-Wendel, Ward, & Twombly, 2007; Ward & Wolf-Wendel, 2005). Surprisingly, the same attention has not been given to how having children affects women administrators. The very nature of administrative work, including long hours and weekend work, would seem to pose a particular challenge for women administrators who have children. The purpose of this study is to understand how women higher education administrators with children make sense of and negotiate their multiple roles and commitments as professionals and parents.

Examining the complexities of managing a career and a family may be particularly important given the perceived lack of qualified individuals in the college and university leadership pipeline. The growing organizational complexity, increasing enrollments, and cutbacks in state and federal funding are just a few of the obstacles facing postsecondary leaders today.

One of the most significant and pending challenges confronting higher education is transition in leadership. Currently, 49% of all college and university presidents are age 61 or older (American Council on Education [ACE], 2007), meaning most will likely retire within the next 10 years. Similarly, key administrative staffs are expected to retire at increasing rates. Twenty-nine percent of chief academic officers (CAO) are 61 or older. Since over 40% of new presidents were former CAOs, the presidential pipeline is greatly affected by the pending retirements of CAOs. These continuous challenges, along with the anticipated retirements of senior-level administrators, leave some believing that developing a new generation of leaders may be one of the greatest challenges facing higher education (VanDerLinden, 2004).

This expected leadership crisis may present an opportunity for women to advance into positions that were previously assumed by men. As the number of women working in college and university administration increases, understanding how they successfully manage work and family are keys to their advancement and retention. Learning from women who have assumed senior-level administrative positions while raising children may provide insights into how others can achieve the same personal and professional successes.

Women in Higher Education

The most comprehensive portrait of college and university presidents and senior-level administrators is provided by the ACE reports: *On the Pathway to the Presidency* (King & Gomez, 2007) and *The American College President* (ACE, 2007). In 2006, 23% of college and university presidents were women compared to 10% in 1986 (ACE, 2007). Also, the ACE study discovered that 89% of male presidents were married compared to only two-thirds of the female presidents. Additionally, 68% of women presidents had children versus 91% of male presidents. Regarding other administrative positions, 45% of all senior administrators were women (King & Gomez, 2008). The percentage of women by position is as follows:

- 38%   Senior Academic Officer
- 36%   Dean
- 43%   VP for Administration
- 49%   VP for External Affairs
- 45%   VP for Student Affairs/Enrollment Management
- 50%   Central Academic Affairs
- 55%   Chief of Staff
- 56%   Senior Diversity Officer

These numbers suggest that colleges and universities have an existing pool of qualified, experienced women to tap into to enhance gender diversity at the presidential level (King & Gomez, 2007). Despite this pool, the question of why few women advance to the presidency still exists. Additionally, of those women who do assume the presidency, why a disproportionate number remain single or childless compared to their male counterparts remains.

Although a growing number of women are assuming senior-level positions, most assume roles such as directors, managers, and coordinators. The National Center for Education Statistics (2003) reports that in 2003 women constituted over half (51%) of the administrative, executive, and managerial positions in U.S. higher education institutions. While the presence of women is noted, women remain disproportionately concentrated in the middle-level rather than senior administrative positions (Chamberlain, 1988; Kaplan & Tinsley, 1989; Rosser, 2000; Sagaria & Johnsrud, 1985; Touchton & Davis, 1991; Twale, 1995). It remains puzzling why in light of the increasing number of women faculty and administrators in academe, so few advance to senior-level position. Studying those who have assumed senior-level leadership positions may provide insight into how others can do the same.

While more research is needed to determine why women are not advancing, scholars speculate that women may be professionally limited either by their own choosing or by higher education's inability to support them adequately (Apter, 1993). Levtov argues that because of "socialized professional standards," women may be led to believe that "the realities of combining a family and a career may be incompatible with the current values of the profession" (2001, p. 17), thus forcing them to choose between career and family. Unfortunately, the research literature is largely silent on whether having children affects women's advancement to senior-level positions in higher education administration.

The work culture in higher education is one that may demand long hours of hard work (Levtov, 2001). Those beginning their careers, especially in student affairs, are generally the first to be asked to commit themselves to evening and weekend engagements, to live on the job, or to otherwise structure their time so that the task of managing a family would be especially difficult (Nobbe & Manning, 1997). The values held by higher education and the realities in the field may contribute to tough decisions for women administrators who have or are contemplating having children.

In addition to being a time-consuming profession, career advancement in higher education often requires relocation, which typically is not an option for women with children in school and in dual-career relationships (Sagaria & Johnsrud, 1985). These realities, coupled with demands from home, may lead women college administrators to question their career choices. As Jones and Komives (2001) wrote:

> While a "balanced life" continues to be an elusive goal for many women professionals, women in senior-level . . . positions must reconcile the great demands of their work and with other interests and responsibilities. The irony in this situation is that successful women leaders often suggest that part of their success is due to the well-rounded lives they lead, which includes time for relaxation and renewal, family, and interests outside the workplace. However, the realities of senior leadership positions do not always support the matching of espoused values with such activities. (p. 242)

As more women join the ranks of higher education administration and advance to senior positions, it is imperative that their needs be assessed in order to support and retain them. While women themselves are primarily responsible for managing work and family and for coping with the many pressures associated with assuming both roles, the need to study and learn from their experiences becomes more urgent. Before any meaningful effort can be made to enhance the recruitment and retention of working women, we need to understand how working affects mothers, their families, and careers. This study provides positive examples and encouragement that indeed women can advance to senior-level administrative positions and also have children. Learning from women who have already successfully balanced their senior-level careers and children provides insights into how others may do the same. This research provides critical perspectives and hope for women who intend to assume similar positions while raising a family.

REVIEW OF THE LITERATURE—WHERE ARE THE CHILDREN?

Although some literature has spotlighted women administrators' career trajectories, advancement, professional development, education, and mentoring (Anders, 1997; LeBlanc, 1993; McDade, 1997; McFarland &

Ebbers, 1998; Nidiffer & Bashaw, 2001; Warner & DeFleur, 1993), there is a noted underrepresentation about the implications of these activities in the careers of senior-level women administrators with children. While the literature addresses various issues of women in administration, all neglect to reference, mention, or consider the competing demands of childbearing and rearing made on female administrators.

More broadly, scholars studied five general topics related to women in higher education administration. First, several, for instance, explored common characteristics associated with the career advancement of women administrators (Earwood-Smith, Jordan-Cox, Hudson, & Smith, 1990; Evans & Kuh; 1983; Ironside, 1981; Kuyper, 1987; Rickard, 1985). Characteristics frequently considered were educational background, employment history, willingness to relocate, presence of role models, and marital status. None included children as a variable in their analyses, providing no information on whether having a family helps or hinders women's advancement into senior-level positions. Other scholars explored attrition as it relates to women administrators (Bender, 1980; Burns, 1982; Hersi, 1993; Holmes, Verrier, & Chisholm, 1983; Richmond & Sherman, 1991). Their findings suggest that women leave the profession because of low pay, limited ability to advance within an institution, burnout due to long hours, and discrimination. Work-family issues were not mentioned or considered as potential reasons why women leave the profession. Still other scholars examined the overall job satisfaction of women in higher education administration (Bender, 1980; Reeves, 1975). This research revealed that women administrators were less satisfied than their male counterparts. This lack of satisfaction was attributed to factors such as lack of support and work-related stress.

Next, researchers explored the barriers that women administrators overcame to achieve professional success (Tinsley, 1985; McEwen, Williams, & McHugh Engstrom, 1991). These studies addressed barriers such as discrimination and the perceived "glass ceiling," but they did not consider whether having a family was a barrier to success. Last, scholars investigated the role that mentoring played in promoting or hindering the professional success and advancement of women administrators (Blackhurst, 2000; Hersi, 1993; Tinsley, 1985; Twale & Jelinek, 1996). Their findings suggested that mentoring was needed to encourage women to obtain advanced degrees, to write for publication, to become involved in professional associations, and to remain in the profession. None discussed mentorship as it related to work-family issues.

Although most of the literature pertaining to women higher education administrators neglects to consider children as a variable, there exists a small body of research on the experiences of women administrators with children. For the most part, the extant literature paints a largely negative picture. For example, a series of articles discussed how women administrators with children had higher levels of stress than those who do not (Berwick, 1992; Blackhurst, Brandt, & Kalinowski, 1988; Scott & Spooner, 1989). These stresses stemmed out of problems with day care arrangements, conflicts between organizational and family demands, and fatigue.

Next, other studies claimed that having a family limited the professional success and advancement of women administrators with children. Warner & DeFleur (1993) suggested that interruptions in careers due to child rearing were impediments to career advancement. LeBlanc (1993) asserted that the advancement of women administrators with children was limited because of the time required by their families. Since higher education administration often requires late night and weekend commitments, scheduling issues become quite complicated for working mothers. Although Marshall and Jones (1990) discovered no significant relationship between childbearing and career development in higher education, the majority of the women administrators in their study believed that childbearing hurt their careers. Nobbe and Manning's (1997) research supported this point. They found that women administrators with children gave up or changed career goals when they added children to their lives.

The current research on women administrators with children is largely negative, outdated, and limited in scope. Much of the research pertaining to women administrators overlooked children as a "variable of interest." Most studies did not offer positive examples of women administrators with children, including their strategies for negotiating multiple roles, advice for others in the same position, or suggestions for improving higher education work environments. In addition, most of the studies available were quantitative in nature. This research did not allow for the sharing of perspectives, experiences, or detailed examples.

To address these voids in the literature, this study provides insights into how senior-level women administrators negotiated the complexities of managing work and family. Understanding the experiences of women who have advanced to senior-level positions while having children offers promising information into how others may successfully navigate both roles. This study provides a deeper understanding and explanation of the realities faced by administrative mothers and also encourages further engagement and research about this increasingly common issue on our nation's college and university campuses.

RESEARCH DESIGN

Purpose

Since little is known about female college and university administrators with children, this study was designed to bring attention to the personal and professional issues in their everyday lives. The purpose of this exploratory study was to understand how women higher education administrators with children made sense of and negotiated their multiple roles and commitments as professionals and parents.

Research Questions

The following research questions informed this inquiry:

1. How does having a family affect the personal and professional realities of women administrators with children?
2. What rewards and frustrations accompany the shared roles of professional and parent?

The findings offer an in-depth look at how being a mother and an administrator has positively and negatively affected the lives of the participants. With an emphasis on the pros and cons of managing work and family, the intent of this paper is to inform its readers of the realities of assuming both roles.

Research Method

Since one of the goals of this investigation was to gain understanding of this underresearched group, a qualitative, narrative inquiry method was used to investigate participants' in-depth perspectives. Qualitative inquiry allows for the study of the work-family phenomenon with greater understanding and detail specifically from the participants' vantage points. More specifically, life story research was conducted. Life story research was effective in that "life stories themselves embody what we need to study: the relation between this instance of social action (this particular story) and the social world the narrator shares with others; the ways in which culture marks, shapes, and/or constrains this narrative; and the ways in which this narrator makes use of cultural resources and struggles with cultural constraints" (Chase, 1995, p. 21). These characteristics of life story research were relevant to this investigation.

SAMPLE

The intent of this research was to contribute to current knowledge on women college and university administrators by including the perspectives of women administrators who also had children. The sample configuration selected supported the ultimate goal of the study, to learn more about how female administrators manage the dual roles of administration and motherhood. Toward this end, 17 participants were selected based their ability to meet the study's criteria.

All participants were (1) female college or university administrators who (2) had children. The women selected were employed at least at the level of dean of a functional higher education unit. All selected participants reported either directly to the president or a vice president. In large part because this study intended to share the insights of administrative women with children who achieved professional success by advancing to a senior-level position in higher education administration, this sampling criterion was pivotal. To be sure, while one may learn a great deal from women entering the field who have children, the purpose of this study was to provide positive examples of female administrators with children who were more established in their careers and had achieved career success. Second, of those women who met the first sampling criterion, only those who had children school-aged or younger were considered for participation in this study. The age of the children was important, as younger or school-aged children tend to have more parental needs than adult children. By investigating women with younger children, current competing demands generated by work and family were explored.

The 17 participants in this study assumed professional positions in academic affairs (5), development (3), finance (1), legal council (1), marketing (1), and student affairs (7). They held the positions of president (2), vice president (6), associate/assistant vice president (7), and dean (2). They were employed at a variety of institutional types from large public research universities to community colleges in six different states.

DATA COLLECTION

Interviewing was the primary source of data collection. From interviews, the stories of others were shared. "If we take seriously the idea that people make sense of experience and communicate meaning through narration, then in-depth interviews should become an occasion in which we ask for life stories" (Chase, 1995, p. 2). Life stories were solicited by asking open-ended and exploratory questions that allowed the interviewee to "tell her story" from her own perspective. Interviews lasted between 90 and 120 minutes and were typically followed up with additional phone calls and e-mails. Interviews were tape-recorded and transcribed. Copies of the transcripts were shared with the participants to verify the content of the transcriptions.

In addition to interviews, a variety of documents were included and analyzed in this study. First, each participant was invited (not required) to share personal materials such as photographs, resumes, awards, published works, or other memorabilia. These documents were used to develop deeper insights into the life of each woman.

Second, institutional documents that referred to work-family issues were also reviewed. The review of these documents occurred before each interview. With prior knowledge of the institution's work-family benefits, each participant's knowledge and utilization of these benefits was examined. Participants were asked about their familiarity with the various policies and their willingness to take advantage of these policies. In addition to institutional work-family documents, campus mission statements were collected and analyzed.

ANALYSIS PROCEDURES

Interviews were analyzed via the constant comparative method (Glaser, 1978; Glaser & Strauss, 1967; Stauss, 1987; Strauss & Corbin, 1990). While using this method, the interviews were simultaneously coded and analyzed in order to develop concepts: "By continually comparing specific incidents in the data, the researcher refines these concepts, identifies their properties, explores their relationships to one another, and integrates them into a coherent theory" (Taylor & Bogdan, 1984, p. 127). While various types of coding categories may be used in qualitative research, in this study coding categories were not predetermined. Instead, codes suggested themselves out of the data. Using this method of analysis, the patterns, themes, and categories of analysis came from the data. They emerged out of the data rather than being imposed on them prior to data collection and analysis (Patton, 1990). These codes came from close and repeated listenings, coupled with careful attentive transcription (Riessman, 1993).

Lincoln and Guba (1985) offer four criteria to help ensure the trustworthiness of qualitative research: credibility, transferability, dependability, and confirmability. In this study, triangulation, member checks, thick description and an audit trail were used to ensure the trustworthiness of the research findings (Lincoln & Guba, 1985).

FINDINGS

There is little dispute that working mothers have complex and often competing roles between their personal and professional lives. While the demands of both a career and children can be challenging, participants also shed light on the many benefits of assuming both roles. The women in this study candidly shared the sacrifices, trade-offs, and tensions that resulted from their responsibilities as parents and professionals. They also communicated the advantages and added meaning to their lives. The two sections below review the realities of managing both a career and a family. The first examines the compromises and downsides. Also included are recommendations for offsetting these negative aspects. The second details the rewards and benefits.

Compromises and Trade-offs

In this section, insights into some of the less than positive realities are discussed. Accordingly, in this section the difficulties participants experienced as mothers and senior-level college or university administrators, focusing specifically on the professional compromises they made, the personal trade-offs they experienced, and the emotional tolls that characterized their lives as working mothers, are examined. While participants noted how their dual roles required hard work and sacrifice, they also recommended strategies for overcoming these problems. Recommendations for recognizing, coping with or surmounting these possible pitfalls are included.

Professional Compromises

Participants in this investigation candidly discussed the varied professional compromises they made throughout their careers. These included accepting only positions that were conducive for their families, foregoing education, limiting their involvement in professional organizations, and making less money.

Always considering the needs of their children first, the women discussed professional positions they accepted and declined based on how well they met the needs of their families. Others simply did not allow themselves to consider positions that forced them to relocate. This finding was consistent with Apter's research (1993) that women sometimes limited their careers by their own choosing.

Hope explained the conscious decision she made not to relocate her family, despite her awareness that this decision limited her career advancement:

> Most people in [administration] move around quite a bit before they get to a top position . . . I made a decision early on that I wasn't going to do that. I didn't want to do all that moving with my children, and my husband had a good job that he liked. It didn't make sense to uproot. I never even looked for other positions. I teach in the graduate program, and I used to be a little jealous when all the new grad students were getting these new jobs. They were excited about moving to new places and then I stayed here. I would go to national conferences and I'd see people who I taught, my students, who were now deans and I was still a director. But, that was okay, because I had to make those sacrifices, and yes it was a conscious decision to do that because of my family.

Besides discussing the trade-offs they made regarding the advancement of their careers, several women noted that they chose to forego advanced education because of their hectic work-family schedules. Lack of time and energy simply did not allow for the added responsibility of graduate studies. In these cases, the women made conscious decisions to defer their educations in order to maintain greater harmony between home and work.

Ruth, for example, explained her decision to not continue her education:

> There's some choices I've made. I don't have a Ph.D. People know that. I mean I'm very clear that I didn't have time to get a Ph.D. I wasn't willing to give up the time to do that based on the way that my life was going. Well, this woman said I would never amount to anything without a Ph.D. I thought, "Well, okay, fine. I'm doing what I like to do so, okay, but [continuing my education is] not something that I can do right now."

Many study participants also discussed the compromises they struck regarding their involvement in professional organizations. Involvement in these groups often meant the obligation to travel and the assumption of additional, time-consuming responsibilities. With overflowing plates, these working mothers simply did not have the time to become significantly involved in professional organizations. Hope shared:

> [Not participating in professional organizations] is a sacrifice I've made. I go to one conference a year, which for me, was primarily to go to rest and just to get away. I never got involved with the associations. That was one thing that I just didn't have time to do . . . There're certain things you have to do if you want to be involved in those national organizations, in terms of contacts you need to make, networking, committees you need to be on; and I just made a choice early on that that was something I couldn't do.

Whether because of passed-up professional opportunities, perceived lack of professional commitment, or unwillingness to work extensive hours, a few women in this study also believed they made less money because of their decisions to have children. Referencing the trade-offs in her life, Megan agreed that she could be making a lot more money but she simply was not willing to accept positions that took too much time away from her family:

> As far as the tradeoffs, I feel like I could be making a lot more money, but I've made the personal decision that I don't want to work for some big company. That's not where I want to be, but that's a trade-off. I don't think I would have made that decision if I didn't have [my daughter].

The professional tradeoffs included limiting career advancement, setting aside educational goals, limiting involvement in professional associations, and earning less money. While these were realities for the participants, most recognized that they could have all these later in life. They made the necessary professional sacrifices while their children were young and parenting was more demanding. They anticipated further advancing their careers, obtaining terminal degrees, increasing their involvement in professional associations, and possibly earning more money once their children were grown. As one participant said, "I will achieve my goals. I just have to prioritize them and know that I can't do it all at the same time." All said, participants emphasized that while understanding the professional downsides associated with being a mother and a senior-level administrator was important, these should be considered alongside the positive aspects associated with both roles.

Personal Trade-offs

The drawbacks of being both a professional and a parent can also be personal in nature. Many interviewees, for example, spoke about their limited personal time, which forced them to sacrifice downtime, sleep, exercise and wellness, and personal friendships. Others noted the marital strain that resulted from their marriages being the third priority in their lives after their children and their careers. Still, others regretted how they had sacrificed time with their children.

Limited Time for Self

With a limited amount of time for personal interests, a number of women shared that their priorities left little time for themselves. These women were first concerned with their children, then their careers, and then their partners. The result was that their needs often came last or were completely neglected.

Several women discussed the trade-off of sacrificing time for themselves. As Laurel, with a full measure of humor, shared:

> The big trade-off is that you can kind of forget about the personal time. All these people say, "Oh, I just need a lot of quiet time." Well, my lord, if you need a lot of quiet time then you just don't ever need to try any of this. I really mean this. I come last. That's been a trade-off because you can lose your soul sometimes. There have been some times when I have gotten lost and get up and look in the mirror, and I don't even know who I am. I am so many different things. I play so many different parts. You know, mom, wife, president, speaker, mentor . . . That's the biggest trade-off.

Another manifestation of "no time for self" was the sleep so many of these women sacrificed. This often led to a lack of energy and mental alertness and exhaustion. Many participants discussed their lack of energy that resulted from sleep deprivation or because their days rarely included downtime. Although they may have received an average amount of sleep, their days were very full and oftentimes overwhelming because they were forced to be mentally alert both at work and at home. That took a toll on their personal health. Leslie explained:

> Even though I sleep, the kids go to bed at 9:00. I go to bed at 10:00. I wake up at 6:00. I get a decent night's sleep; but because you absolutely do not have one second of down time the entire time you are awake, it takes its toll. Even now, lunch hour, because I don't go home. I just think that I am going to go and sit in a parking lot somewhere, wind down the windows, and take a nap; but [instead] you are out buying groceries because you have no other time.

Others commented on how their lack of energy and limited time did not allow for adequate amounts of exercise. Although some women in this study routinely exercised, other women commented on how they sacrificed their health by not exercising. As Mallory conveyed:

> The other thing I don't do is I don't exercise enough, so I don't have enough time for me. I really don't [exercise] because I'm too tired. You know I've thought about exercising and I need to the older I get. Physically I know I need to do that, but trying to fit that in with everything else seems impossible. What usually happens for me is that I put me last and everybody else goes first. Intellectually, I know I shouldn't do that because if I get sick, then believe me, even though my husband is home full-time, everything would fall apart and I don't want that to happen.

A number of participants also discussed how they had little time to pursue their personal interests. This included reading, traveling, visiting museums, or even weeding a garden. They gave up these personal interests because time simply did not allow for them. When they prioritized their days, their personal needs were last, which meant they rarely had time to enjoy the things they liked to do.

Another disadvantage resulting from leading complex lives was the limited time available for personal friendships and dating. Several women, for example, expressed their longing for close female friends. Karen shared how she sacrificed personal friendships because she simply did not have time for them:

> Another downside for me is before children I always had close girlfriends, and that has been pretty much sacrificed. I still have some close girlfriends, but I'm not able to spend the time with them. I miss that female community, and I don't have it here at the university. My husband doesn't need that like I do. He does not have this need for male friendship or companionship. I really miss my time with my female friends, and it's pretty minimalized at this point in my life.

While many interviewees routinely admitted that they compromised many of their personal needs in order to meet the needs of their families and their careers, some did successfully manage a personal life outside of work and family. Some exercised regularly, often in the early morning while others set aside time each day to explore their personal interests and friendships. The key to their successes was to first make their interests a priority. Rather than focus on the needs of their children, home, and work, they purposefully set aside time for themselves. Next, they solicited support from their children, partners, and work colleagues. They reinforced the importance of needed personal time in order to be a better partner, mother, and employee. With the support of these key individuals, participants found the time to reconnect with friends, read, vacation, and exercise.

Marital Strain

> I think there are compromises to my marriage—massive compromises to my marriage—because of the lack of time. None of that is fun stuff. (Gwen)

When referring to trade-offs and tensions, a common theme repeatedly emphasized by respondents was the amount of marital strain experienced. Some attributed this to not having adequate time to devote to their relationships, and others blamed it on their partners' resistance to appreciate their wives' high-profile jobs.

In discussing the strain she experienced in her relationship, Brenda referenced how her multiple responsibilities left little time and energy to devote to her life partner:

> If you have two children and [are] juggling a job, they are high stress. They require all from you both physically and emotionally. It gets better in many regards as [the children] get older because they can dress themselves and feed themselves and can do their own homework, but those first few years you are attending to each of those little details. You are doing what you need to do on the job and having a fulfilling partnership with your spouse is difficult.

Several interviewees also noted their partners' insecurities about having professional wives raised tensions in their marriages. Laurel related that her husband simply did not like being in the shadow of her career. Her perspective was also unique because she was a vice president when she met him, so he knew of her career aspirations from the very beginning.

Interestingly, he chose to stay home with the children. Laurel explained how her husband reacted to her public lifestyle:

> He has a grumpy side. I'll come home from a long day exhausted, and he wants tons of attention. I simply don't have the energy to tend to him. Now again, that's not necessarily of just a president, but can be true of anybody. This is just life. It's not different when you are a president except for the difference is the public life. When we go anywhere, [our town] is sort of a small town with you know, people are lining up to talk with me. It's been very awkward for him. They will ask him what he does and he will say, "Well, I'm a stay-at-home dad." Well, the men in the south just about fall over dead. Of course, in [our previous community] there were four on our street but you know here, it is just a real novelty. That has been real awkward for him. Then he gets wounded and when we get back in the car, instead of enjoying the event, I have to tend to his ego and take care of him. Sometimes I have the energy for that, and sometimes I don't.

Overall, one of the commonly verbalized tensions that resulted from managing their roles as parents and administrators was the strain that resulted on many participants' marriages. They admitted to paying less attention to their partners because of limited time and energy. The demands of their children seemed immediate, and work expectations had deadlines. Caring for their partners and themselves seemed less of a priority.

Some participants were cognizant of the strain on their relationships. To combat this strain they openly communicated their concerns with their partners, sought marital counseling, spent purposeful time together, and made each other more of a priority in their lives. Michelle reinforced this idea:

> The best thing I can do for my children is to love their father. Failing at my marriage is not an option, for me or for them. I lost sight of that for awhile when the kids were little and demanded so much time. We both recognized that we were growing apart and now work very hard to make our relationship a priority. After all, the kids will move out at some point. We need to make sure our relationship is more than about coparenting them.

Other strategies employed by the participants to lessen marital strain included spending an hour together each night after the children went to bed, talking during the day via phone or e-mail, regular adult outings or dates, exercising together, taking adult vacations, and pursuing similar interests.

Missing Out

Missing out was another theme that emerged when study participants discussed the tensions in their lives. Although they enjoyed their careers and preferred to work versus stay at home, they worried about missing out on their children's lives. They were concerned about not spending enough time with their children, fearful that they would grow up quickly and they would feel like they missed out.

Hillary voiced this theme in her interview. With her children almost grown, she reflected:

> There are times when I realize that some of my children's earliest days are kind of a blur, not because I wasn't there but because I was doing so many things. I look at these pictures of when they were small, and it just goes so fast. I'll show you this picture because it seems like just yesterday. This was the day I got my doctorate. I was in my gown and [my daughter] wanted to be in a gown too. Of course, I had to get one for her. She's 4 and he's 8. It seems like just yesterday. [Hillary started to cry.]

Feeling Guilty

> The tension is in my mind a lot of times. I don't feel like I'm doing anybody any good. I feel like I'm doing the best I can at both places, but I don't feel like it's good enough at either place. I feel like [if] I'm doing better at either place, it would probably be at home. I feel like I could do so much more at work, but I'm just too tired. It frustrates me. (Lisa)

For most women in this study, the biggest trade-off they experienced as a result of being both a mother and a senior-level administrator was the emotional toll it took on them in the form of guilt. These women frequently shared their apprehensions about not spending enough time with their children or not dedicating themselves fully to their careers. As the amount of time in each day was limited, women felt conflicted about not giving 100 percent of themselves to either work or home, which often led to feelings of guilt.

The vast majority of women interviewed felt guilty about work and home, especially about not spending enough time with their children. Helen related that she often "suffer[ed] the guilt of always feeling like "I am giving someone my second best. You'll feel like you have done nothing or that you haven't done enough for your kids."

Likewise, Leslie shared a story about the extreme guilt she felt about having someone else spend more time with her children than she did—a realization she reached when she learned that her nanny was teaching her young daughters new things:

> It brings me down a lot. I get depressed about the kids. More so recently because my older daughter is learning so much. I came home one day to feed her dinner, and the nanny left. I'm feeding the baby, and she picked up her cup and started drinking milk out of it. I just cried the rest of the night. I had said, "Let's try it and see if you can use the sippy cup." She just picked it up and I said, "You've done this before." I just balled the rest of the night. Everything changed after that. I'm going to get teary now. Everything changed after that because I knew that she wasn't just learning from me. She says new words when I come home, and I know that I didn't teach her.

The next form of guilt that the interviewees talked about was the remorse they felt about not giving themselves fully to their work. Connie started by sharing the guilt she placed on herself to be a good administrator. Her personality as a perfectionist, her desire to be a good administrator, and her insecurities about not spending enough time with her daughter fueled her guilt:

> I feel very conflicted to tell you the truth. My problem is that I cannot do a mediocre job. I have this expectation that my job is very important and that I have to do it to perfection. If I delegate—and I do delegate a lot—I have to supervise sooner or later.

The respondents offered a variety of suggestions for overcoming the guilt that they felt regarding inadequately dedicating themselves to their children and to their careers. First, they recommended realizing that one was experiencing guilt and then learning to manage the feelings of anxiety. Next, these women advised that working mothers were present for their children more than they realized. Therefore, they should not feel guilty about not making them more of a priority. Hope, who had children ranging in age from 4 to 25, offered her explanation of this strategy:

> Probably I could have spent more time with the kids, and I say that as part of the guilt as a parent. On the other hand, I really have been pretty involved. My oldest daughter is 25, and she constantly says that to me. That it amazes her as she looks back, how I was able to be at all her plays and all her concerts. I went anyway, and I supported her and [my son] too. I was there as much as many other parents who stayed at home. So yeah, maybe I could have volunteered more in school, could have done some of those things, but at the same time I say that I did do a lot of that.

Also, women in this study became more confident about their decisions to work when they saw their children grow into mature young adults. Much of the guilt these women felt about their children stemmed from their concerns that being a working mother would somehow jeopardize their children's successes. Women agreed that most of their guilt about their children dwindled when they saw their children "turning out" okay. As their children grew up, they saw confident, well-behaved, intelligent, and interesting people. Knowing that they raised positive members of society made them feel better about their decisions to work. Karen shared:

> I'm trying very hard to not to [feel guilty], and I think I'm getting so much better. I think one of the reasons I'm getting so much better is my kids are turning out well. I think I felt much guiltier when they were babies because I didn't know if I could be doing permanent damage. Both of my girls have been identified by their teachers to go into the gifted program in their school system. In sitting down with their teachers and counselors and the principal of their school . . . it was very rewarding for me to hear that they were well adjusted. They were leaders in their classrooms. They get along well. Obviously they are good students, hard working, and well mannered. That's the type of thing that you want to hear as a parent. . . . That for me was very rewarding. For professionals to say that my kids are good kids, creative, like school, and bright. It makes me feel good to know that along the way I made some of the right choices.

Next, women in this study talked about developing professional confidence in order to overcome the guilt surrounding their careers and their abilities to give fully to their professions. When Helen recognized that she was good at what she did, she was a valued employee, and not in jeopardy of losing her job, the guilt somewhat subsided:

> Some of it is confidence that you are good at what you do. I think one of the primary reasons that I always felt guilty is because I never really knew until I had some outside signals that I was doing a worthwhile job. You get promoted. You get raises. You get performance appraisals. Then you realize, "They like me." I have to credit this to my husband because he always says, "You know your competency but you don't know your worth. You understand that you are good at your job. You know you are smart. You know that you are competent, but you have no idea what you are worth." He said, "I think that women, especially women who are moms, have a difficult time understanding anything other than their competency." I thought that was very interesting. I think that understanding that I am more than competent has helped me eventually understand and deal with the guilt.

With this confidence, Helen no longer felt guilty about taking time away from work to be with the children. She explained:

> I think the second thing is that you start to see that your children are getting older. I'm recognizing that I have a limited amount of time with them. Work is no larger as important. "Darn it, you can fire me if you want but I'm going to the soccer game." I think you develop some feeling that this is a time-sensitive option that you have and that you aren't going to lose it.

The trade-offs, tensions, or compromises described in this section centered around three themes. The first detailed the many professional compromises women experienced because of the complications of managing career and family. They found themselves selectively choosing their professional positions based on the needs of their families, foregoing their schooling, and limiting their involvement in professional organizations. Second, these women also discussed the many personal sacrifices that resulted from their complicated lives. These included little to no personal time, lack of sleep and energy, marital strain, and "missing out." Last, participants candidly described the guilt they often experienced for not spending more time with their children and not dedicating themselves as fully as they would have liked at work. Some of this guilt was alleviated when these women recognized that their children were "turning out well" and that they were, indeed, good at what they did professionally.

THE BENEFITS

Despite whatever frustrations they felt as working mothers, the women in this study repeatedly reinforced that the benefits and rewards of their dual roles far outweighed any and all trade-offs associated with it. Interviewees often were eager to share their perspectives on the many positive aspects that accompanied being a mother and a senior-level college or university administrator. In this section, participants voiced the personal and professional advantages and benefits to their children as key "rewards" of working motherhood.

Personal Benefits

Participants shed light on the personal benefits associated with being a mother and a professional. These included satisfying incomes, enriching lives, and gratification that came with making others proud. First, although greatly downplayed, women discussed the material benefits they received from working. These included increased income, which enabled them to provide more material goods, after-school activities, and in some cases private education for their children. Megan shared her perspective on having an additional income: "Obviously, materially, we can afford to have her in band and piano lessons that we may not [otherwise have been] able to provide. That's not the most important thing, but it does help."

Interviewees also said that being a professional and a parent made their lives better, more enriched. Most refuted the stereotype that if given a choice all women would stay at home and raise their children and, in so doing, increased others' awareness of the personal and professional satisfaction mothers can receive through their roles as mothers and professionals. They admitted that the rewards they received from both roles were extensive and that they genuinely enjoyed both aspects of their lives. Many detailed the pleasures and joys they received from being a mother. They agreed that being a mother provided them with a richness in their lives that they never imagined possible. As Gwen put it:

> Here's my little secret. I think that nothing in life compares to [having kids]. It's not to minimize the importance of the work that we do, but because I think having children does put things in perspective and help you develop priorities. The trade-offs are, given that I have not won the lottery, I can't imagine a better life. Not everyone has this gift of children. I do. They are so funny. They are so silly. They are so sweet. I am witness to that every day. I am the beneficiary of their love.

Having children also helped these women prioritize what was important in their lives. Many claimed that children gave them perspective, helping them to see that their lives were, in their view, more than just their careers. Reflecting back on a difficult workday this past Halloween, Laurel found joy in coming home to her children:

> I can be at work and be real frustrated and [then] go home. Last night [I saw my daughter] in her Josie Pussy Cat outfit and [I] just melted. I never thought about work again while we were handing out Halloween candy. [My son] has an outfit that bleeds. Little boys love to bleed. It was just gross, but he's so cute. I just have this really rich life besides a career. I have this really rich home life. I love these people, and they love me. We watch movies and pop popcorn and giggle and laugh, and I just have a whole other world. When I was single it was hard to get away from it mentally. When I go home now, I am pretty much focused on little freckles.

One final personal reward participants mentioned was the satisfaction they took in "making others proud." Hearing their children, spouses, or their families talk about their successes was particularly gratifying for these women. Many expressed the joy they received from knowing that their children were proud of them.

Sharon, for instance, shared this anecdote about her son:

> I do remember some conversations with [my son] early on, in fact. One day, he was maybe 5 years old and my husband said to him, "Who do you think is smarter: your mother or your father?" My husband is thinking he's going to say him and he said, "Mom." My husband almost fell off the chair. When he asked him why he said that, my son responded, "Because mom is a teacher. Teachers are smart." I just smiled.

The personal rewards accompanied with being a mother and a professional were immeasurable for the women in this study. While they mentioned the benefits of having more money, they became more passionate as they discussed how their lives were more enriching and satisfying because of working motherhood. As many commented, these personal benefits far outweighed any of the downsides that accompanied assuming both roles.

Professional Benefits

Participants also discussed the professional benefits of being both a mother and an administrator. They shared how being a professional allowed them to have a positive impact on society by helping others. As a result, they had high levels of job satisfaction that positively affected their personal lives. Megan captured this sentiment as well as anyone when she said, "I think I'm a better parent because if I didn't have [a professional] sense of achievement I would just be unhappy and I wouldn't be as good of a parent because I would be an unhappy person. You have to be a happy person to be a good parent." Interestingly, the benefits went the other direction as well. These women likewise noted how being a mother made them better administrators, often by helping them to become more approachable, better organized, and more compassionate.

First, from a professional perspective, many spoke about their love for their careers. They appreciated the opportunity to have a positive impact on others, especially on students. Hope commented:

> I have such close contact with students and a lot of those students have graduated. To know that you were there to help them graduate is very rewarding. I know that I made a difference in their lives. That's been really rewarding to be so personally involved. Aside from being proud of my family, I think it is real important that we all have something that we are proud of that has nothing to do with being a wife and a mother. I can look back on my career and my life and say, "You know, I really did some meaningful things. I helped some neat people. I met some neat people, and I feel good about who I am because of those things that happened." That's important to me.

Next, participants shared how being a mother made them better professionals. Many said that in their roles as mothers, they learned about compassion and understanding. These skills were useful in their work settings, particularly when managing people and working with students, in large measure because having children helped them to understand the needs of others and increased their sensitivity to the individual obligations of those with whom they interacted.

Hillary, for example, shared this story about how being a mother helped her to understand and interact more effectively with others:

> Because I am also a mother, I think that I am a better dean. I'll give you an example from today. I get to work at 7:30. I drop my daughter

off at her school and then I come here. So I am here at 7:30. There were two police cars in front of the building. I came in and there was a student who had nothing on except boxer shorts. An 18-year-old freshman student who was drunk found his way into the building and spent part of the night here. My son is 20 . . . [and this student also felt] like my son in the sense that I had such compassion. Here's a kid who is drunk and needs some support. Another one of my employees was very afraid. In a way, again, because of my mothering skills, I could also understand her fear. I have had an incredible education that has prepared me to plan quality programs, but I think that my experience as a mother enables me to interact with different kinds of employees, students, clients, and nonclients.

Interviewees also pointed out that motherhood helped them to become more sensitive to the individual needs of their colleagues. In Brenda's case, she believed she was more empathetic with those who worked with her:

I think to be an effective administrator you have to be compassionate, understanding, and sensitive to employees. It is very important. Each person who works with you has her own story. The more that you've experienced in your own personal life, the more you are able to understand. I have to be flexible. When I am understanding and empathetic and flexible with their family needs and with them, they will work that much harder when those concerns aren't there.

Finally, when asked about the benefits of being a professional and a parent, many women spoke enthusiastically about how their working had benefited their children. From their vantage points, their lives as university administrators had not only exposed their children to enriching opportunities commonly found on college and university campuses, but it had also provided them with powerful role models.

Several interviewees discussed how working in a university setting provided their children with rich opportunities for growth—opportunities, many believed, that their children otherwise might not have experienced. For example, Rose explained how her son was introduced to greater diversity because of their life on campus:

My job has benefited [my son]. I think he has a wider view of the world. He lives in an environment that is very diverse. He's very comfortable with people who don't speak and don't hear, people in wheelchairs, persons of color, people who speak languages other than English, just because of the environment that we live in. I think that's been the biggest benefit from my perspective.

With similar enthusiasm, Connie shared how her career in academia has influenced her daughter and exposed her to travel outside of the United States:

I have found that my [daughter] is very familiar with the rhythm of the semester. Her vocabulary includes words like *semester, tenure, faculty, Dr. so and so, history,* [and] *anthropology.* The university has been her world. I think my working has added to the richness of her life, her intellectual life, her relationships, and her educational development. She has been to Europe since we teach there in the summer. She's 8. She's been to Europe maybe seven times.

Besides providing their children with enriching opportunities, many interviewees believed that their lives as working mothers have had a positive influence on their children's futures as parents, professionals, and members of society. As Hillary put it:

Frankly, I think my children will be better professionals and parents given what they have been through. I think that my son will be a better father. Both, by the way, want to have children. They also want to have real careers, not just jobs. So that to me suggests an endorsement of my life. They get it, and they in some ways want to emulate it.

Interviewees cited many rewards that resulted from their lives as professionals and parents. They described the personal and professional benefits as well as the rewards that their working had on their children. Many appreciated how having children had helped them to establish priorities and gave them a life outside of work. Additionally, they felt that being mothers made them better professionals by helping them to become more compassionate and sensitive to the needs of others. Finally, they appreciated how their children had benefited from their working. All of these rewards, they believed, made working motherhood satisfying and worthwhile.

DISCUSSION AND IMPLICATIONS

In this paper the advantages and disadvantages of being both a mother and a senior-level administrator were presented. A number of key conclusions regarding the management of work and family may be drawn from the data. Additionally, these conclusions have potential to inform policy and practice. First, the participants all had passionate commitments to work and family. While they each offered testimony that combining a career with children was challenging, their success paved the way for future generations of college and university administrators.

Throughout the course of this investigation, a common denominator was underscored time and time again: The women in this study were among the first to negotiate the work-family dance within senior administrative ranks in colleges and universities. They chose to assume these multiple roles not completely knowing what was in store for them. With few mentors or role models who had previously challenged maternity leave policies, questioned the need for work-family benefits, or expressed frustration with the current status quo, these tasks fell on the shoulders of these trendsetters. As such, these women helped both to start a dialogue on work-family issues in colleges and universities.

The first step toward improving conditions for women administrators is to increase the awareness of the realities associated with managing a career and children. One way to better understand the multiple demands placed on those who manage work and family is by learning from them. Gaining insights, via a directed campus dialogue, offers one promising avenue for understanding more fully how women's needs have been met in the past, and how higher education might better address those needs in the future.

Additionally the need for mentors is apparent. It is imperative women, similar to those in this study, become more proactive in serving as mentors to others. Many professional associations facilitate mentoring programs. It is essential that these organizations work to incorporate administrative mothers as mentors.

A second major finding from this study was that women had great passion for both their families and their careers. While they loved their children a great deal and recognized the downsides of managing both roles, most admitted that they could never be at home with their kids full time because they would miss the intellectual stimulation that work provided. Being a professional made them happy, and this personal satisfaction carried over into their family lives. That said, although these women loved their careers, all clearly stated that if managing a career and a family ever got too complicated, or if in some way they felt like their professional lives were somehow jeopardizing their children, they would quit.

Understanding working mothers' commitments to home and work is essential, especially for supervisors. Supportive supervisors play key roles in the successful management of work and family and the controlling of guilt toward home and work. It is recommended that supervisors empathize with working parents by allowing them the flexibility to occasionally leave work early to attend a child's event or infrequently stay at home to care for a sick child. Supportive supervisors avoid scheduling meetings in the early morning or late in the afternoon in an effort to not conflict with childcare arrangements. They may also offer alternative employment options such as 4-day workweeks, 10-month contracts, and possible part-time work. Those who are able to recognize the multiple demands of working parents are more likely to retain them. As this finding indicates, if the work environment is not supportive and conflicts too much with personal commitments, colleges and universities will lose these valuable and highly trained employees.

Third, each of the 17 women in this study offered persuasive testimony that although their lives as professionals and mothers were complicated and did not come without sacrifice, managing fulfilled lives as senior-level administrators and parents "could be done." To be sure, interviewees candidly shared that their professional success was accompanied by personal and professional sacrifices. Despite the multiple trades-offs from their dual roles, these women were professionally successful and personally satisfied. Their stories not only exemplified the hard work, dedication, passion, and commitment required to be a mother and a senior-level administrator; but they also embodied the many rewards that accompanied both roles. Participants underscored that if a woman aspired to be a senior-level administrator and have children, it could be done and done well. They took pride in being role models for others as proof that women could have successful careers and children and love having both.

Although this is a meaningful message, finding participants for this study was no easy task. When contacting postsecondary institutions, more times than not I was told that no one at the institution met the criteria for the study, meaning either there were no women in senior-level management positions or none had children. Assuming then that these success stories are rare, it is even more important for women to know that indeed there are women in senior administrative leadership positions in colleges and universities who also have children. While the finding that "it can be done" may seem overly optimistic, it is an important statement to make to aspiring women. While they need to know the realities of these dual roles and the pros and cons of assuming both, they also need the inspiration of knowing that while it may not be easy, "it can be done."

Related to the finding that "it can be done," this study reveals implications for women who aspire to senior-level positions and want children. First, women must make their personal needs and interests priorities in their lives. By prioritizing their personal needs, women will better sustain their busy schedules and levels of happiness. Second, administrative mothers must understand their professional and personal competencies. Knowing that they are valued, productive employees and good mothers is the first step toward elevating the guilt often felt by working moms. Another way to possibly lessen the guilt at home is to focus attention at home, when home. When physically home, working mothers should focus on their children, partners, and needs of home; not check e-mail, read papers, or return telephone calls. This allows women to fully enjoy their families rather than be distracted with work. Last, administrative mothers should master the art of delegation and maximizing their time both at home and at work.

The next major finding that emerged from this study was a simple one: There was no one way to achieve personal and professional success, and no one way to manage it all. Time and time again, participants emphasized the uniqueness of their experiences. They did not have predetermined professional plans that they followed to achieve their professional successes. Similarly, they could not predict how having children would affect their lives. They learned how to manage their dual roles based on their own set of circumstances. Although there were commonalities among the data and general conclusions were drawn regarding the realities of managing multiple roles, all emphasized that in order to succeed, women needed to work within their own sets of conditions. They must understand themselves and their priorities, be aware of their support systems and their limitations, and recognize the demands of their professions coupled with the demands of their personal lives.

Next, while efforts have been made to improve the current conditions for working mothers, the culture of higher education remains somewhat unsupportive. Some of this is due to the professional culture of academe and some to the perceptions of society in general. In order to reverse these perceptions, there needs to be a raising of awareness within the profession, increased education that young women can have careers and families, the inclusion of men in the work-family conversation, and the ongoing education of employers that working mothers are valuable investments in the future success of their colleges and universities.

On the whole, the issues surrounding work and family must be more of a priority on college and university campuses and within the profession as a whole. With the increasing presence of women in administrative and faculty positions in academe, the need to develop a supportive culture accompanied by work-family benefits is likely to become a key recruitment and retention issue in the near future.

There are a variety of ways to make work-family a priority on college and university campuses. First, there needs to be an increased awareness of work-family issues and policies at all levels. These issues must be discussed at the departmental, school/college, and senior institutional levels. Second, work-family issues should be discussed proactively. Topics related to work and family, including dual-career hiring practices, should be clearly stated in employee handbooks and discussed during new employee orientation. Human resource professionals, at the very least, should be well versed in these policies to ensure that they can guide and accurately advise new employees about them. Third, benefits and policies related to parenthood should be routinely evaluated for their use and effectiveness. If certain benefits are not used, policy makers should investigate the potential causes for their underutilization.

In sum, senior administrators and policy makers may find this research useful in understanding the conditions for success that are important for these women and, in turn, work to design effective support and outreach systems within higher education to serve them. Once these understandings and systems are established, it is possible that women administrators with children may find themselves remaining in the profession longer and advancing more frequently to its senior levels.

CONCLUDING REMARKS

This qualitative study focused on the life histories of 17 women who were senior-level college and university administrators and mothers of school-aged children. Although they experienced their share of hardships, trade-offs, and compromises, the women in this study emphasized that by believing in themselves and their abilities and embracing their love for their careers and families, they were able to successfully negotiate and enjoy their complex lives.

A major conclusion that can be drawn from this research is that there is no single path for achieving personal and professional success. When women learn of this research, they often ask, "How do women do it?

What's the answer?" Findings from this study will not give women a set of commandments for managing motherhood and career; rather, they offer to women various examples of how others have managed the dual roles of professional and parent. For some readers, simply learning that it "can be done" may be more significant than understanding how women actually do this!

The women in this study did not follow a straight path. Many of them encountered various roadblocks and hurdles along the way. From these perspectives come shared insights or suggestions about how one might approach managing work and family. There is no set way to achieve success. There is no one way to define success. Participants agreed that based on individual circumstances, women who aspire to professional positions similar to theirs will find a way to make it all work.

REFERENCES

American Council on Education. (2007). *The American college president*. Washington, DC: Author.

Anders, J. (1997). Leadership training initiatives for community college administrators. *Community College Review, 24*(4), 27–53.

Apter, T. (1993). *Working women don't have wives: Professional success in the 1990's*. New York: St. Martin's Press.

Bassett, R. H. (2005). *Parenting & professing: Balancing family work with an academic career*. Nashville, TN: Vanderbilt University Press.

Bender, B. (1980). Job satisfaction in student affairs. *NASPA Journal, 18*(2), 2–9.

Berwick, K. R. (1992, January). Stress among student affairs administrators: The relationship of personal characteristics and organized variables to work-related stress. *Journal of College Student Development, 33*, 3–11.

Blackhurst, A. E. (2000). Effects of mentoring on the employment experiences and career satisfaction of women student affairs administrators. *NASPA Journal, 37*(4), 573–586.

Blackhurst, A., Brandt, J., & Kalinowski, J. (1998). Effects of personal and work-related attributes on the organizational commitment and life satisfaction of women student affairs administrators. *NASPA Journal, 35*(2), 86–89.

Burns, M. (1982). Who leaves the student affairs field? *NASPA Journal, 20*(2), 9–12.

Chamberlain, M. (Ed.). (1998). *Women in academe: Progress and prospects.* New York: Sage.

Chase, S. (1995). Taking narrative seriously: Consequences for method and theory in interview studies. In R. Josselson & A. Lieblich (Eds.), *Interpreting experience: The narrative study of lives* (1–26). Thousand Oaks, CA: Sage Publications.

Colbeck, C., & Drago, R. (2005, November/December). Accept, avoid, resist: How faculty members respond to bias against caregiving . . . and how departments can help. *Change, 73*(6), 10–18.

Earwood-Smith, G., Jordan-Cox, C. A., Hudson, G., & Smith, M. U. (1990). Women making it to the top as chief student affairs officers. *NASPA Journal, 27*(4), 299–304.

Evans, N. J., & Kuh, G. D. (1983). Getting to the top: A profile of female chief student affairs officers. *Journal of NAWDAC, 46*(3), 18–22.

Glaser, B. G. (1978). *Theoretical sensitivity.* Mill Valley, CA: Sociology Press.

Glaser, B., & Strauss, A. (1967). *The discovery of grounded theory.* Chicago: Aldine.

Hersi, D. T. (1993). Factors contributing to job satisfaction for women in higher education administration. *CUPA Journal, 44*(2), 29–35.

Holmes, D., Verrier, D., & Chisholm, P. (1983). Persistence in student affairs work: Attitudes and job shifts among master's program graduates. *Journal of College Student Personnel, 24,* 438–443.

Ironside, E. M. (1981). Uncommon women/common themes: Career paths of upper-level women administrators in higher education institutions. *Paper presented at the joint conference of the Southern Association for Institutional Research,* Charlotte, NC.

Jones, S. R., & Komives, S. R. (2001). Contemporary issues of women as senior student affairs officers. In J. Nidiffer & C. T. Bashaw (Eds.), *Women administrators in higher education: Historical and contemporary perspectives* (pp. 231–248). Albany, NY: State University of New York Press.

Kaplan, S., & Tinsley, A. (1989). The unfinished agenda: Women in higher education administration. *Academe, 75*(1), 18–22.

King, J., & Gomez, G. G. (2008). *On the pathway to the presidency: Characteristics of higher education senior leadership.* Washington, DC: ACE publications.

Kuyper, L. A. (1987). Career development of women in administration of higher education: Contributing factors. *Journal of NAWDAC, 50*(4), 3–7.

LeBlanc, D. (1993). Barriers to women's advancement into higher education administration. In P. Mitchell (Ed.), *Cracking the wall* (pp. 41–49). Washington, DC: College and University Personnel Association.

Levtov, A. (2001). Family-friendly? Challenging choices for women in the student affairs field. *The Vermont Connection, 22,* 25–36.

Lincoln, Y. S., & Guba, E. G. (1985). *Naturalistic inquiry.* Beverly Hills, CA: Sage Publications.

Marcus, J. (2007). Helping academics have families and tenure too: Universities discover their self-interest. *Change, 39*(2), 27–32.

Marshall, M. R., & Jones, C .H. (1990). Childbearing sequence and the career development of women administrators in higher education. *Journal of College Student Development, 31,* 531–537.

Mason, M., & Goulden, M. (2002, Nov/Dec). Do babies matter? *Academe, 88*(6), 21–27.

McDade, S. (1997). Intentions of becoming an administrator. *Journal of Continuing Education, 45*(2), 2–13.

McEwen, M. K., Williams, T .E., & McHugh Engstrom, C. (1991). Feminization in student affairs: A qualitative investigation. *Journal of College Student Development, 32,* 440–446.

McFarland, C., & Ebbers, L. (1998). Preparation factors common in outstanding community college presidents. *Michigan Community College Journal, 4*(1), 33–47.

National Center for Education Statistics. (2003, Fall). *Staff in postsecondary institutions, fall 2003, and salaries of full-time instructional faculty, 2003–2004.* Retrieved Summer 2008, from http://nces.ed.gov//pubs2005/2005155.pdf

Nidiffer, J., & Bashaw, C. (2001). *Women administrators in higher education.* Albany, NY: State University of New York Press.

Nobbe, J., & Manning, S. (1997). Issues for women in student affairs with children. *NASPA Journal, 34*(2), 101–111.

Patton, M. Q. (1990). *Qualitative evaluation and research methods.* Newberry Park, CA: Sage Publications.

Perna, L. W. (2005, Summer). The relationship between family and employment outcomes. In J. W. Curtis (Ed.), The challenge of balancing faculty careers and faculty work (pp. 5–23). *New Directions for Higher Education* (no. 130). San Francisco: Jossey-Bass.

Reeves, M. E. (1975). An analysis of job satisfaction of women administrators in higher education. *Journal of NAWDAC, 38*(3), 132–135.

Richmond, J., & Sherman, K. J. (1991). Student-development preparation and placement: A longitudinal study of graduate students' and new professionals' experiences. *Journal of College Student Development, 32,* 8–16.

Rickard, S. (1985). Career pathways of chief student affairs officers: Making room at the top for females and minorities. *NASPA Journal, 22*(2), 52–60.

Riessman, C. K. (1993). *Narrative analysis.* Newbury Park, CA: Sage Publications.

Rosser, V. (2000). Mid-level administrators: What we know. In L . Johnsrud & V. Rosser (Eds.), Understanding the work and career paths of midlevel administrators (pp. 5–14). *New Directions for Higher Education* (no. 111). San Francisco: Jossey-Bass.

Sagaria. M., & Johnsrud, A. (1985). Administrative mobility and gender: Patterns and processes in higher education. *Journal of Higher Education, 59*(3), 305–326.

Sallee, M. W. (2008). Work and family balance: How community college faculty cope. In J. L. Lester (Ed.), Gendered perspectives on community colleges (pp. 81–91). *New Directions for Community Colleges* (no. 143). San Francisco: Jossey-Bass.

Scott, N. A., & Spooner, S. (1989) Women administrators: Stressors and strategies. *Journal of NAWDAC, 52*(2), 31–36.

Strauss, A. (1987). *Qualitative analysis for social scientists.* New York: Cambridge University Press.

Strauss, A., & Corbin, J. (1990). *Basics of qualitative research: Grounded theory procedures and techniques.* Newbury Park, CA: Sage.

Taylor, S. J., & Bogdan, R. (1984). *Introduction to qualitative research: The search for meanings.* New York: John Wiley.

Tinsley, A. (1985). Upward mobility for women administrators. *NAWDAC Journal, 49*(1), 3–11.

Touchton, J., & Davis, L. (1991). *Fact book on women in higher education.* New York: Macmillan.

Twale, D. J. (1995, Summer). Gender comparisons of NASPA Membership. *NASPA Journal, 32*(4), 293–301.

Twale, D. J., & Jelinek, S. M. (1996). Proteges and mentors: Mentoring experiences of women student affairs professionals. *NASPA Journal, 33*(3), 203–217.

VanDerLinden, K. E. (2004). Gender differences in the preparation and promotion of community college administrators. *Community College Review, 31*(4), 1–24.

Ward, K., & Wolf-Wendel, L. (2005, Summer). Work and family perspectives from research university faculty. In J. W. Curtis (Ed.), The challenge of balancing faculty careers and faculty work (pp. 67–80). *New Directions for Higher Education* (no. 130). San Francisco: Jossey-Bass.

Warner, R., & DeFleur, L. (1993). Career paths of women in higher education administration. In P. Mitchell (Ed.), *Cracking the wall* (pp. 4–18), Washington, DC: College and University Personnel Association.

Wolf-Wendel, L., Ward, K., & Twombly, S. (2007). Faculty life at community college: The perspective of women with children. *Community College Review, 34*(4), 255–281.

Evaluation of Sexual Harassment Training Instructional Strategies

Mary Pilgram
Assistant Professor of Communication
Washburn University

Joann Keyton
Professor of Communication
North Carolina State University

> *This field experiment study evaluated a commercially produced online sexual harassment training program used in educational settings. Manipulation of instructional strategies (online, instructor, reading) examined effects on knowledge and behavioral identifications in sexual harassment training for college students. Training did not produce an immediate gain in knowledge scores regardless of training condition. However, reading and face-to-face training conditions predicted the correct answer of case-related questions on the posttest; reading and online training conditions predicted knowledge retention 3 weeks after the training. On video scenarios, participants correctly identified 54% of verbal and 30% of nonverbal sexual harassment cues. Participants overidentified 19% of verbal cues and 16% of nonverbal cues as sexual harassment.*

Much has been written about sexual harassment in the workplace (see Jansma, 2000; Keyton, 1996 for reviews). Moreover claims of sexual harassment in educational settings are also prevalent (see Dziech, 2003 for research review; *Chronicle of Higher Education*, 2006; Hill & Silva, 2005) and have been the setting for three of the eight groundbreaking court decisions about sexual harassment.

Based upon the Equal Employment Opportunity Commission definition (1980), sexual harassment includes harassment in many relationships. Most common is professor to student and student to student, but student harassment of faculty has also been reported (Carroll & Ellis, 1989; Meth & Nigg, 1983) The ramifications of sexual harassment can be serious and costly. Many organizations, including universities, have put training in place to educate employees about sexual harassment and protect themselves from liability. However, the effectiveness of training programs is rarely rigorously evaluated. This field experiment study evaluates an existing online sexual harassment training program and examines the effects of three instructional strategies on knowledge and behavioral identifications in sexual harassment training for college students

SEXUAL HARASSMENT IN HIGHER EDUCATION

Dziech (2003), who reviewed the incidence of sexual harassment over 20 years (1981–2002), found that of the 5,000 complaints received each year by the U.S. Department of Education's Office for Civil Rights, sexual harassment accounts for 70% of discrimination cases filed on behalf of female college students and 39% by male college students (American Association of University Women, 2002 as cited in Dziech). Female students are overwhelmingly targeted, (Fitzgerald & Ormerod, 1991; Struckman-Johnson, 1993). Females are also more likely than males to define specific behaviors as harassment (Hill & Silva, 2005). Student-to-student harassment is evident with as many as 90% of female students experiencing unwanted behavior from male peers (Sandler & Shoop, 1997); moreover, more than one-third of female (41%) and male (36%) students experience sexual harassment in their first year of college (Hill & Silva). Students report that they engage in sexual harassment because they think it is funny (59%), believe the victim liked it (32%), or believe it to be *no big deal* and a part of school life (30%; Hill & Silva).

Faculty-to-student harassment is also prevalent as nearly one-third of female undergraduates reported experiencing sexual harassment from faculty (Charney & Russell, 1994). Female graduate students have reported slightly higher figures (Fitzgerald, 1998; Schneider, 1987). Clearly, sexual harassment is a problem for females in higher education. Studies have also documented sexual harassment in intercollegiate debate (Stepp, 2001), medical school training (Hinze, 2004; White, 2000), and during fund-raising with alumni (Dougherty & Smythe, 2004).

Much has been written about cultural indicators of sexual harassment in business settings (see Keyton, Ferguson, & Rhodes, 2001). Recently,

Dougherty and Smythe (2004) indicated that academic organizations are particularly susceptible to chronic sexual harassment due to the prevalence of traditional sex roles that allocate formal and informal power to men who then marginalize women through a variety of practices. Hill and Silva (2005) note that college is a critical time for young adults. "In a culture marked with contradictory messages about sexuality and sexually aggressive behavior, it is no surprise that college students have different reactions to sexual harassment" (p. 36).

Sexual Harassment Training

The threat of litigation has forced all workplaces, including colleges and universities, to take preventative action by creating sexual harassment policies and reporting procedures and educating students, faculty, administrators, and staff. According to Kirkpatrick (1994), the purpose of training is to increase knowledge, improve skills, and change attitudes whether for present job improvement or for development in the future. However, Knapp and Kustis (1996) admit that many organizations put sexual harassment training in place simply to minimize their liability. Training may provide a level of legal protection, but it does not guarantee that there will be a translation from policy and procedure into changed behavior (Hill & Silva, 2005).

Even though some educational institutions have sexual harassment training available, in most cases it is for university employees, not students. Although many students work, Keyton and Rhodes (1999) found that even those with work experience identified fewer sexual harassment cues than full-time vested employees.

Research indicates how difficult it is to conduct sexual harassment training due to the lack of standards defining specific sexually harassing behaviors (see Keyton, 1996). Jansma's (2000) summary of sexual harassment training suggests that the training should cover three primary elements: (a) training to increase awareness, (b) formal policies prohibiting sexual harassment, and (c) complaint procedures for victims. Keyton et al. (2001) call for training that goes beyond the legal definition of sexual harassment and to giving "employees an opportunity to deliberate about the behaviors that they believe constitute sexual harassment" (p. 5). Effective training programs should enable individuals to distinguish between behavior that is and is not sexual harassment (Paludi & Paludi, 2003), as Keyton and Rhodes (1999) confirmed that some could not identify which verbal and nonverbal cues were sexual harassment. Being able to do so is critical. Dziech (2003) argues that "once people can label unacceptable behavior and language more precisely, they become more forbidding targets" (p. 166).

In the sexual harassment training literature, two primary issues noted are: (a) instructional strategy used and (b) training evaluation.

Instructional Strategy

An influence on the evaluation of training programs is the type of instructional strategy used. Instructional strategies can include both synchronous and asynchronous delivery mediums (Instructional Systems Design [ISD], 2004). Synchronous delivery is defined as real-time learning events in which all participants share the learning experience and may interact with each other, such as in a classroom (face-to-face) setting. Asynchronous delivery is defined as learning events that can be accessed at disparate times. Events can be designed for one person or multiple participants. However, interactions with other participants do not occur in real time (e.g., Web- or computer-based training, print or audio and visual materials with no live instructor present). As demonstrated by the nearly 300 colleges and universities using one online program (New Media Learning, 2005), many institutions are turning to asynchronous delivery mediums to address sexual harassment. However, no studies have been uncovered that have evaluated the effectiveness of sexual harassment training via online asynchronous or synchronous methods. In the few studies where the effects of specific instructional strategies have been isolated, findings have been mixed and inconclusive (Bonate & Jessell, 1996; Perry, Kulik, & Schmidtke, 1998; York, Barclay, & Zajack, 1997).

Evaluation of Sexual Harassment Training Effectiveness

Jansma (2000) indicates that empirical assessments of organizational-level strategies to reduce sexual harassment are rare. Although some evaluation of sexual harassment training has taken place, few studies "actually involve methodologically strong, empirical evaluations of existing policies, programs, and training that purport to have an impact on sexual harassment" (Pryor & McKinney, 1995, p. 609).

Jansma (2000) calls for a multilevel analysis of sexual harassment training, which Kirkpatrick's (1994) model of training evaluation describes. Kirkpatrick recommends that training effectiveness be evaluated on four levels. Level 1 is a reaction measure and assesses if training participants are satisfied with the sexual harassment training (e.g., Did they like it?). Level 2 is a learning/knowledge/attitude measure and assesses if training participants learn what was intended they learn about sexual harassment based on the course objectives (e.g., Can participants distinguish sexually harassing behavior from other behaviors?). Level 3 is a behavior measure and assesses how training participants are applying the knowledge gained about sexual harassment once the training has ended (e.g., If a student tells another student that she has been sexually harassed, how would the student respond to this revelation?). Level 4 is a results measure and assesses if there has been any effect on the institution (e.g., After the training are there more reports of sexual harassment?).

Sexual harassment training has been evaluated for effectiveness in business and educational settings. All studies located had a Level 2 knowledge and/or attitude measure; only two studies had a Level 3 application measure. No studies had Level 4 results measures. If Level 1 measures were conducted, they were not reported. Conducting evaluations of sexual harassment training is difficult and complex and explains why researchers have favored experimental over field methods. Methodological problems relative to sexual harassment research have been noted before (Grundmann, O'Donohue, & Peterson, 1977; Lengnick-Hall, 1995).

PURPOSE OF STUDY

This study advances the examination of sexual harassment training in three ways. First Bingham and Scherer (2001) call for ordinary training programs to be evaluated. Thus, field experiment methodology will be used to evaluate the effectiveness of an online sexual harassment program currently being used by nearly 300 educational institutions and an additional 300 business and government organizations (New Media Learning, 2005). Second, to capture multilevel evaluation in assessing training effectiveness (Jansma, 2000), two knowledge measures and one longitudinal knowledge measure were used. Because scholars (Keyton & Rhodes, 1999; Paludi & Paludi, 2003) have suggested that effective sexual harassment training programs include a component that enables individuals to distinguish between behavior that is and is not sexual harassment, this study includes behavior identification. The third way this study advances the study of sexual harassment is by evaluating content-similar instructional strategies to see if the topic of sexual harassment can be taught more effectively through online instruction, face-to-face instruction, or by reading a pamphlet about sexual harassment. Training content is kept constant across instructional strategies by basing the face-to-face and reading conditions on a commercially available online program used as the sexual harassment training at a 4-year university.

Hypotheses and Research Questions

Generally, the purpose of training is to increase knowledge, improve skills, and change attitudes whether for present job improvement or for development in the future (Kirkpatrick, 1994); these are consistent with the goals and objectives of the online training (New Media Learning, 2005). Thus, hypothesis 1 predicts that, as compared to pretest scores, participants will post a knowledge gain immediately after completing sexual harassment training. The training retention literature indicates retention rates begin to drop significantly after a 3-week period of time (ISD, 2004). Thus, hypothesis 2 predicts that as compared to posttest scores, participants will post a knowledge loss in follow-up scores 3 weeks after completing sexual harassment training.

Considering that instructional strategy could also influence training effects, research question 1 asks: Do posttest knowledge scores and follow-up knowledge scores 3 weeks after the training vary by instructional strategy? In addition to increasing knowledge, it is also possible that training could oversensitize participants, causing them to identify behavior as sexual harassment when it is not. Therefore, research question 2 asks: To what degree do participants identify or overidentify cues as sexual harassment behavior after completing sexual harassment training?

METHODS

The online sexual harassment training program is part of a training initiative at a public, 4-year, coeducational, residential, Midwestern university with a student population of 10,500. This commercially produced online program has been available at the university since 2004 and at the time of the study had been completed by 584 faculty and staff and 140 students employed by the university in student contact roles such as peer mentors, resident assistants, and new student orientation leaders. While all students, faculty, and staff are encouraged to take the online program, some are required to participate in the training. Training objectives include: identify behavior that might be considered sexual harassment, explain the legal and other consequences of sexual harassment, describe your role and responsibility in creating an academic and work environment free of sexual harassment, state what actions to take against sexual harassment, and describe university policies and procedures on sexual harassment.

Content and Evaluation of Online Training Program

The online training program content was designed by New Media Learning for delivery to business, government, and educational institutions. Its content is consistent with the recommendations by Paludi and Paludi (2003) for developing and enforcing effective policies, procedures, and training programs for educational institutions. These recommendations include a legal definition of sexual harassment, behavioral examples of sexual harassment, a policy statement, investigatory procedures, information regarding the effect of sexual harassment on individuals, and referrals for filing complaints and seeking psychotherapeutic support. There is no video or animation in the online presentation. The online content is merely a page-by-page, text and pictures presentation of facts and behavioral cues regarding sexual harassment.

Presently the evaluation of the effectiveness of this training program is done by using a Level 2 knowledge measure through a multiple choice mastery test, provided by the online supplier, taken at the end of the online training. If a participant scores 80% or better on the mastery test, they are sent a certificate of completion by the university's human resources department. If a participant does not score 80% on the mastery test, they have the opportunity to review the information they missed and immediately retake the exam. Failures to score 80% are not reported to the institution. Since the online training program is the existing training program for the university and because over 600 other organizations use the same online training, the online condition serves as the control group for this study.

Participants and Procedures

Students at a Midwestern university who had not participated in the university's online sexual harassment program signed up for time slots. Approximately 20 students signed up for each time slot. Time slots were randomly assigned to one of three training conditions. Participants were 323 undergraduate students (females = 163, males = 160) enrolled in various classes with a mean age of 20.7 (SD = 2.98). Their previous work experience averaged 5.5 years (SD = 2.79). The sample was comprised of 64 freshmen (19.75%), 122 sophomores (37.65%), 70 juniors (21.60%), and 68 seniors (20.99%); one participant did not report year in school. Only 48 (14.81%) had previous sexual harassment training. The sample size obtained (N = 323) exceeded that required for the power analysis (alpha = .05, power = .80, effect size = .20, N = 240).

Professors offered extra credit as an incentive to participate. Each participant came to a designated training room and completed an informed consent form. Participants completed a demographic questionnaire and took a written pretest of 10 factual based items and 5 case-type items (an equivalent version of the posttest that was supplied by the online provider) to assess prior knowledge level of sexual harassment. Next, each group participated in one of three content equivalent training sessions: an asynchronous online sexual harassment training program (N = 91), synchronous face-to-face sexual harassment training program (N = 137), or asynchronous condition of reading a pamphlet about sexual harassment (N = 95). The mean completion times for the three training conditions were: reading M = 39.73, SD = 7.91; online M = 37.96, SD = 6.79; and face-to-face M = 50.00, SD = 0.00. All three training conditions were monitored by the first author. An observer watched each face-to-face training session and provided feedback to ensure the first author was consistent in the delivery of material, presented the same information, and did not provide additional information or use additional activities to reinforce the information.

After completing training, each participant immediately took a written posttest to determine knowledge gain after the training (the same posttest as the mastery test provided by the online supplier). In addition, all participants took a behavioral identification posttest by viewing four video scenarios that showed peers in a work setting. This methodology follows a published protocol (Keyton et al., 1999, 2001); the content of the videos has been validated by Keyton and Menzie (2007) and Keyton (2008). Scenarios between two colleagues were taped in four conditions (friendly, dysfunctional, flirting, and sexually harassing) times two manipulations (sex of harasser). Taping was done to simulate a generalized, professional office setting. The same actors, who wore business casual attire, appeared in all four scenes. As a control, the same scripts were used for both sex manipulations. This choice was based on the literature showing no significant gender differences in communication between men and women (Canary & Dindia, 1998; Wood, 2002). After viewing one sexually-harassing, coercive, flirting, and professional scenario, participants were asked to identify each cue they believed to be sexual harassment by underlining these on a verbatim and nonverbally notated script. The set of videos shown varied to show either the male or female supervisor as the harasser; there were no effects for sex of the harasser. A second knowledge posttest (the same posttest given in the training) was administered via e-mail for each group 3 weeks after the training to test for knowledge retention. This time period was chosen based on the training retention literature indicating retention rates begin to drop significantly after a 3-week period of time (ISD, 2004). The return rate for the follow-up test via e-mail 3 weeks after the training was 82.35% (N = 266).

RESULTS

Hypotheses one and two were tested using repeated measures MANCOVA, with sex and prior sexual harassment training as covariates. Hypothesis one was not supported. Participants did not post a knowledge gain immediately after the training when looking at combined scores for the knowledge test of 10 fact items and 5 case items (pretest M = 12.31, SD = 1.38; posttest M = 11.64, SD = 1.40; follow-up M = 11.21, SD = 1.50). Hypothesis two was supported. Compared to posttest scores, all follow-up scores 3 weeks after the training showed a slight decrease in knowledge retention (see Table 1); there was a main effect for time $F(2, 406)$ = 4.25, p = < .015, r^2 = .02, as scores decreased.

Research question one was measured by repeated measures MANCOVA to determine if posttest scores and follow-up scores varied based on training condition. All combined scores decreased regardless of training condition (see Table 1). In a post hoc analysis, separating the fact scores (items 1–10) from the case scores (items 11–15), the *case scores* were significant for training condition, $F(2, 203)$ = 7.16, p = .001, r^2 = .02 (see Table 1; potential range from 0–5). In the reading and face-to-face conditions there was a short-term training gain from pretest to posttest scores. However, in the follow-up the scores were slightly lower than the posttest scores. Sex and prior sexual harassing training did not affect the dependent variables.

Examining fact scores only (items 1–10, see Table 1; potential range from 0–10) there was a significant time effect, $F(2, 406)$ = 2.98, p = <.052, r^2 = .01, as the scores on the follow-up test went up slightly from the posttest training scores for the reading and online training conditions but went down for the face-to-face condition.

TABLE 1. Knowledge scores by training condition at pretest, posttest, and follow-up.

	Combined Pretest[a]		Combined Posttest[b]		Combined Follow-up[c]	
Condition	M	SD	M	SD	M	SD
Reading	12.49	1.47	11.88	1.40	11.59	1.42
Online	12.47	1.36	11.55	1.38	11.27	1.46
Face-to-Face	12.21	1.34	11.77	1.41	11.13	1.36
	Case Pretest[d]		Case Posttest[e]		Case Follow-up[f]	
Reading	4.37	.83	4.63	.68	4.25	.84
Online	4.30	.68	4.17	.83	3.82	.93
Face-to-Face	4.19	.82	4.42	.72	3.95	.99
	Fact Pretest[g]		Fact Posttest[h]		Fact Follow-up[i]	
Reading	8.12	1.00	7.26	1.09	7.34	1.04
Online	8.17	1.00	7.38	.95	7.45	1.02
Face-to-Face	8.02	.96	7.35	1.09	7.18	.98

Note. Actual range of scores for combined, case, and fact scores.
[a]Actual range = 8–15. [b]Actual range = 7–15. [c]Actual range = 7–15. [d]Actual range = 1–5.

[e]Actual range = 1–5. [f]Actual range = 1–5. [g]Actual range = 5–10. [h]Actual range = 3–10.
[i]Actual range = 4–10.

The second research question asked was: "To what degree do participants identify or overidentify cues as sexual harassment behavior immediately after completing the sexual harassment training?" Overall, participants correctly identified more of the verbal sexual harassment cues (M = 53.88%, SD = 29.84%) than nonverbal sexual harassment cues (M = 29.95%, SD = 27.64%). Participants also *overidentified* more verbal cues as sexual harassment (M = 18.75%, SD = 19.21%) than nonverbal cues as sexual harassment (M = 16.16%, SD = 16.51%). Post hoc analysis ANOVAs revealed that only correct identification of nonverbal sexually harassing cues was predicted, $F(41, 311)$ = 1.67, p = .0096, r^2 = .20, with three main effects: training condition, $F(2, 311)$ = 3.16, p = .0440, r^2 = .02; prior sexual harassment training, $F(1, 311)$ = 4.10, p = .0440, r^2 = .01; and sex, $F(1, 311)$ = 6.09, p = .0142. r^2 = .02. As is shown in Table 2 those in the face-to-face training session correctly identified more nonverbal sexually harassing cues (34.18% correct) than did those in the other two training conditions (online 30.72%, reading 24.61%). Those that had some prior training in the topic of sexual harassment also correctly identified more nonverbal sexually harassing cues (34.73%) than those with no prior

TABLE 2. Percentages of correct identification of nonverbal sexual harassment cues.

Condition	M	SD
Reading	24.61%	24.84%
Online	30.72%	28.94%
Face-to-Face	34.17%	28.21%
Prior Training on Topic	**M**	**SD**
Yes	34.73%	27.37%
No	29.53%	27.66%
Sex	**M**	**SD**
Female	35.67%	28.08%
Male	24.60%	26.04%

training (29.53%). In addition, female participants correctly identified more of the nonverbal sexually harassing cues (35.67%) than did the male participants (24.60%).

DISCUSSION

An intriguing finding is that participants did not post a knowledge gain for the combined scores on the knowledge test immediately after the training. There was a time effect as scores decreased regardless of training condition. It appears that the training or the evaluation items confused participants in certain areas. Examination of the fact questions (items 1–10) shows that 5 were answered correctly in the pretest but missed on the posttest. For example, question 6 on the pretest asks true or false: "It is considered sexual harassment to tell a classmate of the opposite sex that he/she looks nice?" The correct answer is false, and 87% of the participants answered this question correctly on the pretest. However, only 54% answered it correctly on the posttest. Perhaps the training caused the participants to be overly sensitive (Keyton et al., 2001) and more cautious in identifying what constitutes sexual harassment after the training, supporting the complex nature of the topic. Some may have become paranoid, believing that to even pay a compliment to someone could be misinterpreted. Conversely, the evaluation items may not have been adequately written to capture knowledge gain. The goal of sexual harassment training is ultimately to sensitize participants to verbal and nonverbal sexually harassing behaviors, not oversensitize them to the point that participants may stop communication completely with coworkers in fear of offending them. If, as a result of the sexual harassment training, participants examine their own behavior and think carefully before speaking or acting based on their knowledge of sexual harassment, the goal of sensitization was reached.

Item 8 on the pretest asks true or false: "Title IX of the Education Amendments of 1972 extends Title VII of the Civil Rights Act and prohibits sexual harassment in educational settings?" The correct answer is true, and 81% of the participants answered this question correctly in the pretest. However, only 17% answered it correctly in the posttest. The posttest asks an equivalent question stating that Title IX prohibits sexual harassment in *any work setting*. The answer to this question is false. This type of legal minutia may be too much for students to digest, and it is unclear if knowing these types of facts helps individuals describe and identify sexual harassment. Despite the suggestion that sexual harassment training evaluations should focus on sexual harassment behaviors (Keyton et al., 2001), this type of fact-based question is representative of posttests included with many sexual harassment training programs.

Research question 1 asked if posttest knowledge and follow-up scores would vary by training condition. Posttest scores did not vary by training condition when looking at the overall knowledge test. However, the case scores were significant with a main effect for training condition. In the reading and face-to-face training conditions, there was a short-term training gain from pretest to posttest scores. This indicates that the participants understood the content relating to the case questions, and this content is stressed considerably in the training itself. Item 13 was the only case question where the posttest score went down significantly (from 88% correct to 72% correct). This item deals with identifying a hostile work environment. This terminology may have been confusing as participants confuse having a supervisor in a bad mood that yells at the employees and leaves the office in a rage (e.g., showing hostility) as a hostile work environment, even though this is not wholly consistent with the definition of *sexual* harassment. Reading and face-to-face settings are the more common ways of learning in a university setting for educational purposes, so it is not surprising that there was a gain in the posttest scores from those two training conditions.

The scores on the follow-up test went up slightly for the reading and online training conditions, but went down for the face-to-face condition.

This result might be explained by the passive learning experience of a lecture (ISD, 2004). Greater personal engagement is required in the learning process in the reading and online training conditions.

When examining the pretest and posttests (from the mastery test supplied by the online training provider), it is questionable if these items were the most useful for evaluating knowledge. For example, all but one of the questions use a true/false response format. It is possible that pretest scores were high due to this testing format. The one multiple choice item on the pretest was most missed. Choosing a response rather than having a 50/50 guess possibly reflected a truer knowledge base as a starting point to the training. Though it is possible that some of the training content confused the participants, it is likely the format of the items on the pretest, and equivalent posttest and follow-up tests were also a factor.

All instructional design processes stress the importance of evaluation of each learning objective to determine training effectiveness (Dick, Carey, & Carey, 2004; Kirkpatrick, 1994; Mager, 1997). Of the 15 posttest items, most were relevant to the first two course objectives concerning identifying sexually harassing behavior and explaining the legal consequences of this behavior. Even though the training content addresses the remaining three objectives, there are no corresponding test questions. Alternately, every item on the test was covered in the training content. Therefore, for future training sessions, the posttest should include items for all learning objectives. In addition, the course objectives are written to assess knowledge gain at the two lower levels of learning on Bloom's Taxonomy (1956), which are knowledge (recall) and comprehension, which is defined as the ability to grasp the meaning of material. The results show that negotiating the gray area of sexual harassment is difficult. Sexual harassment training should consider instruction on behavior identification skills that require higher order thinking and learning outcomes based on Bloom's Taxonomy.

Case studies describe actual problems that exist in organizations. A major assumption of the case study type questions is that participants are more likely to recall and use knowledge and skills if they learn through a process of discovery. "Cases may be especially appropriate for developing higher-order intellectual skills such as analysis, synthesis, and evaluation" (Noe, 2002, p. 225). The case study items on the pretest, posttest, and follow-up tests do provide for assessment of a higher level learning skill such as application, defined as the ability to use learned material in new and concrete situations. However, the true or false response format limits their effectiveness. Open-ended case questions where participants have to craft a response would be a stronger way to test for this knowledge. An example of such a case-type open-ended item would be: Joe frequently tells sexually-explicit jokes during team meetings. Other students in the group are very offended. They don't think Joe's jokes are so funny. Joe believes his behavior is not at risk because the jokes are all in fun and are not intended to sexually harass anyone. Identify whether this scenario depicts sexual harassment and state why or why not.

This type of open-ended question challenges participants to demonstrate and apply their knowledge of sexual harassment. Modifying all of the case study questions in this way would be a strong addition to the evaluation measure.

Hypothesis two was supported showing that follow-up scores 3 weeks later fell slightly as expected. However, these retention scores are much better than would be expected according to the learning retention literature, which states that only 18% of the content would likely be retained after 3 weeks, as participants will naturally forget information as time passes (ISD, 2004).

Adding the video tapes as an evaluation measure to this sexual harassment training provided the opportunity for participants to demonstrate the transfer of Kirkpatrick's (1994) Level 2 knowledge to Level 3 application. Thus, the second research question asked: "To what degree do participants identify or overidentify cues as sexual harassment behavior immediately after completing the sexual harassment training?" There were three main effects in predicting the correct identification of nonverbal sexually harassing cues: training condition, prior training on the topic of sexual harassment, and sex. Those in the face-to-face training session correctly identified more nonverbal sexually harassing cues than did those in the other two training conditions. Those that had some prior training in the topic of sexual harassment also correctly identified more nonverbal sexually harassing cues than those with no prior training. In addition, female participants identified more of the nonverbal sexually harassing cues correctly (M = 36%) than did the male participants (M = 25%). These findings are in line with Hill and Silva (2005), who found that female students are more likely to be the target of sexual jokes, comments, gestures, or looks; and with Ivy and Hamlet (1996), who found that males expressed a need for a clear-cut, concrete definition of sexual harassment so they could avoid those behaviors. Still, we question if these identification scores are high enough to actually prevent sexual harassment.

As has been noted, those in the face-to-face training condition correctly identified more of the nonverbal sexual harassment cues than those in the other two training conditions. The authors speculate the participants may have been watching the nonverbals of the training facilitator as she presented the training content about nonverbals and sexual harassment, and she likely may have leaked some information about the value of some nonverbals or which types of nonverbals were preferred or not. Perhaps this sensitized participants to the nonverbal cues as this (a live facilitator who was animated in her presentation) was the missing component for the reading and online training groups.

IMPLICATIONS FOR FUTURE SEXUAL HARASSMENT TRAINING

If universities are truly interested in protecting themselves from liability, they would be protected more if the training used was effective at preventing sexual harassment behaviors. Trainees should be able to do more than just regurgitate legal facts and figures. The results suggest that a face-to-face component should be used to train college students about sexual harassment, as students in the face-to-face sessions identified more nonverbal sexual harassment cues correctly than those in the other instructional strategies. The correct identification of nonverbal cues is critical in preventing sexual harassment. Having a face-to-face component is necessary for students to ask questions and for the trainer to ensure that participants can correctly identify sexually harassing behaviors. In addition, having a facilitator present would help address issues around hypersensitive responses to interpersonal interactions (e.g., complimenting someone on his/her outfit and thinking this might be sexual harassment). These fine distinctions can be made and stressed in the training to ensure appropriate workplace behavior. Therefore, a multimodal approach to sexual harassment training is recommended.

Another interesting implication of the findings was how high the pretest scores were for the college population. The participants' high scores suggest that they knew a significant amount about sexual harassment coming into the training session. Therefore, in training this population in the future, it might be appropriate to begin the training session by identifying what they know and building on that versus assuming they know nothing about the topic. Another suggestion would be giving a pretest prior to attending the training session and tailoring the content based on the pretest results.

This study also raises the question about the difference between statistically, practically, and socially significant results. Educational institutions are mandated by law to provide information about the prevention of sexual harassment. Many institutions do this by offering training on the topic. Especially in educational institutions, why is the method of training not evaluated for its effectiveness? From a social standpoint, knowing that young adults may be better informed to prevent sexual harassment is key, especially when college students report a fear of being sexually harassed at the same time they believe sexual harassment is funny and just a part of school life (Hill & Silva, 2005). Knowing the behaviors and how to address those behaviors will be critical in preventing sexual harassment on college campuses and in future workplaces. Perhaps this training should be required and incorporated into new student or freshman orientation.

In future assessments of training effectiveness, evaluations should include higher-order learning rather than simple recall of information. Effectiveness of the training should be measured using case-based questions and behavioral identification measures. The ultimate goal of sexual harassment training should be for participants to demonstrate that they can identify sexually harassing verbal and nonverbal behaviors. This is the piece that will be most important in helping institutions create a culture that fosters a harassment-free environment for women and all those involved in higher education.

REFERENCES

American Association of University Women. (2002). *A license for bias: Sex discrimination, schools, and Title IX.* Washington, DC: Author.

Bingham, S. G., & Scherer, L. L. (2001). The unexpected effects of a sexual harassment educational program. *Journal of Applied Behavioral Sciences, 37,* 125–153.

Bloom, B. S. (1956). *Taxonomy of educational objectives: The classification of educational goals.* New York: Longman.

Bonate, D. L., & Jessell, J. C. (1996). The effects of educational intervention on perceptions of sexual harassment. *Sex Roles, 35,* 751–764.

Canary, D., & Dindia, K. (1998). *Sex differences and similarities in communication.* Mahwah, NJ: Erlbaum.

Carroll, L., & Ellis, K. (1989). Faculty attitudes toward sexual harassment: Survey results, survey process. *Initiatives, 52,* 35–41.

Charney, P., & Russell, R. (1994). An overview of sexual harassment. *American Journal of Psychiatry, 151*, 10–17.

Chronicle of Higher Education. (2006). Retrieved June 1, 2006, from www.chronicle.com

Dick, W. O., Carey, L., & Carey, J. O. (2004). *The systematic design of instruction* (6th ed.). New York: Allyn & Bacon.

Dougherty, D. S., & Smythe, M. J. (2004). Sensemaking, organizational culture, and sexual harassment. *Journal of Applied Communication Research, 32*, 293–317.

Dziech, B. W. (2003). Sexual harassment on college campuses. In M. Paludi & C. A. Paludi (Eds.), *Academic and workplace sexual harassment: A handbook of cultural, social science, management, and legal perspectives* (pp. 147–171). Westport, CT: Praeger.

Fitzgerald, L. (1998). The incidence and dimensions of sexual harassment in academia and the workplace. *Journal of Vocational Behavior, 32*, 152–175.

Fitzgerald, L., & Ormerod, A. (1991). Perceptions of sexual harassment: The influence of gender and academic context. *Psychology of Women Quarterly, 15*, 281–294.

Grundmann, E. O., O'Donohue, W., & Peterson, S. H. (1997). The prevention of sexual harassment. In W. O'Donohue (Ed.), *Sexual harassment: Theory, research, and treatment* (pp. 175–184). Boston: Allyn and Bacon.

Hill, C., & Silva, E. (2005). *Drawing the line: Sexual harassment on campus*. Washington, DC: AAUW Educational Foundation.

Hinze, S. W. (2004) 'Am I being oversensitive?' Women's experience of sexual harassment during medical training. *Health, 8*, 101–127.

Instructional Systems Design. (2004). Instructional systems design (ISD): Specifying instructional strategies. Retrieved December 5, 2004, from www.nedc.nrcs.usda.gov/isd/isd8.html

Ivy, D. K., & Hamlet, S. (1996). College students and sexual dynamics: Two studies of peer sexual harassment. *Communication Education, 45*, 149–166.

Jansma, L. J. (2000). Sexual harassment research: Integration, reformulation, and implications for mitigation efforts. In M. E. Roloff (Ed.), *Communication yearbook 23* (pp. 163–225). Thousand Oaks, CA: Sage.

Keyton, J. (1996). Sexual harassment: A multidisciplinary synthesis and critique. In B. R. Burleson (Ed.), *Communication yearbook 19* (pp. 93–155). Thousand Oaks, CA: Sage.

Keyton, J. (2008). Distinguishing supervisor coercion from sexual harassment. *Journal of Communication Studies, 1,* 5–19. Retrieved August 13, 2008, from http://www.marquettejournals.org/images/JCSVol1No1np.pdf

Keyton, J., Ferguson, P., & Rhodes, S. C. (2001). Cultural indicators of sexual harassment. *Southern Communication Journal, 67,* 33–50.

Keyton, J., & Menzie, K. (2007). Sexually harassing messages: Decoding workplace conversation. *Communication Studies, 58,* 87–103.

Keyton, J., & Rhodes, S. C. (1999). Organizational sexual harassment: Translating research into application. *Journal of Applied Communication Research, 27,* 158–173.

Kirkpatrick, D. L. (1994) *Evaluating training programs: The four levels* (2nd ed.). New York: Berrett-Koehler.

Knapp, D. E., & Kustis, G. A. (1996). The real "disclosure": Sexual harassment and the bottom line. In M. S. Stockdale (Ed.), *Sexual harassment in the workplace,* vol. 5 (pp. 199–213). Thousand Oaks, CA: Sage.

Lengnick-Hall, M. L. (1995). Sexual harassment research: A methodological critique. *Personnel Psychology, 48,* 841–864.

Mager, R. F. (1997). *Making instruction work* (2nd ed.). Atlanta: CEP Press.

Meth, A., & Nigg, J. (1983). Sexual harassment on campus: An institutional response. *Journal of National Association of Women Deans, Administrators, and Counselors, 46,* 23–29.

New Media Learning. (2005). Retrieved September 15, 2005, from www.newmedialearning.com

Noe, R. A. (2002). *Employee training and development* (2nd ed.). New York: McGraw-Hill.

Paludi, C. A., & Paludi, M. (2003). Developing and enforcing effective policies, procedures, and training programs for educational institutions and businesses. In M. Paludi & C. A. Paludi (Eds.), *Academic and workplace sexual harassment: A handbook of cultural, social science, management, and legal perspectives* (pp. 175–198). Westport, CT: Praeger.

Perry, E. L., Kulik, C. T., & Schmidtke, J. M. (1998). Individual differences in the effectiveness of sexual harassment awareness training, *Journal of Applied Social Psychology, 28,* 698–723.

Pryor, J. B., & McKinney, K. (1995). Research on sexual harassment: Lingering issues and future directions. *Basic and Applied Social Psychology, 17,* 605–611.

Sandler, B. R., & Shoop, R. J. (1997). Student to student sexual harassment. *Sexual harassment on campus: A guide for administrators, faculty and students.* Needham Heights, MA: Allyn & Bacon.

Schneider, B. E. (1987). Graduate women, sexual harassment, and university policy. *Journal of Higher Education, 58,* 46–65.

Stepp, P. L. (2001). Sexual harassment in communication extra-curricular activities: Intercollegiate debate and individual events. *Communication Education, 50,* 34–50.

Struckman-Johnson, C. (1993). College men's and women's reactions to hypothetical sexual touch varied by initiator gender and coercion level. *Sex Roles, 29,* 371–385.

White, G. E. (2000). Sexual harassment during medical training: The perceptions of medical students at a university medical school in Australia. *Medical Education, 34,* 980–986.

Wood, J. T. (2002). A critical response to John Gray's Mars and Venus portrayals of men and women. *Southern Communication Journal, 67,* 201–210.

York, K. M., Barclay, L. A., & Zajack, S. B. (1997). Preventing sexual harassment: The effect of multiple training methods. *Employee Responsibilities and Rights, 10,* 277–289.

Program Descriptions

The Alice M. Baldwin Scholars Program

Colleen Scott — Duke University

In 2002–03, University President Nannerl Keohane led The Women's Initiative, a qualitative research project on the status of women at Duke. Focus group discussions were conducted with undergraduate and graduate students, faculty, staff, alumnae, and trustees.

The undergraduate findings were disturbing. The research team, led by Dr. Donna Lisker, found that undergraduate women experience a drop in self-confidence between matriculation and graduation. Students cited a phenomenon called "effortless perfection," which they described as the pressure to achieve both academically and personally; to have straight A's; and to be pretty, thin, and fashionable, all without visible effort. They compared effortless perfection to a duck on a pond, floating gracefully on the surface but paddling madly beneath. Students noted a gap between first-year and upperclass women; because the two groups are housed on different campuses at Duke, their only significant contact is in the classroom or through the sorority system. They lamented the lack of connection and mentoring between women. Further, the researchers found women's campus leadership focused primarily in sororities, community service, and the arts. Male students dominate campus-wide leadership positions in Duke Student Government and Campus Council.

The Women's Initiative results inspired the creation of the Alice M. Baldwin Scholars program. Modeled after the Women Involved in Living and Learning (WILL) program at the University of Richmond, the Baldwin Scholars program seeks to provide a nurturing and challenging environment for women to find their passions and create positive change.

Eighteen first-year women are selected each fall semester. Through a competitive process, interviewers identify women with high self-awareness and leadership potential, women who see themselves as change agents. At this time, the program is limited to 72 total students for financial reasons; an official review in fall 2008 may allow the program to expand opportunities to more women in future years.

The program has four main components: a first-year seminar, a sophomore residential experience, a paid internship, and a senior capstone seminar. The first-year seminar, entitled "Perceptions of Self, Society, and the Natural World," introduces the women to female faculty members and to new areas of study that will push them out of their comfort zones. During their sophomore year, Baldwin Scholars live together in upperclass housing, inviting a non-Baldwin Scholar roommate if they choose. Students complete their internship requirement the summer before or after their junior year; with the support of the Career Center, students find an internship in a field they would like to explore. Funding is provided to support their living expenses. The senior seminar, entitled "Women and the Professions," examines women in careers from historical, current, and future perspectives.

In addition to these main components, the program offers lectures, dinner discussions, retreats, and other activities that help the women connect with each other and network with faculty and alumni. There is also a mentoring component where each first-year Baldwin is assigned to a sophomore, junior, and senior in the program; the mentor-mentee groups are encouraged to meet informally but regularly.

The staff designed an assessment instrument that the Scholars complete before they start the program, at graduation, and 5 years after they graduate. The survey is also administered to women who expressed interest in the program but did not apply, and women who applied but were not selected.

Since the first class of Baldwin Scholars graduated in May 2008, this instrument has only collected one set of "post-program" data. The graduating Baldwin Scholars reported much higher self-confidence, self-knowledge, and belief in the possibility of change than did their peers. They grew in confidence speaking in public even when they knew their views would be unpopular. They demonstrate greater awareness of women's issues, and they see themselves as highly qualified leaders. Their peers tended to stay the same or even decline slightly in all these markers. Their mean cumulative GPA was also significantly higher than either of the control groups.

Contact: Colleen Scott   colleen.scott@duke.edu

REAL Collaborative: Research for the Educational Advancement of Latin@s

Iliana Alanís, Kimberley K. Cuero, Mariela A. Rodríguez —
The University of Texas at San Antonio

Earning a terminal degree and securing tenure-track positions within research institutions has proven to be a difficult path for Latinas to follow (Contreras, 1995; Aguirre, 2000; Padilla, 2003). Of the more than 145,000 assistant professors identified in 2001, fewer than half were women; Latinas held only 2,200 of those positions (National Center for Education Statistics, 2005). Historically, Latinas have encountered barriers to success and have struggled to have their voices heard within the walls of the ivory tower (Luna, 2000; Turner & Myers, 2000). Given these dismal statistics, we believed it was important to form a community of researchers who studied issues in education pertinent to Latina/os in public schools and institutions of higher learning.

Research for the Educational Advancement of Latin@s (REAL) is an interdisciplinary research collaborative housed in The Women's Studies Institute at The University of Texas at San Antonio (UTSA). It is primarily comprised of Latina tenure-track faculty from UTSA and Trinity University who are interested in researching Latina/o issues in education from various perspectives (e.g., educational leadership and policy studies, bicultural/bilingual studies, curriculum and instruction, special education, and educational psychology). The purpose of REAL is to represent the voices of a new generation of Latinas in the academy and to document their journey through specific values of support, persistence, and legitimacy. The primary goals of this collaborative are: to engage in active interdisciplinary research with a focus on Latina/o issues, to present collaboratively at national and international conferences, and to provide collegial support through the tenure-track process.

Members of REAL engage in multiple activities that contribute to both the collaborative and the larger educational community. A primary role of founding members is to recruit and mentor newly hired Latina junior faculty interested in similar issues and to schedule informal seminars where senior Latina faculty interpret and legitimize the matriarchical influences that shape REAL members' research agendas. To further develop their scholarship, REAL holds quarterly writing retreats. These 3-day retreats (at a member's home) provide extended periods of time to prepare manuscripts for peer-reviewed publications. Many of these are collaborative research projects where REAL members engage in multiple projects that strengthen their commitment to Latina/o education and to each other. Additionally, members participate in presentations in relation to joint research and REAL's mission at national, regional, and local conferences. Finally, REAL also seeks professional development grants for intensive faculty professional growth opportunities to serve as an impetus for developing existing research agendas.

REAL members are equally and strategically committed to including others in their research and writing. In this sense, most of their work is coauthored with other scholars within the REAL collaborative. Consequently, achieving academic success is not an individual endeavor; it involves building community and community uplift as they extend the dialogue related to women in the academy and make contributions to the field of education.

Contact: Dr. Iliana Alanís   iliana.alanis@utsa.edu

REFERENCES

Aguirre, Jr., A. (2000). *Women and minority faculty in the academic workplace: Recruitment, retention, and academic culture.* San Francisco: Jossey-Bass.

Contreras, A. R. (1995). The odyssey of a Chicano academic. In R.V. Padilla & R. Chávez Chávez, *The leaning ivory tower: Latino professors in American universities* (pp. 111–129). New York: SUNY Press.

Luna, C. M. (2000). Narratives from Latina professors in higher education. *Anthropology & Education Quarterly, 31*(1), 47–66.

National Center for Education Statistics. (2005). *Educational attainment of the population 15 years and over, by age, sex, race, and Hispanic origin: 2004.* U.S. Census Bureau, Current Population Survey. Available at www.nces.ed.gov.

Padilla, R. V. (2003). Barriers to accessing the professoriate. In J. Castellanos & L. Jones (Eds.), *The majority in the minority: Expanding the representation of Latina/o faculty, administrators, and students in higher education* (pp. 179–204). Sterling, VA: Stylus.

Turner, C. S., & Myers, S. J. (2000). *Faculty of color in academe: Bittersweet success.* Boston: Allyn & Bacon.

Young Women Leaders Program

Edith Lawrence, Keonya Booker, Lauren Germain —
The University of Virginia

The Young Women Leaders Program (YWLP) is a yearlong youth mentoring program that has operated at the University of Virginia since 1997 and has recently expanded to other sites. To date, it has trained more than 900 college women to be mentors and has served more than 800 middle school girls. The program focuses on supporting the developmental and leadership needs of both college women and middle school girls within the context of a university-community partnership. It is distinguished from other mentoring programs by its: (1) research-based curriculum, (2) combination of one-on-one and group activities, (3) emphasis on mentor training and weekly supervision, and (4) commitment to ongoing program evaluation. Although programs that incorporate a higher number of research-supported mentoring program practices such as these have been found to have larger outcome effect sizes, the degree to which YWLP also meets the needs of both university and community stakeholders may be more relevant to its sustainability as a successful partnership.

The first step in the development of YWLP was an investigation by faculty at the University of Virginia of the mentoring needs of the youth in the community. Meetings with area middle and high school personnel and, later, parents of youth this age, identified the need for a mentoring initiative that helped at-risk middle school girls. Once the community need was determined, university faculty and students reviewed the literature on adolescent development and risk behavior prevention in order to identify evidence-based practices in mentoring. The YWLP curriculum focuses on enhancing both the middle school girls' and college women's self-worth and perceptions of themselves as leaders by nurturing their existing competencies, providing them with meaningful opportunities for connections, and highlighting their ability to be independent thinkers.

During the year of mentoring, the college women meet each week with the seven other mentors from their group and a facilitator to review the curriculum and discuss group and mentoring issues. The facilitator, a former YWLP mentor herself, is responsible for organizing the weekly mentoring and supervision group meetings, as well as providing individual problem-solving consultation should a pair have difficulties. This weekly peer supervision not only bonds the women to each other and to the program, but also provides an adequate level of monitoring. Finally, to ensure that the mentors have a comprehensive understanding of the issues underlying the group curriculum, YWLP requires that they enroll in a course taught by qualified faculty. The course explores the various biological, psychological, social, and cultural issues affecting adolescent girls and college women and, then, integrates this learning into what is known about "best practices" in mentoring.

By providing all the college participants with numerous opportunities to test their theoretical knowledge and its application through supervised service learning, YWLP clearly meets the needs of the university. At the same time, restricting the opportunity to mentor and supervise to those who are trained and supervised themselves enables YWLP to also meet the needs of the community.

Contact: Edith Lawrence   wlawrence@virginia.edu

Book Reviews

Through the Labyrinth: The Truth About How Women Become Leaders

by Alice H. Eagly & Linda L. Carli. Boston: Harvard Business School Press, 2007. 336 pp. ISBN-13: 978-1-4221-1691-3 (hardcover)

Reviewed by Paige Haber—University of San Diego

Through the Labyrinth is an engaging and thorough analysis of women's leadership. It examines key questions that illustrate women's leadership of the past, present, and future. Accessible to readers from various disciplines and backgrounds, it reflects a strong balance of rich research, relatable examples, and clear discussion.

Focusing primarily on women leaders in organizational leadership, the book addresses the issue of the scarcity of women in powerful leadership roles. The labyrinth is a metaphor the authors introduce to describe the underrepresentation of women in top executive roles. As opposed to more conventionally used metaphors, such as the concrete wall (women are not allowed) and the glass ceiling (women are allowed to a certain point but no further), the labyrinth explains how some women have broken through and gained access to top leadership positions. The authors demonstrate how women must navigate a labyrinth of twists, turns, barriers, and dead ends that men often do not. Research indicates women leaders are emerging through the labyrinth at higher rates today than ever before and are predicted to continue to progress in leadership attainment.

A number of forces are presented as explanation of the increasing presence of women and the continued dominance of men in leadership roles. Through extensive literature review and research, the authors identify a number of key findings. Rejecting the evolutionary stance that leadership capacity is inherent in men but not women, Eagly and Carli find the traits contributing to leadership are not dominantly one sex or another; rather, they tend to equally reflect masculine and feminine traits. Examining domestic work, research shows that men are increasingly taking on more responsibility with housework and childcare. Despite this, women still have considerably more domestic responsibility than men, a fact that holds them back in leadership attainment.

Additionally, women face disadvantages in the workplace in both promotion and wage categories. By examining gender role associations and stereotypes, the authors highlight the disadvantage women have due to people's mental models of what constitutes a leader (mostly masculine qualities) and the resulting resistance to women leaders. The collaborative leadership styles of women are an advantage and highly desired in today's complex organizations. Regardless, organizations, which are often led by men, tend to reflect more hierarchical leadership and encompass norms that disadvantage women. This helps explain why many women in top positions are entrepreneurs or work in newer industries (such as technology). The book concludes with strategies that may be used to navigate the labyrinth and a hopeful, yet realistic, look at what the future may hold for women's leadership.

The strengths of this book greatly overshadow any limitations. Strong on methodology, the authors synthesize a plethora of research studies, government data, anecdotal pieces, mainstream news, and literature into the book that span different disciplines (40 pages of endnotes and a 15-page author index!). The integration of sources is clear, and the authors create a coherent picture of women's leadership today. Additionally, the book's organization facilitates the progression of the discussion; each chapter focuses on a different question (i.e., Is discrimination still a problem?). This is helpful for readers who are looking for specific information. Also, each chapter can be read on its own. By separating the arguments by chapters, the authors are able to fully dissect an argument, draw on relevant literature, and provide a strong discussion leading to overall conclusions.

The book's primary focus is business leadership, which is a valuable frame for college student educators who help prepare students for life after college. Studies highlighted in the book on high school students resulted in leadership being shared about equally among men and women. In contrast, college men have tended to take on leadership more often in small group studies than college women, and the disparity is even greater after. This speaks to the importance of the college environment in providing opportunities for women to engage in and gain confidence in leadership. To that end, this book can provide valuable knowledge for college student educators to understand. In turn they can educate college women about the labyrinth they are likely to face and strategies for navigating it. Finally, women working in higher education can benefit from understanding the labyrinth in which they themselves may be operating as they strive for senior leadership positions.

Although the issues discussed in the book are relevant to all women, the heavy business leadership focus may not provide as much insight to leadership in other vocations. Additionally, the view of leadership as positional can be limiting in understanding the presence of leadership outside of a positional role. A positional definition of leadership is often challenged by leadership studies scholars (Heifetz, 1994; Komives, Lucas, & McMahon, 2007; Rost, 1991), who emphasize leadership as a group process. With that said, this book is inarguably a significant contribution to our understanding of women in top leadership roles in our society, discrimination toward women, and how women leaders are viewed.

This work serves as a welcome complement to the existing women's leadership literature. Heffernan's (2007) *How She Does It* focuses on success stories of women entrepreneurs, and Helgesen's (1990) *The Female Advantage* studied four successful business women. *Through the Labyrinth* provides a strong macro view that these books do not. Kellerman and Rhode's (2007) *Women and Leadership* is a valuable compilation of essays on women's leadership from different scholars. In comparison, *Through the Labyrinth* pulls together much research to create a comprehensive whole with generalizable findings.

College student educators working with female students in many capacities, especially leadership programs and career counseling, will benefit from the comprehensive nature of this book. It is a must-read for people interested in women's leadership and management, and it has applications across many career fields. *Through the Labyrinth* is a gold mine of valuable information and a considerable contribution to many fields of study and practice.

REFERENCES

Heffernan, M. (2007). *How she does it: How women entrepreneurs are changing the rules of business success.* New York: Viking.

Heifetz, R. A. (1994). *Leadership without easy answers.* Cambridge, MA: Harvard University Press.

Helgesen, S. (1990). *The female advantage.* New York: Doubleday.

Komives, S. R., Lucas, N., & McMahon, T. R. (2007). *Exploring leadership: For college students who want to make a difference* (2nd ed.). San Francisco: Jossey-Bass.

Rost, J. C. (1991). *Leadership for the twenty-first century.* Westport, CT: Praeger.

Challenges of the Faculty Career for Women: Success and Sacrifice

by Maike Ingrid Philipsen. San Francisco: Jossey-Bass, 2008. 341 pp. ISBN: 978-0-470-25700-5 (hardcover)

Reviewed by Jeni Hart—University of Missouri

Challenges of the Faculty Career for Women: Success and Sacrifice by Maike Ingrid Philipsen is a rich qualitative analysis of the experiences of 46 women faculty at various stages in their careers, with varying life circumstances, and working for five markedly different institutions within one Mid-Atlantic state. The foreword by Mary Deane Sorcinelli reinforces the book's intent, which is to discover the nature of women's faculty lives, the complex challenges they confront, and the mechanisms they use to navigate work and personal lives. Philipsen identifies challenges through the voices of her study participants and highlights the "relative success" (p. 136) of the faculty in her research. Ultimately, she found that the women in her study were resilient and persisted, despite the obstacles they confronted. The relative nature of their success was predicated upon the fact that they did face challenges and often had to make difficult choices that came at a cost to themselves, their families and friends, or aspects of their academic careers.

The book is divided into five chapters and preceded by an introduction that describes the methods used for her study. The introduction is a comprehensive explanation of Philipsen's qualitative research design and includes an autoethnographic perspective that enhances the reflexivity and trustworthiness of her analysis. The first three chapters follow the three stages of a faculty member's career: early, mid, and late career. Through participant narratives and supporting scholarship, each chapter presents salient themes for the women faculty she interviewed at particular stages of their careers. The primary themes coalesced around life and identity characteristics, like being single, having an academic partner, having children, caring for partners or parents, and being a nonnative born scholar. Each chapter identifies three or four challenges or sacrifices experienced by women faculty in her study, most of which are shaped by the unique life and identity characteristics described above; each chapter concludes with how faculty cope and manage challenges and sacrifices.

Chapter four compares the themes found throughout the career stages. Philipsen found that while many things have improved for women faculty over time and the span of a career, problems still exist, particularly sexism (both subtle and overt), increased workload demands, and ongoing inequities between the genders in terms of family care. The themes did not differ greatly based upon the faculty members' discipline or field of study, and very little difference was described based upon institution type. Thus, it is likely that her findings are strongly transferrable to other women academics.

Chapter five highlights recommendations made by the participants in Philipsen's research. First, participants make general and specific recommendations to transform academe into an environment that better supports its entire faculty. Second, she shares advice from her study participants intended to help women faculty and graduate students navigate the existing academic system. Finally, Philipsen concludes the book with a summary and points out some of its unique contributions.

This book makes several contributions to the existing scholarship about women faculty. First, the study uses powerful narratives to describe the personal and professional lives of women faculty. While I challenge Philipsen's assertion that firsthand accounts are missing from the extant literature (for example, see Coiner & George, 1998; Kolodny, 1998; Monroe, Ozyurt, Wrigley, & Alexander, 2008; and chapters from edited books by Bracken, Allen, & Dean, 2006; and Jacobs, Cintrón, & Canton, 2002), her study does complement other faculty narratives and provides a strong method to ground her analysis.

Second, the study looks at the experiences of women faculty in a variety of institutional types. Often, studies focus on faculty in one type of institution, most often research universities. Philipsen's study provides some insight into the lives of women faculty at an historically Black university, a community college, a public research university, a private comprehensive university, and a large urban research university. However, she did not disaggregate her analysis by institution type. This sort of analysis would have been an interesting and valuable contribution, although it may have been outside the scope of the study.

Third, themes and narratives that address the experiences of immigrant scholars, single faculty, faculty doing eldercare, lesbian faculty, mid-career faculty, and faculty considering retirement are underrepresented in the existing literature on women faculty. Philipsen's perspectives on these faculty are valuable contributions. The racial make-up of her participants, especially for "colonized minorities" (Moody, 2004, p. 3), is somewhat homogenous, despite her claim that she sought out racial/ethnic diversity. Understanding the experiences of historically underrepresented women faculty in the United States also may have been outside the scope of her study, but including some of these women as part of her "purposeful sample" (p. 7) would have strengthened the overall transferability.

Fourth, Philipsen offers some creative recommendations that would transform faculty work. She proposes an exemplar model for tenure that would accommodate faculty who have myriad demands on their lives, either as a consequence of work, family, or a combination of the two. As she states, most of the other recommendations are not unique; however, they do serve to challenge and repair the academic system, not to "fix the women," as so many of the other approaches to improving the lives of women faculty do. However, some of the advice shared by her participants falls much more in line with the "fix the women" approach. For example, participants said that women need to learn to be more assertive and women need to carefully plan when to have a baby. Yet, Philipsen's primary emphasis is on critiquing and changing academe and its entrenched rules; this focus is both refreshing and noteworthy.

Overall, *Challenges of the Faculty Career for Women: Success and Sacrifice* is a rich, well-organized, easily read text that provides a solid overview of the nature of the lives of women faculty throughout academe. In addition, the book is a robust example of a qualitative study. Women faculty and other historically underrepresented faculty will likely find that the narratives reflect aspects of their own experiences throughout their careers. Graduate students, both male and female, can benefit from reading this book due to its breadth and depth, especially for those who are considering careers as faculty members. Administrators, those participating in faculty governance, members of faculty unions, and faculty activists will also learn a great deal from Philipsen's analysis. Although some of the stories shared and the recommendations offered are not revolutionary (for similar examples, see Caplan, 1994; Cooper & Stevens, 2002; and Moody, 2004), she has added some new perspectives to the conversation about women faculty and the need for institutional transformation that can serve as an empirical foundation to improve the academy for everyone.

REFERENCES

Bracken, S. J., Allen, J. A., & Dean, D. R. (Eds.). (2006). *The balancing act: Gendered perspectives in faculty roles and work lives.* Sterling, VA: Stylus.

Caplan, P. J. (1994). *Lifting a ton of feathers: A woman's guide to surviving in the academic world.* Toronto: University of Toronto Press.

Coiner, C., & George, D. H. (Eds.). (1998). *The family track: Keeping your faculties while you mentor, nurture, teach, and serve.* Urbana: University of Illinois Press.

Cooper, J. E., & Stevens, D. D. (Eds.). (2002). *Tenure in the sacred grove: Issues and strategies for women and minority faculty.* Albany: State University of New York Press.

Jacobs, L., Cintrón, J., & Canton, C. E. (Eds.). (2002). *The politics of survival in academia: Narratives of inequity, resilience, and success.* Lanham, MD: Rowman & Littlefield.

Kolodny, A. (1998). *Failing the future: A dean looks at higher education in the twenty-first century.* Durham, NC: Duke University Press.

Monroe, K., Ozyurt, S., Wrigley, T., & Alexander, A. (2008). Gender equity in academia: Bad news from the trenches, and some possible solutions. *Perspectives on Politics, 6,* 215–233.

Moody, J. (2004). *Faculty diversity: Problems and solutions.* New York: RoutledgeFalmer.

Unfinished Agendas: New and Continuing Gender Challenges in Higher Education

by Judith Glazer-Raymo (Ed.). Baltimore: The Johns Hopkins Press, 2008. 299 pp. ISBN-13: 978-0-8018-8862-5

Reviewed by Kathryn M. Moore—North Carolina State University

When I was a young scholar beginning my career at Cornell University in the early 1970s, I offered a graduate seminar entitled "Academic Women." Quite possibly, it was one of few in the country at that time. The principle challenge my graduate students and I faced was finding sufficient materials. We had Jessie Bernard's work, and that of Helen Astin on the woman doctorate, but we felt like explorers in seeking out things to read and ponder. In the end, we decided to do our own research on the few women emeritus faculty at Cornell. I still recall our work and our colleagueship as a highlight of my own career as an academic woman. Fortunately, for all of us in higher education the scholarship has burgeoned in the ensuing decades. Yet, the sense of bold discovery still prevails, and regrettably so do many of the conditions that the emeritae told us about.

Unfinished Agendas arrives at another important time for examining and advancing academic women's place and contribution in the academy. It is a sequel to Glazer-Raymo's *Shattering the Myths: Women in Academe*, published in 1999. While it revisits several of the themes and topics of the earlier volume, it provides a fresh assessment of current conditions and brings some new perspectives to bear. Framed as "an intergenerational and interdisciplinary discourse," the authors focus on a broad spectrum of higher education institutions and the intersections of gender, race, ethnicity, and social class that are found there. Overarching all of the chapters is a concern for the changing economic, political, and social climate in the United States that in Glazer-Raymo's words, "now threatens to reverse many of women's hard-earned gains of the past thirty-six years" (p. xii).

Make no mistake, women have made major strides. They are now the majority of undergraduate students in the nation, and in many professional and graduate fields they are also a majority or near majority, reflecting their numbers in the population far more accurately than in any past decade. For example, in the 1970s at Cornell or anywhere, it was rare for a woman to be part of an entering class in Veterinary Medicine; now nationally women are the majority—though not of veterinary faculty. And herein lies part of the enduring conundrum of U.S. higher education: despite rapid increases in numbers of students across nearly all fields in the last 2 decades, faculty and administrative positions still remain stubbornly male dominated. Moreover, while women in general have seen gains, they are by no means equally distributed across racial, ethnic, social class, or type of institution. In some cases, numbers are flat or declining and the policy environment is turning unfriendly, if not directly hostile, to women's concerns.

The book is organized into 11 chapters whose topics range from women faculty in research universities to women in community colleges, women on governing boards and women in the presidency, women of color, and women as scientists and mathematicians. The writers use a rich variety of research methods and analytic and theoretical perspectives. Some of the chapters, such as Stage and Hubbard's analysis of baccalaureate origins of recent mathematics and science doctorates, are exemplars of their genre of research. Others, such as Aleman's discussion of faculty productivity and gender, and Metcalfe and Slaughter's work on the differential effects of academic capitalism on women in the academy, pose provocative theoretical and analytic perspectives that deserve careful reading and discussion. There are also pieces that combine the personal and the scholarly in a commonly feminist blend of the personal and the political. These include chapters by Ropers-Huilman on women faculty and the dance of identities and Ward and Wolf-Wendel's study of varying perspectives on work and family in faculty careers. There is some in-depth work on women in research universities by Terosky, Phifer, and Neumann that like Stage's work builds on earlier work and is clearly part of a detailed and ongoing research agenda by these scholars.

And this is the point after all: namely, that women have the right and responsibility as members of the academy to conduct intellectual work that contributes to disciplinary knowledge, policy, and practice. This is the traditional and honored role of the scholar in society, and women no less than men are asserting their place in that tradition. Some of the authors, including Terosky et al. and Ward and Wolf-Wendell, worry that a variety of academic duties—such as in teaching and administration, or responsibilities in the home like motherhood and other caregiver roles—may distract or even derail women's potential and actual presence as academics. Still, this volume and others like it are testimony to the opportunities women scholars are seizing to conduct serious academic work across many disciplines and to take their rightful places as shapers of their subjects of study and of the academy writ large.

It is my fond hope that this volume will find its place in many courses and seminars, perhaps even in seminars dedicated to academic women. The quality of the scholarship and of the discourse in these chapters deserves serious study in a variety of other venues as well. These may include task forces on women, study groups and conferences on diversity and leadership, as well as in discussion of the contemporary history and social policy of the university. Moreover, there is a global community of scholars working in this area, such as Mary Ann Danowitz Sagaria's edited volume *Women, Universities and Change: Gender Equality in the European Union and the United States* (Palgrave MacMillan, 2007). Their work contributes to a much broader understanding of women's roles and contributions in higher education worldwide. Women in the United States are not alone in their struggles nor in their refining work in their disciplines. And that is decidedly good news.

REFERENCES

Astin, H. S. (1969). *The woman doctorate in America: Origins, career and family.* New York: Russell Sage Foundation.

Bernard, J. (1964). *Academic women.* University Park, PA: Pennsylvania State University Press.

Danowitz Sagara, M. (2007). *Women, universities, and change: Gender equality in the European union and United States.* New York and London: Palgrave MacMillan.

Glazer-Raymo, J. (1999). *Shattering the myths: Women in academe.* Baltimore: Johns Hopkins University Press.

Guidelines for Authors

The *NASPA Journal About Women in Higher Education* seeks scholarly essays and research-based manuscripts that illuminate important issues related to women in higher education and that make an original contribution to the knowledge base about these women. The journal welcomes manuscripts that look at women in non-U.S. higher education settings as long as connections are drawn between the manuscript's topic and related studies about U.S. women.

Additionally, the journal seeks book reviews and brief program descriptions. To submit a book review, please contact the editors for advance approval and guidelines. Books being reviewed must be on a topic relevant to women in higher education and have been published in 2008. Program description submissions should be 500-word descriptions highlighting an innovative program designed for women in higher education.

Style Guidelines

All manuscripts must adhere to the 5th edition of the *Publication Manual of the American Psychological Association.* Depending upon the type of article, manuscripts should be at least 15 pages, and no more than 25 pages, double-spaced in 12-point Times New Roman font. Page length includes tables and figures, but does not include title page, abstract, or references.

Manuscript Review Process

Manuscripts are judged using a blind review process, each by at least two reviewers. The genre of the paper is taken into consideration when being critiqued. Criteria related to some modes of inquiry are noted below, but these are suggestive, not definitive or exhaustive.

- **Research Paper:** Consider the use of theory and the available literature; the design, sampling, and data gathering procedures; appropriateness of the method for the question; the treatment and interpretation of data; the importance of results; the practical and substantive implications of results.

- **Professional Practice Paper:** Consider the validity of the description of the problem and its context; the clarity of assumptions; the discussion of alternative solutions; the defense of the chosen course of action; practical or theoretical implications.
- **Best Practices Paper:** Consider the adequacy of the description of the practice or program, the uniqueness of the case, the method for gathering data about the program, the implications of the program for other colleges and universities.
- **Scholarly Essay:** Consider the importance of the problem, thoroughness of coverage of relevant literature, and logical development of the essay.
- **Literature Review:** Consider its scope, coherence, and impartiality; the development of meaningful insights for the practitioner; its suggestions for necessary scholarship.

Each manuscript is evaluated on the paper's form and content. Form includes writing style and readability, logical development, length, and relation of author's objectives to those appropriate for the genre. Content includes originality of topic or approach, significance of the subject, and significance to the readers.

The manuscripts published in the *NASPA Journal About Women in Higher Education* are selected by the editors in consultation with the reviewers.

How to Submit

To submit a manuscript, please send an electronic copy in Microsoft Word to jawhe@naspa.org, with "JAWHE Manuscript Submission" in the subject line. A title page, abstract, and author(s) biography (40 words maximum) should be included with the manuscript. Please include manuscript title; name and title of author(s); and submitting author's address, phone number, and e-mail address on the title page.

Submission Deadline

The *NASPA Journal About Women in Higher Education* is published annually in March. Manuscripts are due no later than March 15 for publication consideration. Visit www.naspa.org/pubs/journals/jawhe for deadline information.